TERTULLIAN AND THE CHURCH

Was Tertullian of Carthage a schismatic? How did he view the church and its bishops? How did he understand the exercise of authority within the church? In this study David Rankin sets the writings of Tertullian in the context of the early third-century church and the developments it was undergoing in relation to both its structures and its self-understanding. He then discusses Tertullian's own theology of the church, his imagery and his perception of church office and ministry. Tertullian maintained throughout his career a high view of the church, and this in part constituted the motivation for his vitriolic attacks on the church's hierarchy after he had joined the New Prophecy movement. His contribution to the development of the church has often been misunderstood, and this thorough exploration provides a timely reassessment of its nature and importance.

TERTULLIAN AND THE CHURCH

BY

DAVID RANKIN

CAMBRIDGE
UNIVERSITY PRESS

Published by the Press Syndicate of the University of Cambridge
The Pitt Building, Trumpington Street, Cambridge CB2 1RP
40 West 20th Street, New York, NY 10011–4211, USA
10 Stamford Road, Oakleigh, Melbourne 3166, Australia

First published 1995

Printed in Great Britain at the University Press, Cambridge

A catalogue record for this book is available from the British Library

Library of Congress cataloguing in publication data

Rankin, David (David Ivan), 1952–
Tertullian and the church/by David Rankin.
p. cm.
Includes bibliographical references.
ISBN 0 521 48067 1 (hardback)
1. Tertullian, ca. 160–ca. 230. 2. Church – Authority – History of
doctrines – Early church, ca. 30–600. 3. Montanism. I. Title.
BT91.R36 1995
262′.013′092 – dc20
94–24375 CIP

ISBN 0 521 48067 1 hardback

VN

To my wife Julie and children Nicole and Michael

Contents

x   *Contents*

Acknowledgements

I would like to acknowledge the considerable debt owed by me to my teacher and supervisor, the Revd Professor Eric F. Osborn, for his advice, encouragement and support over many years, and particularly so during the preparation of this book. His wise counsel, humour and kindness have been a constant source of strength to me.

I also wish to acknowledge my appreciation to the Revd Professor Ian Breward for his valuable advice and encouragement over the years; to the Principal and Faculty of the Uniting Church Theological Hall, Melbourne, and to the Committee of Post-graduate Studies, for their generous provision of financial and other assistance; to Dr Lawrence McIntosh of the Joint Theological Library, Ormond College, Melbourne, for his counsel and encouragement; to the Principal, staff and students of Wesley House, Cambridge, where my family and I spent a most enjoyable year in 1987; to Mr Saul Bastomsky of the Department of Classical Studies, Monash University, for his assistance in translating some of the more difficult passages from Tertullian's text; to the Revd Dr Neil Byrne of Pius XII Provincial Seminary, Brisbane, and a colleague in the Brisbane College of Theology, for reading the manuscript and making some valuable suggestions for its improvement; and to Mr Alex Wright of Cambridge University Press for his advice and counsel.

And, finally, to my dear wife Julie I express my heartfelt love and gratitude for her patience, encouragement and the many well-placed words of gentle humour which often saw me through the more difficult moments of the last few years.

Abbreviations

ACW	Ancient Christian Writers, Westminster, Maryland, 1946-
A-NCL	Ante-Nicene Christian Library, Edinburgh, 1870-
CCL	Corpus Christianorum. Series Latina, Turnhout, Belgium, 1953-
GCS	Griechischen christlichen Schriftsteller der ersten drei Jahrhunderte
LCL	Loeb Classical Library, Cambridge, Mass., 1912-
PL	J-P.Migne, Patrologia Latina, Paris, 1940-
AC	*Antike und Christentum*
AJPh	*American Journal of Philology*
ALMA	*Archivum Latinitas Medii aevi*
AnFLetN	*Annales de la Faculté des Lettres et Sciences humaines de Nice*
CH	*Church History*
CQR	*Classical Quarterly Review*
ExpT	*Expository Times*
IER	*Irish Ecclesiastical Record*
JEH	*Journal of Ecclesiastical History*
JRS	*Journal of Roman Studies*
JTS	*Journal of Theological Studies*
KerDo	*Kerygma und Dogma*
RScRel.	*Revue des Sciences Religieuses*
REAug.	*Revue des études Augustiniennes*
REG	*Revue des études grecques*
RHE	*Revue de l'histoire ecclésiastique*
ScotJTh.	*Scottish Journal of Theology*

SE	*Studia Evangelica*
SP	*Studia Patristica*
TheolStuds	*Theological Studies*
VC	*Vigiliae Christianae*
ZKG	*Zeitschrift für Kirchengeschichte*

A note on chronology of texts

The criteria normally used for determining the chronological order of Tertullian's writings include doctrinal development, stylistic variation, disciplinary rigour, attitudes towards the Catholic church and the New Prophecy movement, historical allusions and references to other writings. Some involve considerable difficulty. With regard to the first – doctrinal development – it is generally accepted that, whatever the attitude towards it in the fourth and later centuries, the New Prophecy of the late second and early third centuries was doctrinally orthodox; and, while the third – disciplinary rigour – is generally useful as an indicator, in some cases, for example, *De Idololatria* (see below), it may not be so.

Of the many attempts to construct a feasible chronology for Tertullian's writings two of the most recent, those by Fredouille (1972) and Barnes (1984 – a revision of his seminal 1970 work) offer the most useful starting points.[1] While there is a considerable degree of harmony between the two, Fredouille, unlike Barnes, insists on a rigid division of the writings into three distinct periods of Tertullian's Christian life: 'période catholique' (197-206), 'sous l'influence montaniste' (207-12) and 'rupture avec l'Eglise' (213-). Barnes, having earlier established 207/8 as the first datable manifestation of Tertullian's Montanism, now

---

[1] J.-C. Fredouille, *Tertullien et la conversion de la culture antique* (Paris, 1972) pp.487f.; T. D. Barnes, *Tertullian: a historical and literary study*, 2nd edition (London,1984) , pp. 325f. Unfortunately I have had no access to R.Braun, 'Chronologia Tertullianea: Le De Carne Christi et le De Idololatria', Hommage à P. Fargues, *Annales de la Faculté des Lettres et Sciences humaines de Nice* 21 (1974).

believes that this date must be shifted beyond 208.[2] Too precise datings are in any case both problematic and unnecessary, as are assumptions of a definite rupture with the Catholic church on the part of Tertullian.

Barnes identifies eight ideas or expressions distinctive of Montanist beliefs; with only one exception,[3] he assigns to the later part of Tertullian's career only those writings which exhibit one or more of these marks: (1) the naming of Montanus or one of his female associates, or appeal to a Montanist oracle; (2) specific reference to the New Prophecy or the rebuttal of charges of 'pseudoprophetia' or of 'nova disciplina'; (3) commendation of the ecstatic state; (4) mention of spiritual gifts as possessed only by Montanists; (5) description of the Holy Spirit as 'Paracletus'; (6) 'nos' or 'noster' used to describe persons or things peculiarly Montanist;(7) 'vos' or 'vester' used to contrast Catholic and Montanist; and(8) abuse of Catholics as 'Psychici'.[4] Only in *De Ieiunio* do all eight marks appear; in *De Pudicitia* there are seven.[5]

Barnes' schema demonstrates significant variations from that of Fredouille with regard to four writings: *De Idololatria, Scorpiace, De Pallio* and *De Carne Christi*. Despite the obvious rigour of its disciplinary stance (it is, for example, far more rigorous than the admittedly Montanist *De Corona Militis*), Barnes places *De Idololatria* very early in Tertullian's career. Fredouille, like many others, dates it later, to 211-12. Yet Barnes finds support both from van der Nat, who dates it before the persecution of 197, and

---

[2] Barnes, *Tertullian*, p.328.

[3] *Ad Scapulam* which, although it contains none of these Montanist 'marks' and resembles more the *Apologeticum* from Tertullian's Catholic period, must be dated, by universal agreement, to 212 by virtue of precise historical references (e.g. 3,2 and 4,5).

[4] The Latin word 'psychicus' – a loan-word from the Greek – literally means 'of the soul'. Tertullian uses it as a contrast with 'spiritualis' (spiritual) which is consistent with the use of the Greek '*psuchikos*' in the New Testament (e.g. 1 Cor. 2,13; 15,14; James 3,15; Jude 19) as a contrast to '*pneumatikos*'. The Lewis and Short dictionary translates 'psychicus' as 'animal, carnal, carnally inclined', using Tertullian's *De Monogamia* 1 as an example. Most of the older translations of Tertullian's works – A-NCL for example – also consistently translate 'psychicus' as 'carnal'. While some might properly prefer 'unspiritual' as a more correct translation in the context of its standing over against 'spiritualis', and given that 'carnal' or 'carnally inclined' might not be seen to accord with the literal meaning of the word, I shall nevertheless here follow the well-established tradition.

[5] Barnes, *Tertullian*, pp. 43f.

Rordorf, who has no doubts that it predates *De Corona*.[6] It is also worthy of note that Johannes Neander, in his 1824 work on Tertullian, also placed *De Idololatria* among Tertullian's pre-New Prophecy works. While Fredouille (along with others) dates *Scorpiace* to 211-12, Barnes places it early in the first decade of the third century. He argues plausibly that Tertullian's appeal to Matthew 16,18 to support the concept of the transmission of the disciplinary power of the keys through Peter to the church (10,8), is more consistent with the argumentation of the Catholic *De Praescriptione (Haereticorum)* (22,4) than with that of the New Prophecy *De Pudicitia* (21,9).[7]

Most commentators place *De Pallio* very late; Fredouille puts it beyond 217 and posits it as Tertullian's last extant writing.[8] Barnes, who would not go so far as Constanza in placing it as early as the time of Tertullian's conversion (perhaps in 193),[9] places it in the middle of the first decade of the third century. It contains no Montanist 'marks' (see above) and there are no historical allusions or signs of doctrinal progression which require a later date. Fredouille places *De Carne Christi* in the period 208-12, 'sous l'influence montaniste'. Barnes originally dated it to 206 (a year or so after *Adv. Hermogenem*), but later suggested an even earlier date. It contains no Montanist marks and for the divine 'Word' Tertullian employs the Latin 'verbum' rather than the more dynamic 'sermo'; the former is typical of his earlier writings, the latter his consistent practice from *Adv. Hermogenem* onwards. The early date is reinforced also by the arguments of Mahé.[10] The only real difficulty for this early dating – the clear reference at 7,1 to *Adv. Marcionem* IV,19 – is dealt with quite adequately by Braun. He suggests that Tertullian

---

[6] P. G. van der Nat, *QSF Tertulliani De idololatria*, part I, (Leiden,1960), p.14; W. Rordorf, 'Tertullians Beurteilung des Soldatenstandes', *VC* 23 (1969), pp.118f.

[7] 'Tertullian's Scorpiace', *JTS* ns 20 (1969), p.116. In this book I have also chosen to refer to *De Praescriptione (Haereticorum)* – although more often by the abbreviated *De Praescriptione* – rather than to *De Praescriptionibus*. The former is preferred by the editors of CCL and is that found in the earliest two manuscripts of the work, the ninth-century *Codex Parisinus Latinus* and the eleventh-century *Codex Paterniacensis*.

[8] *Tertullian*, p. 488.

[9] S. Constanza, *Tertulliano, De Pallio* (Naples, 1968), p. 35.

[10] J.-P. Mahé, *Tertullien: La Chair du Christ*, Sources Chrétiennes CCXVI-CCXVII (1975), vol. I, pp. 27f.

wrote *De Carne Christi* in his earlier period, but published it only some years later, along with its companion piece *De Resurrectione Mortuorum*, retouching it only superficially and adding the present preface and conclusion.[11]

Barnes plausibly places the following writings in the period before the middle of the first decade of the third century (with Fredouille in generally broad agreement, save for the exceptions discussed above) and in the following order:[12] *De Cultu Feminarum* II (Fredouille places this with book I), *Ad Nationes* I and II, *Adv. Judaeos*, *Ad Martyras*, *Apologeticum*, *De Spectaculis*, *De Idololatria*, *De Testimonia Animae*, *De Baptismo*, *De Oratione*, *De Paenitentia*, *De Patientia*, *Ad Uxorem* I and II, *De Praescriptione*, *De Carne Christi*, *Adv. Hermogenem*, *De Pallio* and *De Cultu Feminarum* I.

He places the following, which exhibit one or more of the Montanist 'marks', in the period beyond 207, and probably most of them much later: *Adv. Valentinianos*, *De Anima*, *De Resurrectione Mortuorum*, *Adv. Marcionem* (I and II and III in 207/8; IV and V later), *De Corona*, *De Exhortatione Castitatis*, *De Fuga*, *De Velandis Virginibus*, *Adv. Praxean*, *De Monogamia*, *De Ieiunio*, *De Pudicitia* and *Ad Scapulam*.[13] For the purposes of this book this chronological ordering of Barnes will be, unless otherwise indicated, that followed.

[11] According to Barnes, *Tertullian*, p. 326.

[12] Barnes is not so concerned as are others with precise datings and acknowledges in his second edition that his earlier Montanist datings were far too tight.

[13] While Barnes had originally regarded *Ad Scapulam*, dated to 212, as the latest extant writing of Tertullian, he is now more open to Fredouille's schema which assigns some of the more vitriolic anti-Catholic works to the latter half of the second decade of the third century.

Introduction

The writings of Tertullian of North Africa which bear on the nature of the church and of Christian ministry mark an important stage in a development from the fluid ecclesial concepts of the second century to the more fixed structures of the third. This is a shift from a dominant concern for the preservation of authentic apostolic doctrine to one for the validation of a regular, prescribed apostolic office.

Until the end of the second century nowhere is there in Christian thought – neither in the West nor the East – evidence of a clearly defined ecclesiology; that is, no extant Christian document of the period possesses a coherent and comprehensive doctrine of the church. It might be said that prior to the end of the second century the existence and the nature of the church were taken for granted. There is little evidence that any Christian writer before Tertullian had given attention to the question of the church's essential marks or notes. None appears to have gone beyond the reproduction of biblical images such as 'the body of Christ' and 'the bride of Christ'. Yet, by the middle of the third century, in the writings of the most prominent Western churchman of the time, Cyprian of Carthage, a highly developed ecclesiology had emerged. Questions of apostolic orthodoxy and a due order in Christian ministry and office aside, the church simply was. Its raison d'être was its existence. It was, at most, a means to an end, and no end in itself.[1]

---

[1] Hans von Campenhausen's *Ecclesiastical authority and spiritual power in the church of the first three centuries* (London, 1969), provides already a more than adequate coverage both of the development of ecclesial structures and the inherent tension between the demands of the Spirit and the prerogatives of office within that process of development during

While a sharply defined, absolutist monoepiscopacy (rule by a single bishop) seems to have prevailed in parts of the Eastern church from early in the second century[2] two thirds of the way through the second century there is no evidence in the Latin West for anything other than a moderate form of monoepiscopacy. In the writings of Irenaeus of Lyons, for example, who clearly was a single bishop exercising jurisdiction over the Christian communities of Lyons and Vienne, the bishop is still only 'primus inter pares' and the episcopal office which he occupies is at times barely distinguishable from the presbyterate. Towards the end of the second century – at the time of the Quartodeciman Controversy and as reflected both in Hippolytus of Rome and Tertullian himself – there is, however, a single bishop exercising a jurisdiction independently of the presbyterate at Rome.[3] Yet it is not until the middle of the third century, as evidenced by the writings of Cyprian of Carthage, that an absolutist, and not merely functional, monoepiscopacy becomes the unquestioned norm in the West. That such a transformation in the episcopate took place in the West within seventy years is remarkable; it was the result of a process of development for which the opening years of the third century were crucial. There was at that time a significant increase in the relative proportion of Christians in Roman society and a bitter dispute was beginning over the administration of penitential discipline within Christian communities.

Tertullian played a major but largely unacknowledged role in this process of development and his writings also closely reflected and influenced this development. An attempt to uncover the extent of his contribution in this area is well

the second century of the Christian era. I have for the most part followed his findings and will comment only where I find myself in significant disagreement with them.

[2] By 'absolutist' I mean the effective concentration of power and jurisdiction in someone who exercises complete authority over matters doctrinal and disciplinary and is accountable to noone this side of heaven. We might also note that the evidence of the letters of Ignatius of Antioch, while substantial and important, is largely uncorroborated by other contemporary sources.

[3] The letter of Ignatius of Antioch to the church at Rome, unlike those to other churches, reflects the governing of that church not by a single bishop but by the presbyterate. The suggestion that this reflects only an interregnum at Rome is an unnecessary rationalisation.

overdue. Two related issues must also be considered. The first concerns Tertullian's relationship to the Catholic church: was he a schismatic who abandoned the church for a Montanist conventicle? The other is that of his relationship to the New Prophecy movement. Tertullian was no schismatic. Reports of a breach with the Catholic church have been exaggerated. The extent of the influence of Montanism on Tertullian has also been overstated. Tertullian – particularly the New Prophet – is the object of some suspicion among many Anglo-Catholic commentators who view with unease his apparent anti-clericalism, his advocacy of the New Prophecy and the suggestion of a hint of pre-Nicene unorthodoxy. Some Protestants are equally discomforted by the so-called 'Catholic' Tertullian for his seemingly uncritical support of the historic episcopate and for such matters as his apparent repudiation of marriage as an ideal state for the Christian. The former, however, appreciate what they perceive to be his support for the doctrine of apostolic succession and, however mistakenly, for the primacy of Rome; the latter appreciate his outpouring of vitriol on the occupants of clerical office.

There is no explicit formulation in Tertullian of the marks, notes or attributes of the authentic church. Implicitly present, however, are indications of those notes which appear in later formalised ecclesiologies. The Reformed emphases on preaching truly (the proclamation or handing on of a verifiable, authentic apostolic doctrine), administering the sacraments rightly (see *De Baptismo* and *De Exhortatione Castitatis*) and the maintenance of a godly discipline are present in Tertullian's thought. Of Paul Minear's four Master Images for the New Testament church – the People of God, the New Creation, the Fellowship in Faith and the Body of Christ – the last two are clearly present. The Fellowship of Faith is emphasised in Tertullian's early period, particularly with regard to the questions of unity and apostolicity (see *De Praescriptione*). The Body of Christ is perhaps the most important ecclesial image in the New Testament. While it does not at first appear dominant in Tertullian's thought, it soon becomes obvious that it is so. Of the five ecclesial models offered by Dulles, those of the church as Institution and as Herald (promoting apostolic doctrine) are relevant to Tertullian's presentation; Tertullian's view of the authentic church as constituted by the presence of spiritual persons exhibiting prophetic and apostolic evidences and able, therefore, to forgive sin, may point to the church as Sacrament.

There is in his extant writings no explicit affirmation of the later credal formula of 'one, holy, catholic and apostolic church'. And yet the seeds of such a formula are present. Thus I have also explored Tertullian's thought on the nature of the church by an investigation of the extent to which this later credal form provides a convenient framework. This impression of the presence in Tertullian of the traditional 'notes' of the church is more than confirmed by such investigation. It is also clear that Tertullian's thought on these matters undergoes no significant shift in his transition from staunch defender of the Catholic system to one of its most vocal critics.

Tertullian's understanding of authentic Christian ministry involves the nature of church office. This, in turn, revolves around the three-tier system of bishop, presbyters and deacons, which is validated for him by history rather than by theology. It is important also to consider here two other matters. The first is Tertullian's consistency of thought, particularly with reference to his transition from Catholic to New Prophet. The second is his understanding, particularly in the latter period, of the nature and legitimate exercise of 'potestas'.

In the General Conclusion I have demonstrated that Tertullian betrays, with one exception, no major shift in his thinking on the nature and authority of Christian ministry. This exception concerns the greater emphasis which he places, during the latter period, on the role of the Christian prophet. With regard to both major questions Tertullian preserves in both periods of his Christian life a 'high' view of the church and of the ministry, while still maintaining a healthy scepticism towards the claims of some within the Catholic hierarchy. In his New Prophecy period he displays no desire to repudiate the traditional three-tier system, nor the unity, holiness, catholicity or apostolicity of the church, but rather a vigorous affirmation and defence of both.

Tertullian's writings reflect the existence in Christian thought of a shift from a major emphasis on doctrine to one on discipline. They reflect a shift in understanding office from a historically validated guarantee of apostolic doctrine to something which has an independent authenticity and which in part constitutes the nature of the true church. Consequently, office becomes itself an article within the body of apostolic doctrine.

There is general appreciation both of Tertullian's contribution to the development of trinitarian terminology and of his steadfast stand against heretics like Marcion and Valentinus.[4] However, suspicions aroused by his attachment to the New Prophecy, by some rather unorthodox views (such as on the corporeality of the soul and the ban on second marriages), by his alleged rejection of philosophical culture, and by his abrasive and sometimes spiteful language, have hindered a rational consideration of his contribution to concepts of ecclesial office and ecclesiology in general. Tertullian the schismatic has been viewed as an unreliable contributor to theological debate in any forum. Some deny to him significant patristic status, while others doubt that he ever has anything of real worth to contribute.[5] In more recent years, commentators like Fredouille, Sider, Barnes, Frend and von Campenhausen have sought to redress this imbalance and to rehabilitate his tainted reputation.[6] The underlying purpose of this book is to seek to continue their work into the area of his ecclesiology.

---

[4] This is particularly so of his early writings though of course much, if not all, of his monumental *Adversus Marcionem* was written in the later period.

[5] 'Im eigentlichen Sinne kann Tertullian nicht als Kirchenvater betrachtet werden' contends P. van Beneden, 'Ordo. Über den Ursprung einer kirchlichen Terminologie', *VC* 23 (1969), p. 162, note 5; 'Tertullian is the greatest classical Latin writer of the beginning of the third century. The things he says are not to be trusted but nevertheless he makes wonderful reading' asserts T. Merton, 'The face: Tertullian and St Cyprian on virgins', *Cistercian Studies* 6 (1971), p. 334.

[6] Fredouille, *Tertullien*; R. D. Sider, *Ancient rhetoric and the art of Tertullian* (Oxford, 1971); Barnes, *Tertullian*; W. H. C. Frend, *The Donatist Church* (Oxford, 1952); von Campenhausen, *Ecclesiastical authority.*

PART I

The historical questions

CHAPTER I

The church in North Africa

CARTHAGE

The origins of the Christian church in North Africa are shrouded in obscurity. The reasons for this are not clear. It cannot be said, for example, that the region was a backwater of the empire, easily by-passed by the movements of the day. Very little indeed has been written on the Carthage of Tertullian's day. B. H. Warmington's *Carthage*, one of the most comprehensive works on Carthage in recent times, effectively deals only with the history of Carthage up to the time of the city's destruction at the end of the Third Punic War in 146 BC.[1] North Africa was, as the granary of Rome, a significant region of the empire, both militarily and economically; Carthage probably was the second city of the empire after Rome. Herodian, who wrote during the first half of the third century AD, asserted that 'the city is the next after Rome in wealth, population and size, though there is rivalry for second place between it and Alexandria in Egypt'.[2]

Why is there so little information about the origins of the church in one of the most important regions of the empire? If the thesis of Walter Bauer were in part correct – that 'in some areas the initial form of Christianity was actually heretical according to later standards, and that orthodoxy as defined by the church councils triumphed at a relatively late date'[3] – one might speculate that the first Christian communities there were later

[1] B. H. Warmington, *Carthage* (London, 1960).
[2] Herodian, *History of the Empire from the time of Marcus Aurelius* (LCL,1970, transl. by C. R. Whittaker), vii, 6, 1.
[3] W. Bauer, *Orthodoxy and heresy in earliest Christianity*, 2nd edn, ed. R. A. Kraft and G. Krodel (Philadelphia, 1971).

9

adjudged as less than orthodox. Earlier records may not then have survived the rigorous scrutiny of a later age.

EARLY HISTORY OF THE CHURCH IN NORTH AFRICA

Although it is widely agreed that there was no universal or systematic persecution of Christians by the Roman authorities until the reign of Decius in the mid-third century, official persecution was by no means sporadic in the provinces of Africa towards the end of the second and the beginning of the third centuries. It has been appropriately remarked that the history of the North African church during its first 500 years is, in great part, a history of martyrdom. Frend calls the African church 'a church of martyrs'.[4] Thus, it is appropriate both that the earliest extant records of its existence should concern martyrs and also that its first celebrated Father should be one who was so preoccupied with the question of martyrdom. On 17 July 180, during the first year of the reign of the Emperor Commodus, there took place at the court of the Proconsul Vigellius Saturninus the trial and subsequent execution of twelve Christians from the otherwise unknown village of Scillium in Proconsular Africa.[5] The twelve – Speratus, Nartzalus, Cittinus, Veturius, Felix, Aquilinus, Laetantius, Donata, Secunda, Vestia, Januaria and Generosa – all refused the command of the Proconsul to swear by the 'genius' of the Emperor, rejected his offer of a stay of thirty days in which to 'think the matter over', and were summarily executed.

This was not only the first recorded instance of a trial of Christians in North Africa, but probably the first conducted there. We have the claim of Tertullian himself that Vigellius Saturninus was the first Roman official 'qui primus hic gladium in nos egit'.[6] Eusebius' suggestion – with reference to an outbreak of persecution at Lyons and Vienne in Gaul some three

---

[4] W. H. C. Frend, 'The North African cult of martyrs: from apocalyptic to hero-worship (plates)', in *Jenseitsvorstellungen in Antike*, ed. T. Klausner and E. Dassmann (1982), p. 154.
[5] *Passio Sanctorum Scillitanorum*; the text can be found in O. von Gebhardt, *Acta Martyrum Selecta*, pp. 22-7.
[6] *Ad Scapulam* 3, 4.

years earlier than the Scillitan trial[7] – that this former persecution resulted from a decree of the Emperor Marcus Aurelius may also apply to the latter events in North Africa. And yet there is no other record of such an edict; it is more likely either that Marcus Aurelius had simply reissued Trajan's earlier advisory Rescript to Pliny, the Governor of Bithynia in the second decade of the second century, or that the Proconsul himself, perhaps both on the basis of Trajan's Rescript and in connection with the accession of Commodus to the throne, had simply acted on his own initiative. The legal basis, if such existed, of the trials of Christians has never been satisfactorily explained.[8] Two comments of the historian T. D. Barnes are worth noting in this connection. He asserts both that 'the legal position of Christians continues exactly as Trajan defined it until Decius', and, perhaps even more significantly, that 'it is in the minds of men, not in the demands of Roman law, that the roots of the persecution of Christians in the Roman Empire are to be sought'.[9]

The circumstances of the Scillitan martyrs – both their location and their nomenclature – suggest that the first African Christians were not Greek-speaking immigrants living in large urban centres (as was often the case in places like Gaul), but rather came from among the indigenous rural population which gathered itself around the smaller market-towns.[10] Monceaux's claim that the extant account of the trial displays traces of Montanism cannot be maintained on the evidence of the text as it stands.[11] It is often presumed that the treatise *Ad Martyras*, one of Tertullian's earliest extant writings, was occasioned by a later bout of persecution, perhaps in Carthage itself, in the closing years of the second century. Leclerq considers that this treatise, along with the *Apologeticum* and the *Ad Nationes*, was written

[7] *Ecclesiastical History* (LCL, 1980, transl. by J. E .L. Oulton), v, i, 47.

[8] Most commentators agree that it was probably both the refusal of Christians to participate in the imperial cult and the fact that the church was, technically at least, an illegal society – A. N. Sherwin-White, *Letters of Pliny*, (Oxford, 1966) pp. 778f. contends that this was so particularly in the second century – which formed the legal basis for prosecution. See also A.N.Sherwin-White, *Roman society and Roman law in the New Testament* (Grand Rapids, 1978).

[9] 'Legislation against the Christians', *JRS* 58 (1968), p. 48; ibid. p. 50.

[10] G. Charles-Picard, *La civilisation de l'Afrique Romaine* (Paris, 1959), p. 38.

[11] P.Monceaux, *Histoire littéraire de l'Afrique chrétienne* (Paris, 1901), vol. i, p. 81.

prior to the purported issue, during an imperial visit to Alexandria in 202, of an edict forbidding conversions to both Judaism and Christianity.[12] Rordorf, on the other hand, maintains that the occasion of *Ad Martyras* and the events depicted in the *Passio Perpetuae et Felicitatis* belong to the same period, a persecution in Carthage in early to mid 203.[13] Barnes, however, questions the historicity of this 202/3 edict, labelling it as 'demonstrably fictitious', and discounting any Severan persecution in that year as 'myth'.[14] A biographer of Septimius Severus, A. R. Birley, likewise condemns the existence of any such edict as 'a piece of fiction'.[15] The arguments of both are attractive, if not compelling, but the issue is far from settled. Braun argues, against Rordorf, that 'benedicti martyres designati' at *Ad Martyras* 1,1 does not refer exclusively to catechumens, and further, that the 'praesentia tempora' referred to by Tertullian in the same treatise (6,2) does not mean the same thing as 'notre époque'.[16] Barnes supports the position taken by Braun when he refutes the notion that any 202/3 persecution was exclusively directed against proselytising by pointing out that 'in the *Passio Perpetuae* the charge is still being a Christian, not having become one'.[17] The question of whether there was further official persecution in North Africa between the events recorded at Scillium and the trials and executions at Carthage in 203 must remain unresolved.

On 7 March 203 the well-born Perpetua, only recently become a mother, the slave-girl Felicitas, their fellow-disciples Revocatus, Saturninus and Secundulus, and their teacher Satyrus, were arraigned and convicted before the court of the Proconsul Hilarianus. Five of the six were subsequently put to death in the public arena. The sixth died while awaiting execution. The five were, of course, not the only martyred Christians in this period and region. Cyprian records the names

[12] H. Leclercq, *L'Afrique chrétienne* (Paris, 1904), p. 123.
[13] W. Rordorf and R. Braun, 'Dossier sur l'Ad Martyras de Tertullien', *REAug* 26 (1980), pp. 3f.
[14] T. D. Barnes, 'Pre-Decian Acta Martyrum', *JTS* ns19 (1968), p. 526.
[15] A. R. Birley, *Septimius Severus, the African emperor* (London, 1971), p. 209.
[16] Rordorf and Braun, 'Dossier sur l'Ad Martyras', pp. 14f.
[17] Barnes, 'Legislation', p. 40.

of at least two other groups of Carthaginian martyrs – the brothers Laurentius and Ignatius and their mother Celerina, as well as a group which included Aemilius and Castus.[18] Both groups met their deaths sometime after Perpetua, Felicitas and company. This persecution began under the Proconsulship of Minutius Timinianus who was succeeded on his death by Hilarianus. According to Tertullian, there was already considerable hostility against the Christians which led, inter alia, to calls for the closure of Christian burial areas,[19] itself proof of the relative organisational stability of the Christian community at Carthage. This, added to the popular devotion to the god Serapis at Carthage,[20] provided sufficient impetus for an edict of Severus, if such existed, to be carried out with merciless efficiency and enthusiasm. The occasion of the treatise *De Corona*, in which Tertullian recounts the refusal of a Christian soldier to wear a triumphal laurel, may have been this particular persecution. Barnes, however, suggests that the occasion of the former was the giving of a donative in celebration of the accession of Caracalla and Geta to the throne. Severus died in early February 211, while Geta was murdered, on his brother's orders, in late December of that same year.[21] S. L. Greenslade gives the date of *De Corona* as 'certainly of 211'.[22]

The account of the martyrdom of Perpetua and her friends has an undeniably Montanist ring – though Tertullian himself was probably not, as sometimes suggested, its editor[23] – and suggests that the New Prophecy movement was at that time very active in the Carthaginian church. Visions were not, of course, as D'Alès points out,[24] a Montanist monopoly, but the theological

---

[18] The first group at *Ep.* 34,3 and the second at *De Lapsis* 13.

[19] *Ad Scapulam* 3,1.

[20] This devotion was rivalled only in Alexandria where another major persecution took place at the same time. J. G. Davies contends that it is no great coincidence that the two chief centres of persecution at that time were also major centres for the worship of the imperial favourite Serapis, 'Was the devotion of Septimius Severus to Serapis the cause of the persecution of 202-3?', *JTS* ns 5 (1954), pp. 73f.

[21] Barnes, 'Legislation', p.37.

[22] S. L. Greenslade, *Early Latin theology*, The Library of Christian Classics v, (London, 1956), p. 81.

[23] See below the discussion on Tertullian's relationship to the New Prophecy movement.

[24] A. D'Alès, *La théologie de Tertullien* (Paris, 1905), p. 443.

character of the work is, as Barnes puts it, 'Montanist through and through'.[25] Tabbernee suggests that the account of these martyrdoms provides clear evidence of 'factional' tension in the church at Carthage, though there is no suggestion of actual schism.[26]

From this time until that of the Proconsul Scapula the church experienced a decade of relative peace. Scapula Tertullus assumed the mantle of Proconsul in 211 and served through two successive terms until 213. His time as Proconsul coincides with the first years of the sole reign of Severus' elder son, and fratricide, Caracalla. Though nursed as a child by a Christian, the new Emperor was not enamoured of the Christian faith, and his African Proconsul launched a renewed persecution of the Christians in Carthage. This new wave of persecution, for which no immediate motive is known, occasioned the writing of the treatise *Ad Scapulam*. However, few details of this particular anti-Christian pogrom are known.

Thus, in the more than thirty years from the accession of Commodus, through the reign of Septimius Severus, and into that of his son Caracalla, the Christians of North Africa experienced three, and possibly four, persecutions. This is more than other Christian communities experienced in this period. These persecutions were, it seems, mainly directed against the laity. Tertullian seems to imply that the North African church leadership was largely left untouched, unlike their colleagues in contemporary Gaul.

Towards the end of Tertullian's life – and certainly after the time of his extant writings – a Council was held in Carthage under the leadership of the Carthaginian bishop Agrippinus.[27] The most hotly debated issue at this Council was apparently the re-baptism of heretics, which practice was approved.

The church in North Africa, centred on the 'second' city of the

[25] Barnes, *Tertullian*, p. 77.
[26] W. Tabbernee, 'Remnants of the New Prophecy: literary and epigraphical sources of the Montanist movement', *SP* 21 (1989), pp. 5 and 7.
[27] Tertullian's reference to the Greek provincial councils at *De Ieiunio* 13,6 implies that such gatherings were at that time unknown in North Africa. Cyprian at *Epp.*71,4; 73,3 implies that Agrippinus was the virtual primate of North Africa. The traditional date for the council is 217.

empire, was well established and displayed a similar process of organisational consolidation as was taking place elsewhere. While this development had not yet seen the advent of the absolutist episcopacy which we find in Cyprian's time, the process is well advanced. The traditional rigorism and conservatism of the North African Christian were evidently present in Tertullian's time, for Cyprian reports that in the episcopal generation prior to his own there were a number of bishops in the province who took a hard line on the readmission of adulterers to communion.[28] According to Cyprian,

Et quidem apud antecessores nostros quidam de episcopis istic in provincia nostra dandam pacem moechis non putaverunt et in totum paenitentiae locum contra adulteria clauserunt non tamen a coepiscoporum suorum collegio recesserunt aut catholicae ecclesiae unitatem vel duritiae vel censurae suae obstinatione ruperunt, ut quia apud alios adulteris pax dabatur, qui non dabat de ecclesia separaretur.

(Ep. 55,21)

(And, indeed, among our predecessors some of the bishops here in our province thought not to grant peace to adulterers and shut the gate completely against giving repentance to adultery. They did not, however, withdraw from the assembly of their fellow bishops, nor break the unity of the catholic church by the steadfastness of their severity or censure; so that because peace was being given by some to adulterers he who did not so grant it might be separated from the church.)

Following the 217 Council there is what Leclerq calls a 'profound silence'[29] over the next three decades of North African church history until the coming to the throne of the Emperor Decius – and the first universal persecution of Christians in the empire – and the elevation to the episcopate at Carthage of Cyprian.

Even less accessible to the historian than the early years of the church in North Africa are the circumstances of its original settlement. The observation of Charles-Picard that the first Christians in North Africa were probably not Eastern immigrants

---

[28] Cyprian actually names none of these bishops, though it is tempting to suggest that many of them came from the hinterland, the home of many of the later Donatists; see Frend, 'The North African cult of martyrs', passim.

[29] Leclerq, *L'Afrique chrétienne*, p. 162.

(because of the Punic names of the Scillitan martyrs) still tells us nothing about those from whom they learnt their faith. Passing Christian traders or soldiers stationed in the province probably played some part. The original impetus probably also came from Rome. The ties between Rome and Carthage were very strong, as Tertullian suggests at *De Praescriptione* 36,2 when he asserts that the church in Carthage looked to Rome for inspiration and 'authority', 'habes Romam unde nobis quoque auctoritas praesto est. (You have Rome from whence is at hand for us the authority [sc. of the Apostles]). Later, at 36,4, he speaks of the special relationship between the Roman church and the North African, 'videamus quid didicerit [sc. the Roman church], quid docuerit: Cum Africanis quoque ecclesiis contesseratis' (See what she has learned, what she has taught: what fellowship is had even with our African churches). In the absence of evidence to the contrary, one can safely assume that the church in North Africa was first settled either directly from Rome, or indirectly through the agency of another Roman 'daughter' church.

According to Platnauer, 'the reign of Severus marks almost the beginning of a period of considerable moral, intellectual and spiritual ferment' in the empire, and an era, especially for provincials, of 'peace and prosperity'.[30] For Guignebert, 'a l'époque de Tertullien, il y avait dans le monde antique une inquiétude des âmes très profondes et des aspirations religieuses très sincères'.[31] Christianity found a fertile ground in what Charles-Picard calls the 'tendances spirituelles profondes de la nation africaine'.[32] The natural rigour and fervour of African religious expression was a natural seed-bed for a severe, extreme form of Christianity and church life.[33] 'The Berber, like his Coptic contemporary,' says Frend, 'was always a dissenter'.[34]

---

[30] J. Platnauer, *The life and reign of the emperor Lucius Septimius Severus* (Oxford, 1918), pp. 156 and 203.

[31] Ch. Guignebert, *Tertullien. Etude sur ses sentiments à l'égard de l'Empire et de la société civile* (Paris, 1901), p. 275.

[32] Charles-Picard, *La civilisation de l'Afrique Romaine*, p. 319.

[33] See Frend, 'The North African cult of martyrs', especially chapter 8, 'Factors relating to the conversion of North Africa to Christianity', pp. 94-111.

[34] Ibid., p. 106.

Social condition and status of the church in Tertullian's time

The African Lucius Apuleius, a native of Madaura, had little
time for Christians and offers a scathing caricature of one, the
wife of a village baker, whom he describes as 'saeva, scaeva,
ebriosa, in rapinis turpibus avara, inimica fidei, hostis pudicitiae
. . .'[35] (violent, spiteful, a drunkard, mean in petty thefts, hostile
to faith, an enemy to chastity. . .).

Tertullian was evidently well-educated and displays a disdain
for the 'rude' and 'simple'.[36] The martyr Perpetua's high social
standing – she is described as 'honeste nata'[37] – though worthy of
comment, was not, it seems, unusual for a Carthaginian
Christian. According to D'Alès, mixed-class marriages were
common within the Christian congregations at both Carthage
and Rome.[38] Groh senses in Tertullian a profound dismay at the
sight of Christians, well schooled in the customs of Roman social
climbing, who seek the traditional goals of 'ambitio' and 'gloria'
rather than more appropriate Christian ones.[39] De Labriolle
asserts that the edict of the Roman bishop Callistus on the
readmission of adulterers to communion which so enraged
Hippolytus (and perhaps also Tertullian?) 'marque une phase
importante de l'adaptation de la discipline ecclésiastique aux
conditions réelles de l'humanité'.[40]

Certain of Tertullian's remarks in the treatise *De Idololatria*
imply that there were Christians in Carthage wealthy enough to
undertake significant civic responsibilities. He writes, 'Hinc
proxime disputatio oborta est, an servus dei alicuius dignitatis
aut potestatis administrationem capiat, si ab omni specie
idololatriae intactum se aut gratia aliqua aut astutia etiam

---

[35] *Metamorphoses*, ix, 14; see also the comprehensive work on the social make-up of the
Carthaginian church of G. Schoellegen, *Ecclesia Sordida? Zur Frage der sozialen
Schichtung frühchristlicher Gemeinden am Beispiel Karthagos zur Zeit Tertullians* (Münster,
1985), which I regret I have not seen. I have seen the largely favourable review of it by
Dennis E. Groh in *The Catholic Historical Review* 76 (1990), pp. 99-100.
[36] T. P. O'Malley, *Tertullian and the Bible* (Utrecht, 1967), p.168.
[37] *Passio Perpetuae et Felicitatis*, para.2.
[38] D'Alès, *La théologie de Tertullien*, p. 375.
[39] D .E. Groh, 'Tertullian's polemic against social co-optation', *CH* 40 (1971), p. 7.
[40] See *De Pudicitia* 1; P. de Labriolle, *Tertullien, De Paenitentia, De Pudicitia. Texte et
tradition* (Paris, 1906), p. XXXVII; also see Hippolytus, *Refutation of all Heresies*,IX,12,20-3.

praestare possit . . .' (17,2) (Hence there arose lately a dispute
over whether a servant of God should take on the administration
of any dignity or authority if he is able, either by special grace or
by adroitness, to keep himself undefiled by any species of
idolatry). Tertullian would surely not bother to deny expressly
to Christians the right to exercise the magisterial 'potestas vitae
necisque' (*De Idololatria* 17,3) unless there were significant
numbers of Christians qualified to do so. Murphy points out that
the financial burdens placed on the decurionate in the Late
Empire were onerous, and as such greatly resented.[41] Was the
reluctance of some wealthy Christians to undertake their civic
responsibilities another source of irritation to the wider public?
Many of Tertullian's writings suggest then that the church was
now confronted with social situations not at issue when the
church was drawn primarily from the poorer classes.

Tertullian's attack on those who avoid martyrdom by bribery
indicates that there were Christians, even whole congregations,
with sufficient resources to do so.[42] His description of a free-will
offering taken up during church services indicates moreover a
church with funds sufficient to aid the poor and destitute, slaves,
the shipwrecked, and the confessors.[43] The development of the
office of 'senior' in the African church was probably occasioned
by the necessity forced upon the church of having to deal with
the coming into its possession of substantial property and money.[44]

Barbara Aland sees evidence in the *Octavius* of the African
Minucius Felix – a contemporary of Tertullian – that the
church had begun to penetrate the upper echelons of Roman
society.[45] Though the ranks of the Christians would have
included many well-educated persons (Tertullian and Minucius
Felix are examples), the *Octavius* itself, however, does not
provide solid proof of this. Those addressed by the *Octavius*,
Aland says, 'know their Seneca and Cicero' (i.e. they are
well-educated).[46] These addressees were, however, educated

[41] G. J. Murphy, *The reign of the emperor Lucius Septimius Severus from the evidence of the inscriptions* (Philadelphia, 1945), p. 54.   [42] *De Fuga* 13,3.
[43] *Apologeticum* 39,5.6.   [44] See the section on 'seniores'.
[45] B. Aland, 'Christentum, Bildung und römische Obersicht. Zum "Octavius" des Minucius Felix', in *Platonismus und Christentum*, ed. H. D. Blume and F. Mann (1983), p. 30.   [46] Ibid. p. 16.

pagans and not Christians. The *Octavius* says more about the people Christian apologists sought to reach, than it does about the Christians themselves.

Military service for Christians appears to have become a major issue for the church during the time of Tertullian. The treatise *De Idololatria* is, by general agreement, earlier than the *De Corona*.[47] And yet, in complete contradiction to the pattern normally discernible in Tertullian's polemical writings, it is appreciably more rigorous and uncompromising in tone than *De Corona*. This Rordorf correctly explains as the result of the changing face and role of the army under the Severans.[48] *De Idololatria* was written before the radical militarisation of the empire under Severus had fully taken hold. Christian recruits joining the army or serving soldiers being converted were as yet the exception rather than the rule. Tertullian could afford to be uncompromising in his approach since the issue was still predominantly an academic one for most Christians. By the time of the writing of *De Corona*, however, the situation had altered dramatically. Christians in large numbers were being faced with both military service and a tradition of Christian non-involvement; upper-class Christians, in particular, faced formidable personal and social dilemmas. Tertullian, in the face of this social transformation, had either to offer realistic advice or find himself marginalised in the debate. Tertullian was passionate and generally uncompromising, but no fool. He could display, when appropriate, a certain pragmatism. Harnack argues that the young Christian soldier in *De Corona* may have been claiming for all Christian soldiers, of whom there were by now a considerable number, the same privileges as those granted to the adherents of the cult of Mithras.[49] This cult is probably that referred to as the 'camp of darkness' at various points in Tertullian's writings.[50]

---

[47] See my earlier note on the chronology of Tertullian's writings.

[48] W. Rordorf, 'Tertullians Beurteilung des Soldatenstandes', *VC* 23 (1969), p. 118.

[49] See Tertullian's reference to the 'fratres' of this soldier 'qui se duobus dominis servire posse praesumpserant' (1,1); see A. Harnack, *Militia Christi:the Christian religion and the military in the first three centuries*, (Philadelphia, 1983) p.83.

[50] J. Helgeland, 'Christians and the Roman army AD173-337', *CH* 43 (1974), p. 152.

THE SEVERANS

Any consideration of the reign of the Severans and the development of the North African church must pose the following questions: what impact did the elevation to the imperial throne of the African, Lucius Septimius Severus, have on the North African church? Did the rise to power of this African create a 'favourite son' consciousness among the subjects of the province? Did it make them more 'loyalist' than usual? And, did this create new problems for those who, like the Christians, were perceived as less than loyal? The North African veneration for the imperial favourite Serapis and the significance of this factor in the early-third-century persecution at Carthage (see above) makes this last proposition worth consideration.

The reign of Septimius Severus witnessed the conclusion of a development which had been in progress for nearly two centuries, the movement from the Principate established by Augustus to the absolutism of the Severans and their successors. In this process, says Hammond, Septimius Severus was 'a key figure in the transition from the early to the later Roman empire'.[51] It is clear that S. Severus displayed during his reign no marked preference for his native province.[52] There was, after all, according to Haywood, no African 'nationalism', no particular sense of 'African-ness' among people of the province.[53] Loyalties, such as they were, were given to towns, villages, or the various tribal groupings. S. Severus was himself a native of Leptis Magna, a town on the coast of what is now Libya, and not particularly an 'African'.

S. Severus was in many ways more Italian than Punic, having received the bulk of his formal education in Rome.[54] He did, it

---

[51] M. Hammond, 'Review of G .J. Murphy, *The reign of the emperor Lucius Septimius Severus from the evidence of the inscriptions*, 1947', *AJPh* 71 (1950), p. 202.

[52] T. D. Barnes, 'The family and career of Septimius Severus', *Historia* 16 (1967), p. 97; R. M. Haywood, 'The African policy of Septimius Severus', *Transactions of the American Philological Association* 71 (1940), p. 175; M. Benabou, *La résistance africaine à la romanisation* (Paris, 1976), p.166; Murphy, *The reign of S.Severus*, p.48.

[53] Haywood, 'African policy of S. Severus'.

[54] Barnes, 'Family and career of S. Severus', p. 94.

must be admitted, appoint a disproportionate number of his imperial officials from among his African compatriots. His Praetorian commander and, for a time, the second most important man in the empire after Severus himself was Plautianus, an African related to the Emperor through the latter's mother Fulvia Pia.[55] But this particular preference for Africans in the imperial service was common among his predecessors (none of whom was an African), with the exception only of Commodus.[56] Indeed, some Africans had been among his most vigorous opponents during the civil wars.[57] Provincials everywhere were enthusiastic for Severus, but this resulted more from an imperial anti-Italian policy which indirectly favoured them. Under Severus, maintains Benabou, there was 'une remarquable accélération du processus de romanisation'.[58]

Severus was interested and well versed in legal affairs. The greatest jurist of the period, Papinian, was an intimate;[59] Severus was also quite proficient in both Latin and Greek, even if he never lost his African accent.[60] Hammond questions the traditional view that Severus was primarily a military man who took to armed despotism like 'a fish to water'.[61] He argues that Severus, prior to his elevation to the imperial throne, was very much a career bureaucrat. Westermann and Schiller, while suggesting that the papyri evidence does not support Hammond's argument, contend, however, that it is most likely that Severus was a typical career politician who gradually worked his way up the imperial ladder through a series of administrative rather than military posts.[62] Barnes contends that, far from being a formidable military figure who was early identified as having

[55] Herodian iii,x,v.
[56] Haywood, 'African policy of S. Severus', p. 183.
[57] *Apol.* 35,11; Barnes, 'Family and career of S. Severus', p. 98.
[58] Benabou, *Résistance africaine*, p. 166.
[59] K. Hannestad, 'Septimius Severus in Egypt', *Classica et Mediaevalia* 6 (1944), p. 216.
[60] Dio Cassius, *Roman History* (LCL, 1969,) 76,17,2; Aelius Spartianus, *Scriptores Historiae Augustae* (LCL),19,10.
[61] M. Hammond, 'Septimius Severus, Roman bureaucrat', *Harvard Studies in Classical Philology* 51 (1940), pp. 137-73.
[62] W. L. Westermann and A. A. Schiller, *Apokrimata; decisions of Septimius Severus on legal matters* (New York, 1954), pp. 34 and 63.

leadership potential, it may have been the mediocrity of Severus which secured for him the crucial governorship of Pannonia Superior under Commodus.[63] His successes against both Niger and Albinus, and his policy of outright militarisation which so radically altered the face of the empire, have combined to produce the image of the old soldier, tried and tested on the field of battle, who was then called to discard his military cloak in the hour of the empire's greatest need and rise to her defence and reconstruction. Yet, as Socrates once observed, it is not always the best soldier who makes the most successful general, but rather the best administrator who knows how to organise, delegate, and maximise his resources.[64] While the available evidence might not permit complete agreement with Hammond's view, it represents a serious challenge to the more traditional ones.

There is a general agreement that army life after the accession of Severus became much more relaxed.[65] Soldiers' pay increased and families were allowed to live in the barracks. Yet, by the early third century military service occupied a position of low and diminishing public esteem.[66] A soldier was more likely to see action while breaking up a public brawl than he was on the field of combat. The military increasingly took on police and public order responsibilities. The army was provincialised. Severus' advice to his sons to 'be harmonious, to enrich the soldiers and to scorn all other men'[67] was indeed a mark of his own style. Severus, reports Dio, 'placed his own safety in the strength of the army'.[68] Murphy speaks of the 'military absolutism' of Severus.[69] And yet, says Herodian, the largesse of Septimius Severus 'undermined the discipline of the army',[70] and thus lowered its efficiency and morale.

In the area of social legislation Severus demonstrates some enlightened views. His legislation on such diverse matters as abortion, the rights of minors, and the status of slaves, reflects mildness, equity and a recognition of the inherent value of

[63] Barnes, 'Family and career of S. Severus', p. 94.
[64] Xenophon, *Memorabilia Sokratis* iii, 4,6.
[65] E.g. H.M.D. Parker, *A history of the Roman world from* AD *138-337* (London, 1935), p. 86.
[66] Harnack, *Militia Christi*, p. 84.   [67] Dio Cassius 76,15,2.   [68] 75,2,3.
[69] Murphy, *The reign of S. Severus*, p. 36.   [70] III,8,5.

human life.[71] His anti-adultery legislation is also of some interest. The young Severus was allegedly charged with though he was later acquitted of adultery.[72] His own wife Julia Domna is reported – here Aelian is supported by Herodian – as having been notorious ('famosa') for her adulterous liaisons.[73] The Alexandrians referred to her as 'Jocasta', believing her guilty of incest with one or both of her quarrelling sons.[74] Since adultery laws had existed since the time of Augustus it is unlikely that Severus himself introduced such legislation. However, he does appear to have strengthened the hand of the courts in enforcing the law. While Severus eventually gave up the cause, Dio maintains that he personally saw some 3,000 indictments prepared against Roman citizens for adultery.[75] Tertullian himself makes reference to the existence of these adultery laws and Dolger contends that one of the reasons for Tertullian's obsession with the sins of adultery and fornication was his indignation and regret that Catholic bishops appeared to take these matters less seriously than did the Roman authorities.[76]

Despite his provision of a Christian nurse for the young Caracalla and the church's enjoyment of a period of comparative freedom from official persecution under Severus (and his son), 202 and 203 saw major persecutions in both Carthage and Alexandria, followed by another in Carthage under the Proconsulship of Scapula, in the first year of Caracalla's reign.[77]

On the question of the divinised status of the emperor, Murphy contends, on the basis of official inscriptions, that Severus was the first Roman emperor to be commonly called 'dominus noster'.[78] Caligula, Nero and Domitian had, in their time, claimed such a title, and Antoninus had been called 'Kyrios' in some Eastern provinces; yet for none of them did the title 'Lord' become a permanent appellation. McCann's study of the images and portraits of the era provides strong support for Murphy's claims.[79] In many of his portraits for example,

---

[71] Parker, *History of the Roman World*, p. 75; see also Platnauer, *Life and reign of S. Severus*, p.181.   [72] Aelian ii,2.   [73] xviii,8.   [74] Herodian iv,9,3.   [75] 76,16,4.

[76] *Ad Nationes* 1,6,3; see F. J. Dolger, 'Achtung des Ehebruch in der Kultsatzung', *AC* 3 (1932), p. 147.

[77] *Ad Scapulam* 4,5; see Parker, *History of the Roman World*, p. 137.

[78] Murphy, *The Reign of S. Severus*, p. 102.

[79] A. M. McCann, *The portraits of Septimius Severus* (Rome, 1968).

Severus is shown as having adopted the corkscrew locks of the god Serapis.[80] Says McCann, 'Previous studies have indicated that the idea of the emperor as divine is not new to Roman thought, but for no previous emperor is there such an array of portrait types with divine connotations'.[81] Severus is even said to have claimed – with allusion to Hercules – to have been the cosmocrator (ruler of the world) of the lower world.[82]

This claim to 'Lordship' had implications both religious and social, and the master-slave relationship of the ruler and the ruled in the empire became most pronounced under the Severans. Tertullian's comment in the *Apologeticum* – the context is his discussion on the appropriateness of a Christian calling the emperor 'dominus' – that 'ceterum liber sum illi' (34,1) (In all else I am a free man as far as he (i.e. the Emperor) is concerned) takes on a particular significance. For Tertullian, the God of the Christians is alone the absolute Lord.[83]

MITHRAS

Finally, in any consideration of the reign of the Severans and the situation of the church in the late-second/early-third centuries, there must be reference made to the cult of Mithras. In the same way as orthodox Christians of the same period still seem to have feared the Marcionite churches as the most significant threat from among the heretics to the position of the Catholic church, so it appears did they fear the cult of Mithras as the major threat from among the pagans. In an age of increasing militarisation a predominantly male and military cult must have loomed large in the background of Christian apologetics. The similarities of certain of its ritual forms to those of Christian practice were remarked upon by Tertullian himself.[84] The contention that Tertullian's 'camp of darkness' was indeed the cult of Mithras has much to commend it.[85] Vermaseren points out that Mithraic temples were dark and windowless and Tertullian in *De Corona*

---

[80] Ibid., p. 56.   [81] Ibid., p. 57.   [82] Ibid., p. 52.
[83] For Tertullian 'potestas' is consistently an attribute of God alone and can only be delegated to others.
[84] *De Praescriptione 40,4*; see Guignebert, *Tertullien*, p. 237, note 1.
[85] Helgeland, 'Christians and the Roman army', p. 152.

asks wryly how the followers of Mithras can worship a god of light in the darkness![86] The cult's belief in an eternal struggle between the powers of light and darkness – reflecting its Iranian origins – had much in common with Christian perspectives, and it would have appeared an attractive alternative to many waverers in Christian ranks, particularly among those serving in the army.

Renan, in a celebrated statement on Mithraism, asserted that 'si le christianisme eût été arrêté dans sa croissance par quelque maladie mortelle, le monde eût été mithraiste'.[87] Speidel, speaking of the spread of the cult, states that it 'engulfed the Roman empire during the first four centuries of the Christian era. Mithraic sanctuaries are found from Roman Arabia to Britain, from the Danube to the Sahara, wherever the Roman soldier went. . .'[88] Speidel speaks of it offering 'a highly developed religious life' and 'establishing a comprehensive and detailed view of the cosmos and man's rule in it, in this life and beyond'.[89]

Renan's assertion, once widely accepted, is now very much disputed. Brandon questions it and doubts whether there even existed a formal statement of Mithraic beliefs or any fixed description or form for its cultic practices.[90] Simon, too, in a most thorough treatment of the matter, questions whether the cult was in fact ever a serious rival to Christianity,[91] though this does not mean that it cannot have been perceived as such by Tertullian and others in North Africa. Vermaseren clearly offers us the most comprehensive treatment of the cult presently available.[92] He provides conclusive proof of the vast and powerful Severan patronage of the cult, and demonstrates how the Severan preference for the worship of Serapis was linked to that of Mithras.[93] Worship of and reverence for Serapis was

---

[86] M. J. Vermaseren, *Mithras, the secret god* (London, 1963), p. 38. See *De Corona* 15,3.

[87] *Marc-Aurèle*, p. 579.

[88] M. P. Speidel, *Mithras – Orion: Greek hero and Roman army god* (Leiden, 1980), p. 1.

[89] Ibid. p. 47.

[90] S. G. F. Brandon, 'Mithraism and its challenge to Christianity', *Hibbert Journal* 53 (1954/55), p. 111.

[91] M. Simon, 'Mithra, rival du Christ?', *Etudes Mithraiques* (Leiden, 1978), pp. 457-478.

[92] Vermaseren, *Mithras*.   [93] Ibid., p. 34f.

adopted by many worshippers of Mithras, and Serapis was associated with the latter in a number of inscriptions and images dating from the time of the Severans. We see this at the Aventine Mithraeum in Rome, at the Mithraeum in the Baths of Caracalla at Rome, and at the Walbrook Mithraeum in London.[94]

Vermaseren also highlights a number of similarities with Christian practice, some clear and direct, others obscure and indirect. An inscription from the Aventine – dated to the first decade of the third century AD – shows that those initiated into the cult were regarded as having been 'born at first light' ('natus prima luce').[95] The head of each Mithraic community was called the 'pater' and the members 'fratres'.[96] Another inscription at Rome refers to the divine 'refrigerium' (refreshment) as one of the benefits of participation in the cult.[97] Tertullian, in the *Apologeticum*, likewise refers to the 'refrigerium' acquired by Christian believers.[98] Vermaseren also offers other comparisons.[99] And yet he, like many others, dismisses Renan's claim as 'too sweeping'.[100] It has even been suggested that Tertullian was himself once an initiate of the cult.[101]

---

[94] Ibid., pp. 44, 49 and 54f.
[95] Ibid., p. 44 and 75. 25 December was the date of the annual Mithraic festival when the birth of the god was celebrated along with the advent of the new light.
[96] Ibid., pp. 79, 129 and 153.
[97] This is found on the walls of the Aventine Mithraeum at Sancta Prisca, ibid., p. 88.
[98] *Apol.* 39,16.
[99] He compares the Mithraic community meal with the Christian eucharist (p. 129), and speaks of the Mithraic myth of the Ascension of the god himself (p.130). Among the worshippers of Mithras, and certainly among their priests, remarriage was not permitted, reminiscent indeed of rigorist Christians like Tertullian (p. 131)! As part of their initiation rites, the 'miles' – or third grade in their hierarchy, for which a scorpion was the symbol – took a 'sacramentum' or oath. Vermaseren, *Mithras*, p. 187, also speaks of the attractions of an oriental cult 'which establishes personal relationships with the chosen deity' and a sense of personal salvation from all the turmoil of this life, but without all the exotic manifestations normally associated with such cults. Such was also, in part, one of the attractions of the Christian faith.
[100] Ibid., p. 188.
[101] De Labriolle, *History and literature of Christianity from Tertullian to Boethius* (London, 1924), p. 61 raises a most interesting suggestion when he considers the possibility that Tertullian himself, prior to his conversion, may have been an initiate into the cult of Mithras; this would explain both Tertullian's detailed knowledge of the cult's practices and his considerable aversion to it. De Labriolle wonders whether there is in Tertullian's words in *De Praescriptione*, 'et, si adhuc memini Mithrae, signet illic in frontibus milites suos' (40,4), an 'enigmatic allusion' (p. 61. note 5) to such a time in the African's life. This presents a most intriguing possibility indeed!

CHAPTER 2

Tertullian's relationship to the Catholic church

The relationship between the question of Tertullian's association with the Catholic church of his time and that with the New Prophecy movement is crucial. Neither question can be dealt with adequately without taking the other into account. Thus, while each will be given a separate treatment, there must be some overlap.

INTRODUCTION: THE PROBLEM

It has been a commonplace over the years to assert or simply to accept as given that at some time, probably the middle years of the first decade of the third century, Tertullian defected from the Catholic church and joined a schismatic conventicle comprised of Carthaginian adherents of the Phrygian New Prophecy movement; and further, that from this new base he launched his savage, vitriolic attacks on the Carthaginian Catholic hierarchy. Numerous passages from his writings which would appear, on the surface, to provide evidence of such a separation – along with remarks by Jerome, Augustine and others – are marshalled into line to support such contentions. Alternative interpretations will be suggested here for those passages which bring into question the reliability of Jerome and Augustine in this matter, and other evidence adduced, both from the writings of Tertullian and elsewhere, to support a contrary proposition, to the effect that Tertullian probably never left the Catholic church at all.

Nowhere in his extant writings, except in the most vague terms, does Tertullian give a description of the nature or the inner workings of the sort of conventicle or Montanist 'church'

to which he is alleged to have belonged; that is, unless the
reference to the expulsion of a person from the church for
adultery at *De Pudicitia* 7,22 is to a formally constituted New
Prophecy group. How one wishes that we possessed Tertullian's
treatise *De Ecstasi* – now unfortunately lost – for it was ecstasy,
according to Tertullian 'de quo cum inter nos et psychicos
quaestio est' (*Adv. Marcionem* IV,22,5)(concerning which there
is a matter of dispute between us and the carnally minded).
Nowhere does he urge anyone, not even his Catholic friends
whom he evidently addresses in a number of his later 'Montanist'
works, to leave the Catholic church and join his own group.[1]
Nowhere, not even when he repudiates particular Catholic
bishops – as he does on occasion – as being unworthy pastors of
the people of God (despite, or perhaps because of, what one
commentator calls his 'grand respect for the hierarchy'[2]), does
he actually repudiate or even challenge the notion of a Catholic
hierarchy as such. Indeed, there are a number of passages from
his later works – his 'Montanist' period – which will support a
contention contrary to that traditionally adopted; namely,
that Tertullian never left the Catholic church, but rather
continued his fight for a more vigorous and disciplined Christian
discipleship from within the Catholic church itself; and further,
that the so-called 'Psychici', whom Tertullian so maligns, are
not to be identified with the Catholic church and its hierarchy
in toto, but rather with a particular element within that
church.[3] Moingt asserts that the 'Psychici' are not necessarily
to be identified with the 'simplices' and that the former
apparently kept aloof from the struggles with 'Praxeas'.[4] That
Tertullian was not alone within the North African church in
repudiating what he perceived as a compromising approach,
particularly with respect to the matter of penitential discipline,
is clear both from his own writings and from comments made

---

[1] E.g. *De Exhortatione Castitatis* 1, *De Fuga* 1,1.
[2] Monceaux, *Histoire Littéraire*, p. 394.
[3] At 1 Corinthians 2,14 Paul attacks the '*psychikos anthropos*'; Tertullian employs this
term of abuse exclusively – apart from two references in *Adv. Marcionem*, two in *Adv.
Praxean* and one in *De Pallio* – in *De Monogamia* (ten times), *De Pudicitia* (six) and *De
Ieiunio* (five). See note 4 in my earlier note on the chronology of Tertullian's writings.
[4] J. Moingt, *Théologie trinitaire de Tertullien.* Vol.1, (Paris, 1969), pp. 120 and 122.

by Cyprian.[5] Tertullian's 'breakaway' from the Catholic church
need not be exaggerated; for he fought only on the narrow
front of penitential discipline.[6]

THE EVIDENCE: THE TEXT

At *Adv. Praxean* 1,7 Tertullian states that on account of their
acknowledgement and defence of the Paraclete ('agnitio Paracleti
atque defensio') he and some unnamed associates separated
from the 'Psychici'. This 'disiunxit' does not imply a formal act
of schism from the Catholic church. It is more likely that by
'Psychici' Tertullian means only one particular element in the
life of the church, and not the whole hierarchy and general
membership. Apart from this use of 'disiungere', Tertullian uses
it at least twenty times.[7] In fifteen of these – *Adv. Marcionem* I,4,1;
IV,34,6; 34,2.7 (twice); V,7,6.7 (twice); *Ad Uxorem* I,3,1.4,2; II,2,7.8;
De Patientia 12,5; *De Monogamia* 9,1.4;10,8; *De Exhortatione
Castitatis* 1,5; *De Ieiunio* 1,1 – it is used of the dissolution of a
marriage, while in the other five – *De Resurrectione Carnis* 59,7; *De
Anima* 27,2; 57,2; *De Carne Christi* 10,2 – it is used of the
separation and distinction of natures in philosophical debate. If
Tertullian saw his separation from the 'Psychici' as a kind of
'marriage' dissolution, this need not imply an act of formal
schism, but at most a decision to distance himself from an
element within the church with which he had perhaps at one
time been closely identified. Nowhere, for example, does Tertullian
say that the Catholic church leadership was in its entirety
'carnally minded', and indeed at *De Ieiunio* 16,3 he acknowledges
the existence in the Catholic church of spiritually minded
bishops, 'haec erunt exempla et populo et episcopis, etiam
spiritualibus...' (These will be warnings both to the people and
to bishops, even spiritual ones...).

Cyprian speaks likewise of bishops of a previous generation
from his own province who adopted a position similar to that

[5] Ep. 55,21.
[6] M. Bévenot, 'Tertullian's thoughts about the Christian priesthood', in *Corona
Gratiarum* (1975), p. 131.
[7] G. Claesson, *Index Tertullianeus* (Paris, 1974/75).

advocated by Tertullian concerning the readmission to communion of adulterers and fornicators, and yet who did not see it as
necessary to secede from the church.[8] Tertullian cannot have
been alone, nor, what is more, need he have looked outside of the
Catholic church for influential support. Above all, we need to be
particularly wary of adopting a view of the early third-century
church as some sort of monolith.

Elsewhere in his treatise against the modalist heresy of
'Praxeas', Tertullian makes reference to 'nos', by which he
clearly means both himself and his fellow adherents of the New
Prophecy. In earlier days Tertullian had always referred to the
church of which he was then a most staunch defender as 'nos', as
opposed to the 'vos' who were the heretics and pagans. He seems
now to use the latter with telling effect against those with whom
he was, by his own admission, formerly associated. At *Adv.
Praxean* 2,1 he maintains that 'we' (i.e. he and his New Prophecy
colleagues) have been better instructed (sc. than other Christians)
by the Paraclete ('nos...instructiores per Paracletum') in
understanding the precise nature of the Godhead. At 3,1 he
describes how they (i.e. the New Prophets) are accused by the
'simplices' – that is, the unlettered majority of church members
who are too easily led astray by the beguiling teachings of this
'Praxeas' – of preaching two, or even three, Gods, '...itaque
duos et tres iam iactitant a nobis praedicari, se vero unius Dei
cultores praesumunt...' (...therefore they make a show that
there are two and three gods preached by us, while they presume
themselves to be the worshippers of the one God ...). In neither
of these references is there any evidence of schism. Both suggest
more the flavour of a select group within the church – an
'ecclesiola in ecclesia' – undertaking the self-appointed task of
'saving' the orthodox from the dangers of heterodoxy. Barnes is
right when he says that 'the *Adv. Praxean* exemplifies a paradox.
Tertullian helped to rescue the Catholic church from theological
heresy precisely because he was a Montanist'.[9] Further, while
the 'nos' at 13,5 undoubtedly refers to the New Prophecy group,
the 'apud nos' at 8,3 – placed in the context of a series of

---

[8] Ep. 55,21.   [9] Barnes, *Tertullian*, p. 142.

scriptural quotations referring to the relationship of the Father
and the Son and designed to refute a Valentinian heresy – the
'nos' at 11,2, the 'nostrorum' at 5,3, and the 'praescriptio nostra'
at 11,4 seem to make no distinction between Catholic and New
Prophet. Further examples of the first person plural in *Adv.
Praxean*, such as 'nobis omnes scripturae' at 24,3, 'invenimus' at
27,10 and 'videmus' at 27,11 are nothing more than an
impersonal 'we', and say nothing of factional preferences.

At *De Pudicitia* 1,10 Tertullian speaks figuratively of the
indictment which he would personally enter 'adversus meae
quoque sententiae retro penes illos (sc. Psychicos) societatem...'
(against that fellowship of opinion which I previously enjoyed
with them...). This does not require the conclusion of formal
schism. It means only that Tertullian no longer regards himself as
'at one' with that element in the church which, in his renewed
desire for greater discipline and rigour in the life of the church, he
now brands (in the language of the New Prophecy) as 'Psychici'
or 'carnally minded'. In classical Latin 'societas' can have the
meaning either of a formal association or alliance, or of a close
relationship or affinity. In the passage in question, the latter is the
more likely to represent accurately Tertullian's thought. Later in
the same passage Tertullian speaks of the 'plures' and the 'pauci'
– and of his own identification with the latter – as indicating a
division into 'majority' and 'minority' positions over the matter
of penitential discipline, the former supporting a less rigorous
position. This suggests a single factionalised church rather than
two formally separated ones. And again, we have Cyprian's
witness that Tertullian need not have gone outside the Catholic
church to find support for his rigorous views.

At *De Pudicitia* 1,20, after stating that remarriage 'post fidem'
is not permitted among adherents to the New Prophecy ('nobis'),
Tertullian continues, 'et ideo durissime nos infamantes Paracletum
disciplinae enormitate digamos foris sistimus...' (and for that
reason we expel the twice-married as bringing dishonour upon
the Paraclete by the irregularity of their discipline...). While
this passage could suggest a formal, separated discipline, it
actually requires no more than the existence of an 'ecclesiola in
ecclesia'. Translation of 'foris sistimus' as 'we excommunicate'

has a more formal tone than the sense requires. Something akin to the earlier 'societatis repudium' (1,10) is more likely to be implied here. 'Repudium' – like 'disiungere' – often can bear the meaning of a marriage dissolution in Tertullian, though nothing quite so formal is necessarily implied here. A similar interpretation can equally well be applied to the 'penes nos' at *De Pudicitia* 4,5 whereby secret extra-ecclesial marriages are condemned by the New Prophets as being virtual adultery. The notion of the 'dissolution' of Tertullian's 'marriage' with the 'Psychici' again does not entail the conclusion of what is regarded by some as a formal 'rupture' with the church, that is, as schism.

At *De Pudicitia* 5,12 Tertullian asserts that 'etiam apud Christianos non est moechia sine nobis' (Even among Christians there is no adultery without us). By this he means not that the New Prophecy group provides the prime examples of fornicatory behaviour, but rather that unless they expose and condemn such practices, the latter would probably go unnoticed and unchecked within the Catholic church! While this claim recognises the New Prophecy group as a distinct entity within the wider Catholic community, it does not require the assumption of a separated church. The phrase 'nostra esse' at *De Pudicitia* 5,15 likewise conveys merely the sense of 'taking sides' in a dispute, not of schism.

At *De Pudicitia* 10,12 Tertullian condemns the *Shepherd* of Hermas for its alleged compromising attitude towards the reconciliation of adulterers, and claims that the work has been condemned as well 'ab omni concilio ecclesiarum etiam vestrarum' (by every council of the churches, even of yours). Leaving aside the question of the accuracy of this assertion, this passage does not require the conclusion of two separated churches, let alone of two separate sets of councils. First, there is little likelihood that the New Prophecy movement held formal councils of its own; there is, moreover, no necessary contrast here of 'your churches' against 'our churches'. Second, all that Tertullian requires is that the 'Psychici' own the uncompromising decisions of those church councils with which they would normally associate themselves. That there were, however, no exclusively African councils in Tertullian's own time is clear from his own testimony. The phrase can, however, indicate both particular African ecclesial assemblies (albeit not councils in any formal sense) and also an emphatic demand on the part of Tertullian for the 'compromisers' to heed previous 'conciliar' decisions much as he himself implicitly claims to do.

At *De Pudicitia* 12,9 Tertullian speaks of a 'nobiscum pactus Spiritus sanctus' as a very special 'relationship' enjoyed by the Spirit and the New Prophets. There is here no sense of a formal schism, but only of an especially 'gifted' group within the church, much as even today some Christian groups refer to 'Spirit-filled ministries' as opposed to the more traditional ones.

What was said earlier concerning the deliberations and determinations of ecclesial councils can be said also with regard to Tertullian's rather pointed question to the 'Psychici' at *De Pudicitia* 21,16 (in relation to the power of forgiving serious sins), 'Quid nunc et ad ecclesiam, et quidem tuam, psychice' (What now [has this to do] with the church, and indeed your [church], Carnal man?). The blunt 'your (church)' has probably again a pejorative emphasis – and no evidence of formal separation – although Powell's contention that Tertullian means here to contrast the 'Psychics'' concept of the church and its claimed authority with his own view of an authentically 'spiritual' church[10] has some appeal.

At *De Pudicitia* 1,7-8, where Tertullian speaks of the 'edict' issued by the 'bishop of bishops' and read in the church, it is clear that he means the Catholic church. His description of this church as 'virgo', as 'sponsa Christi', and as 'vera... udica ... sancta' would surely not suit one who had utterly repudiated that church and formally withdrawn from it. Further, at *De Pudicitia* 1,5, Tertullian states that 'nostrorum bonorum status iam mergitur...' (It is now the position of our own good things which is sinking...), in which by 'nostrorum' he clearly includes both Catholics and New Prophets. At *De Pudicitia* 19,5 Tertullian also seems, by the expression 'apud nos' – within a reference to the practice of receiving heretics into the orthodox church by way of (re)baptism – to include both Catholics and New Prophets. It must be acknowledged that Tertullian does speak

---

[10] D. Powell, 'Tertullianists and Cataphrygians', *VC* 29 (1975), p. 35.

at times as if he were outside the Catholic church but only 'as if'. Tertullian is not outside it. To speak in this way is not unknown in the best of families!

At *De Monogamia* 12,3 Tertullian complains to the 'Psychici' that 'digami [episcopi] praesident apud vos' (Twice-married [bishops] preside over you). There is no evidence here of two formally separated churches, but only the allegation that most Catholics accepted without protest twice-married (does not mean bigamist) bishops as leaders of their church. From these persons Tertullian preferred publicly to dissociate himself. The extent to which such appointments applied in the North African church is unknown, but Tertullian's well-known penchant for exaggeration cannot be discounted here.

At *De Monogamia* 11,2 – as at *De Pudicitia* 1,7-8 – Tertullian's manner of speaking of the church as 'virgo' and as 'sponsa Christi' would be unusual for a formal schismatic who denies the legitimacy of that church.[11] Now, while his use of the first person plural at 1,2 of the treatise – 'penes nos' – and at 4,1 – 'mentio Paracleti, ut nostri alicuius auctoris' (the mention of the Paraclete, as of some authority of our own) – clearly indicates the New Prophecy movement, that at 9,8 – 'nobis . . . ne nubere quidem licebit . . .' (to us . . . even marriage indeed is not permitted . . .), in opposition to pagan Roman practice – denotes orthodox Christians in general.

The treatise *De Ieiunio* contains some of Tertullian's most vitriolic attacks on the Catholic leadership. For example, at 12,3, where he refers to one disreputable Pristinus as 'vester non Christianus martyr' (yours, not a Christian martyr), he seems almost to deny to the non-adherents of the New Prophecy the status of Christian altogether. This, however, is polemic-inspired exaggeration, and not a reflection of Tertullian's true position. At *De Ieiunio* 1, 4-5, where Tertullian defends the doctrinal orthodoxy of the New Prophecy movement, he maintains that the latter teaches more frequent fasting than marrying – unlike the 'Psychici'! – and continues, 'arguunt nos, quod ieiunia propria custodiamus, quod stationes plerumque in vesperam

---

[11] In *De Monogamia* Tertullian is probably addressing a Catholic friend.

producamus' (they charge us with maintaining fasts of our own, with prolonging our stations often into the evening). Such charges would probably only make sense if they were directed against a somewhat exclusivist group, yet one still clearly within the church 'fold' – a third-century 'Holy Club' – rather than against a formally separated conventicle.

At *De Anima* 9,4 Tertullian writes of a New Prophecy 'sister' who experienced visions during regular worship services and 'post transacta sollemnia, dismissa plebe, quo usu solet nobis renuntiare quae viderit' (After sacred services are concluded, and the people have been dismissed, by regular custom she recounts to us what she has seen). Tertullian describes here a New Prophecy group staying behind, after the bulk of worshippers have been dismissed, to listen to a 'sister's' report. One assertion, that the worship service was a New Prophecy one and that Tertullian was one of the Montanist clergy who met with the woman to evaluate the authenticity of the purported vision is baseless conjecture.[12] There is no schism here, but rather clear evidence of faction. Further, Tertullian's first person plural references at 7,1 – 'ad nostros [sc. magistros]', as over against pagan officials – and at 43,6 – 'apud nos', as over against pagan philosophers – are references to orthodox Christians generally, with no specific differentiation between Catholics and New Prophets.

At *De Virginibus Velandis* 2,2 Tertullian discusses the varied customs of the churches in the matter of veils. He declares that 'una ecclesia sumus' (We are one church). This is surely not the declaration of a schismatic. At 3,1 he refers to the fact that 'apud nos ad usque proxime' (until very recently among us) the veiling or non-veiling of virgins was a matter of personal and local

---

[12] J. H. Waszink, *Tertullian's De Anima*, p. 169, argues that Tertullian's description of the scrupulousness of the examination of the woman's visions, 'nam et diligentissime digerentur, ut etiam probentur' (for they are examined most scrupulously so that they may be confirmed), would not have been necessary had the service been a Catholic one; he did so to emphasise the probity of Montanist practice. Such emphasis would, however, be appropriate even if Tertullian were speaking only of a New Prophecy group meeting after a regular Catholic service. It is interesting to note that Waszink, despite De Labriolle's claim that the expression 'de anima disserveramus' demonstrates that Tertullian was the preacher at this service, does not accept that Tertullian was a presbyter.

choice. 'Apud nos' cannot here refer to the New Prophecy movement alone; it must refer to the whole church. Such identification of New Prophets and Catholics as 'we' belies formal schism. At 11,6, after speaking about certain heathen customs and practices, Tertullian again refers to related practices 'apud nos'. Again, he clearly means by this 'nos' all orthodox Christians. The same is true for the passage at 17,3 where he says 'nobis Dominus etiam revelationibus velaminis spatia metatus est' (to us the Lord has even by revelations measured the spacing of the veil), though, soon after, his comment 'nam cuidam sorori nostrae' (shades indeed of *De Anima* 9,4!) is clearly a reference exclusively to the New Prophecy group.

As regards *De Exhortatione Castitatis* 12,6, however, I am not as convinced as Powell that the 'someone from among the brethren' ('quendam ex fratribus') must be a Catholic.[13] It is not clear whether Tertullian is criticising the 'brother' for taking a second wife (barren or not) – in which case a Catholic would be meant – or whether he is praising the example set by a New Prophet who has shown the right path by taking a 'spiritual' wife. However, while it is probable that the latter interpretation is correct, it is possible also that Tertullian is speaking fraternally of a person not belonging to his New Prophecy coterie. Further, with respect to Tertullian's employment of the first person plural as a possible indicator of division in *De Exhortatione Castitatis*, his use of it twice at 12,1, 'non enim et nos milites sumus' (for are we not soldiers?) and 'non et nos peregrinates – in isto saeculo – sumus' (and are we not travellers in this age?), and twice at 12,5, 'praecipue apud nos' and 'puto nobis', probably includes all orthodox Christians.

At least one other such reference from a later work of Tertullian, at *De Corona* 5,1, 'puto autem naturae (dominus) deus noster' (But I think that our God is the lord of nature), also refers clearly to Christians generally. The evidence for Tertullian's supposed schism provided by Jerome is so obviously drawn by inference from Tertullian's writings that its independent value is negligible.[14] Likewise, the value of the comments on Tertullian's

---

[13] Powell, 'Tertullianists', p. 34.
[14] *De Viris Illustribus* 53. Barnes has already decisively demonstrated the negligible value of this as evidence; see *Tertullian*, pp. 3f.

career to be found in Augustine's *De Haeresibus* and in *Praedestinatus* is equally open to question.[15] The source for Augustine's assertion that Tertullian was a schismatic is no better placed than Jerome's and may well be based on nothing other than his own inference from the existence of the previously schismatic 'Tertullianistai' in his own day. The existence of such a group nearly two centuries after Tertullian's own time tells very little about Tertullian's own particular allegiances. That such a group formally separated themselves from the Catholic church and took as their eponym one whose ideas, in their view, demanded such action, is not improbable, but tells us nothing about Tertullian himself. The parallels with John Wesley and his early followers who remained, in their own view, convinced and loyal members of the Church of England, but whose activities clearly precipitated the eventual breakaway of the Methodist connexion, are helpful here.[16]

Finally, we have the testimony of Cyprian, the first major Western theologian to maintain both in practice and in theory no real distinction between heresy and schism.[17] He attacks the Cataphrygians (Montanists) of his own day as heretics and was, it is reported, at the same time a frequent reader and great admirer of Tertullian, his 'Master'.[18] This information comes from the for-once reliable Jerome who, on this occasion at least, bases his account on a named and verifiable source.[19] The question then arises: would Cyprian, the arch-foe of schismatic and heretic alike, have so highly regarded a schismatic who had lived in his city only a generation or so earlier?

We might also note the views of three eminent scholars on this issue. De Labriolle, who also makes much of Tertullian's employment of 'nos' to designate even non-New Prophecy Christians (i.e. Catholics) in his later 'Montanist' works, states that 'il est visible qu'il [sc. Tertullian] tend, de plus en plus, à séparer sa vie morale de celle de l'Eglise'.[20] This, then, is

---

[15] i, 86; i, 86.
[16] Tertullian/Wesley probably died a Catholic/Anglican whatever separated conventicle/ church ('Tertullianist' or 'Methodist') developed later out of his work and teachings.
[17] See, e.g., his 'habere iam non potest Deum patrem, qui ecclesiam non habet matrem', *De Unitate Ecclesiae* 6; see also *Epp.* 44,2; 49,1; 52,2 and 74,7.
[18] *Ep.* 75,7.   [19] *De Vir. Illustr.* 53.
[20] De Labriolle, *La crise montaniste* (Paris, 1913), pp.356 and 418.

Tertullian's 'divorce' from the 'Psychici'. It is a movement of the mind rather than of the body, one of attitude rather than of a physical separation. Monceaux is of the view that Tertullian's argument was with 'les chefs de l'Eglise' more so than with the church itself, and that it was against the former that he turned rather than against the latter.[21] Moingt's assertion that 'alors même qu'il [sc. Tertullian] avait cessé de fréquenter les réunions cultuelles de son église, il ne laissait donc pas de se sentir rattaché à elle par la communauté de la foi et de la tradition' makes a crucial point.[22] Tertullian's previous personal attachment to the church would not have been so easily broken as some would have us believe.

Tertullian probably knew nothing of the later schismatic (and even heretical) 'Montanism' (a term never actually used by him) but rather only the original, orthodox and loyal New Prophecy.[23] His own was a loyalty which was to be severely tested, but Tertullian's earlier assertion at *De Baptismo* 17,2 that 'episcopatus aemulatio scismatum mater est' (Envy of the episcopate is the mother of schisms) would have been a sentiment from which he would ultimately not have retreated, whatever the perceived provocation. We must rethink Tertullian's relationship to the Catholic church and thereby our understanding of his doctrines of church and ministry. But we must also reconsider the question of his relationship to the New Prophecy movement of the day, and to the ideas of the Montanists generally, before we can have before us the whole picture. Such a task will be ours in the succeeding section. First, however, we must consider the question of Tertullian's presbyteral status.

WAS TERTULLIAN A PRESBYTER?

The primary evidence for an answer in the affirmative to this particular question can be found in Jerome's admiring paragraph on Tertullian.[24] There is also the suggestion that the first person plural at *De Anima* 9,4 – 'disserveramus', a reference to an act of preaching in a regular service of worship – implies that it was

[21] Monceaux, *Histoire littéraire*, p. 134.　　[22] Moingt, *Théologie trinitaire*, p. 134.
[23] Powell, 'Tertullianists', passim.　　[24] *De Vir. Illustr.* 55.

Tertullian himself who was the preacher, and therefore at least a presbyter. Waszink adopts this view, but insists that the service in question was in fact a Montanist one; and that Tertullian, far from being a Catholic cleric, was actually a Montanist one.[25] An impressive array of authorities align themselves on the side of those who consider Tertullian to have been a presbyter in the Carthaginian Catholic church, or at least to have been one prior to his alleged 'rupture' with that church.[26] They do so particularly with their interpretation of Tertullian's meaning at *De Exhortatione Castitatis* 7,3, 'Nonne et laici sacerdotes sumus?' (And are not we laypersons also priests?) – normally a proof text for those who wish to maintain a lay status for Tertullian (myself included); this sentence they translate as 'Est-ce que, même laics, nous ne sommes pas prêtres?', that is, as a proof text for the opposite contention. Too many of their own preconceptions are read into the sentence; a simple reading of it surely provides proof of Tertullian's lay status. A few commentators, alone among the greater names in patristic scholarship who have ventured an opinion on this question, reserve their judgement.[27] Barnes, as part of a very effective demolition of the evidentiary value of Jerome, casts grave doubts on Tertullian ever having held clerical status, while Teeuwen finds it odd that a supposed priest makes so little use of 'der Kultussprache'.[28]

Jerome's evidence is not particularly helpful and seems to rely

[25] Waszink, *De Anima*, p. 169.
[26] Quasten, *Patrology II: the ante-Nicene literature after Irenaeus* (Maryland, 1984), p. 246, de Labriolle, *La crise montaniste*, p. 306 on the basis of *De Anima* 9.4 and of *De Exhortatione Castitatis* 7,3 (see below) – though elsewhere he has been more cautious about Tertullian's status, 'Tertullien, était-il prêtre?', *Bulletin d'ancienne littérature et d'archéologie chrétiennes* 3 (1913), p. 61 – Monceaux, *Histoire littéraire*, p.182 and van Beneden, *Aux origines d'une terminologie sacramentelle* (Louvain, 1974), p. 26 are in no doubt that the African was a presbyter. The last-named also supports de Labriolle (see above) and Mohrmann, *Tertullian Apologeticum* (1952), p. xxxvii, in their translation of *De Exhortatione Castitatis* 7,3.
[27] Von Campenhausen, *Ecclesiastical authority*, p. 175, does not doubt that Tertullian was a layman. H. Lietzmann, *The founding of the church universal* (London, 1953), p.219, contends that Tertullian probably was a presbyter, yet one who, strangely, never refers at all to his clerical status. This is not so strange if he didn't have any on which to comment! B. Altaner, *Patrology* (London, 1960), p.166, regards it as improbable ('unwahrscheinlich') that Tertullian was a priest.
[28] Barnes, *Tertullian*, p. 3; St W .J. Teeuwen, *Sprachlicher Bedeutungswandel bei Tertullian* (Paderborn, 1926), p. 35. He also dismisses Jerome's evidence as untenable.

far more on his own reading of Tertullian than on any other
independent sources. The passage from *De Anima* 9,4 does not
require the sort of construction put upon it by those arguing for
Tertullian's 'priestly' status, unless one is seeking simply to
confirm a previously determined position. As indicated earlier,
the passage from *De Exhortatione Castitatis* 7,3, read simply,
implies only that Tertullian (and those he was addressing) were
of the 'laici', albeit with 'priestly' obligations (especially that of
monogamy).

CHAPTER 3

Tertullian's relationship to the New Prophecy movement

Tertullian probably never broke away from the Catholic church, but carried on his campaign against what he saw as the decreasing rigour in its life from within its bounds (if only on the disaffected periphery). Tertullian clearly did, however, belong to a Montanist 'ecclesiola-in-ecclesia' (though Tertullian preferred 'New Prophecy' to 'Montanist') within the Catholic community. To what extent this 'ecclesiola' embraced formal structures of organisation, membership and activity independent of the official Catholic congregation is not clear; it is certain, however, that it involved more than a simple discussion group. Tertullian speaks of particular New Prophecy practices and activities which are clearly distinguishable from the traditional Catholic ones; there is no real suggestion, however, that the New Prophets did not involve themselves in the latter as well. One clear example is that of longer and more rigorous fastings. Another is a measure of 'internal' discipline promoted within the Carthaginian New Prophecy group; this included a prohibition on second marriages and the exclusion from the fellowship of adulterers. And this discipline was more than simply the New Prophecy movement's manifesto for the wider church; it appears also to have been implemented within its own fellowship. Such differentiation of practice and activity does not, however, equate with formal schism.[1]

The main issue here is the extent to which either Tertullian's adherence to the New Prophecy affected the development of his

---

[1] The Charismatic Renewal movement within certain Western churches – Catholic and Protestant alike – as opposed to the more formally structured, independent Pentecostal churches, offers a most useful modern parallel.

41

theology, or his association with the movement rather reflected previously determined positions; that is, did he adopt a particular position because he was edged towards it through the influence of the New Prophecy, or did he simply find in the New Prophecy a congenial 'home' for his increasingly isolated views within the Catholic church?

Four issues will be examined here: the views of particular scholars on Tertullian's relationship to the New Prophecy movement; Tertullian's own understanding of the history and development of the movement; the impact of New Prophecy teachings on Tertullian concerning doctrine and discipline, scripture and tradition, and his relationships with and attitudes towards those who did not choose to embrace the discipline of the New Prophets; and, finally, Tertullian's relationship to the published account of the martyrdom of Perpetua and her colleagues in 202 in Carthage, the *Passio Perpetuae et Felicitatis*.

The assertion by Ayers that Tertullian was never really a 'fully fledged Montanist' hardly requires further proof or defence.[2] Nor does that by von Campenhausen that '"Tertullian-as-Montanist" was not wholly different from "Tertullian-as-Catholic"'.[3] O'Malley claims that 'Tertullian elaborated a way of looking at reason, revelation and the world which we can trace throughout his work, and which is consistent with his eventual passage to Montanism'.[4] These properly suggest that Tertullian found a measure of congeniality in Montanism, rather than that he was particularly influenced by it. He actively canvassed a number of Montanist causes, ecstatic experience, the ban on second marriages, the prohibition against flight in time of persecution, the holding of extended fasts, and a more rigorous approach to Christian discipline among them. And in his at times strained adherence to

[2] R.H. Ayers, 'Tertullian's "paradox" and "contempt for reason" reconsidered', *ExpT* 87 (1976), p. 309.
[3] Von Campenhausen, *Ecclesiastical authority*, p. 227, who speaks of Tertullian's 'conversion' to Montanism, can also say that 'im Grunde ist Tertullian als Montanist kein anderer geworden als er immer schon', 'Tertullien' in *Gestalten der Kirchengeschichte*, Alte Kirche I, p. 116. For Braun, *Deus Christianorum* (Paris, 1962), p.523, however, 'elles (i.e. la pneumatologie et l'ecclésiologie du Carthaginois) ont été, on le sait, profondément marquées par son passage au montanisme', ibid.
[4] O'Malley, *Tertullian and the Bible*, p. 120.

mainstream ecclesiastical structures, he stood clearly within the tradition of Montanus and his followers, who themselves had supported the maintenance of such structures within their own communities.[5]

The assertion that Tertullian's pneumatocentric theology 'was not the product of a diluted Montanism, but the logical consequence of his whole approach'[6] has much to commend it. Tertullian brought his natural rigorism to the cause of the New Prophecy. Barnes doubts the influence of Montanism upon Tertullian. Of *De Fuga*, a 'Montanist' writing, he maintains that, despite the presence of two Montanist oracles at 9,4, Tertullian 'studiously avoids' Montanist terminology and argues independently of Montanist convictions when he is speaking to a non-Montanist audience.[7] This, however, reinforces the well-documented view that Tertullian deliberately employs the language of his immediate opponents in each of the various controversies in which he becomes engaged.[8] Wolfl asserts that 'im übrigen bringt der Montanismus Tertullians keine Veränderung seiner theologischen Grundanschauungen, seines theologischen "Systems" '.[9] The differences discernible in the 'later' Tertullian – whatever the influence of the New Prophecy upon him – were generally those of tone and style, and not of substance.

According to Epiphanius of Salamis, Montanism first appeared in Phrygia in the nineteenth year of the reign of the emperor Antoninus Pius, that is, in AD156. Suggestions of a later date, however, do find some support.[10] A dating to the sixth decade places Tertullian some two generations after the time of Montanus and his prophetesses. The 'Montanism' which came to North Africa in about AD 200 was probably, according to Lietzmann, only a movement of 'modified enthusiasm' – as with many reform movements the Phrygians had lost their initial burst of

---

[5] F. E. Vokes, 'Montanism and the ministry', *SP* (1966), p. 308.
[6] G. L. Bray, *Holiness and the will of God* (London, 1979), p.73.
[7] Barnes, *Tertullian*, p. 181.
[8] O'Malley, *Tertullian and the Bible.*, p. 2; see also J. E .L. van der Geest, *Le Christ et l'ancien Testament chez Tertullien* (Nijmegen, 1972), p.57, 'C'est une de ses habitudes caractéristiques d'accorder sa terminologie à celle de ses adversaires.'
[9] K. Wolfl, *Das Heilswirken Gottes durch den Sohn nach Tertullian* (Rome, 1960), p. 269.
[10] Von Campenhausen, *Ecclesiastical authority*, p.181, note 15.

vigour – but 'was very much alive in maintaining the rigour of
the early Christians' eschatological, moral code'.[11]

Given that the African religious style tended towards the
severe, it is probable that Montanism found a congenial 'home'
among sections of the population there.[12] For some Montanism
was a protest against the laxity which had begun to creep into
the church everywhere;[13] for others a protest against an
ecclesiastical organisation which was itself a response to the
heresy of Gnosticism.[14]

The Montanists of Phrygia possessed a regular, graded
ministry, the standard three-tiered structure to which were
added patriarchs (the orthodox 'metropolitans') and '*koinonoi*';
these latter officials, like the 'seniores' of the later African
church, oversaw financial matters. Such would confirm the
image of the early Montanists as standard-bearers for both a
primitive, apostolic Christianity and an orthodox ecclesiology.[15]
De Labriolle asserts that Montanus and his company never
applied the title 'ecclesia' to 'la collectivité montaniste' and that
'ce n'est pas de côté montaniste que viendra la rupture'.[16] The
original Montanists were undoubtedly loyal to the Catholic
church. Such was an attitude which commended itself to the
New Prophecy 'collective' in Carthage and to Tertullian himself
in the early years of the third century AD.

At *Adv. Praxean* 1,5 Tertullian claims that prior to the
intervention of the modalist Praxeas, the bishop of Rome had
'acknowledged' (agnoscentem) the prophetic gifts of Montanus,
Prisca and Maximilla and had 'bestowed peace' (pacem
inferentem) on the Montanist churches of Asia. The passage is
very important for our purposes for a number of reasons. First, it
indicates that though the form of the New Prophecy championed

---

[11] Lietzmann, *The founding of the church universal*, p. 193. This is especially so with
reference both to the original Phrygian movement and to that version which came to
North Africa; ibid. p.222.

[12] Frend, *The Donatist Church*, passim.

[13] E.g. B. Poschmann, *Penance and the anointing of the sick* (London, 1964), p. 36.

[14] J. S. Whale, 'The heretics of the Church and recurring heresies', *ExpT* 45 (1934),
p. 497. See also J. G. Davies, 'Tertullian, De Resurrectione Carnis 63: a note on the
origins of Montanism', *JTS* ns 6 (1955), p. 92.

[15] Vokes, 'Montanism and the ministry', p. 308.

[16] De Labriolle, *Le crise montaniste*, pp. 60 and 136.

by Tertullian may have differed in some crucial respects from the 'Montanism' of contemporary Phrygia, its adherents in North Africa yet saw themselves as providing a continuity of sorts with the founders of the movement. Second, it shows that Tertullian was keen to establish the doctrinal and ecclesiastical orthodoxy of the movement. Third, the context of Tertullian's personal struggle with 'Praxeas' was not Rome in the time of Montanus, but at Carthage in his own. The New Prophecy and the modalist heresy confronted one another on new soil. It was at this time, says Tertullian, as a result of his and others' 'acknowledgement and defence' (agnitio atque defensio) of the Paraclete, that they parted company with the 'Psychici'.[17] Elsewhere, as we have seen earlier, he claims that it was essentially the issue of ecstatic experience which separated the 'Spirituals' from the 'Carnally minded'.[18]

Some commentators make the fundamental error of confusing Montanism with Enthusiasm, and of contending that the New Prophets, and Tertullian in particular, were concerned more with the latter than the former.[19] A clear distinction can be made between Cataphrygianism (as Montanism came later to be known to those orthodox Christians who branded it heretical) and its manifestation in North Africa (and elsewhere) known as the New Prophecy. A distinction is more likely to be found in an inherent dilemma at work within Montanism itself. For von Campenhausen Montanism was characterised by a type of legalism from the start, despite the proclaimed emphasis on enthusiasm;[20] the enthusiast Tertullian himself welcomed the clamp of authority. At *De Scorpiace* 2,1, for example, he says,

auctoritas divina praecedit, an tale quid voluerit atque mandaverit deus, ut qui negant bonum non suadeantur accommodum, nisi cum subacti fuerint. Ad officium haereticos compelli non inlici dignum est. *Duritia vincenda est, non suadenda* ...

(The question of a divine warrant goes first, whether God has willed or commanded such a thing, so that those who deny that it is good are persuaded otherwise, save when they have been compelled. It is proper

[17] *Adv. Praxean* 1,7.   [18] *Adv. Marcionem* 1,22,4.
[19] E.g. T. D. Barnes, 'Tertullian's Scorpiace', *JTS* ns 20 (1969), p. 105.
[20] Von Campenhausen, *Ecclesiastical authority*, p. 188.

that heretics be driven to duty and not enticed. Obstinacy must be conquered, not coaxed...).[21]

During his early period Tertullian was primarily concerned with the question of doctrine, and only later with that of discipline; the Paraclete was for him concerned primarily with the latter. Pelikan maintains that the Paraclete, according to Tertullian, was a teacher of discipline, and that Tertullian was drawn to the New Prophecy, not by theological novelty, but by its moral zeal.[22] Jansen asserts that 'Montanist rigour affects the interpretation of particular texts, but its primary influence is on discipline, not on the authority of Scripture or Tradition'.[23]

Others question this convenient early/doctrine–late/discipline division. R. F. Evans argues that for Tertullian 'the Holy Spirit works not only at the level of discipline but of doctrine as well'.[24] For example, a comment of Tertullian at *Adv. Praxean* 2,1, where he maintains that he and his fellow New Prophecy adherents are 'instructiores per Paracletum' (better instructed by the Paraclete), demonstrates that that understanding of the Trinity which Tertullian outlines in the treatise has come to him directly by way of a revelation from the Holy Spirit. And, yet, at *De Monogamia* 3,9 he is equally adamant, in answer to a charge of doctrinal innovation, that 'nihil novi Paracletus inducit' (the Paraclete introduces nothing new).

Further, his understanding of the key terms '*monarchia*' and '*oikonomia*' receive confirmation, though not determination, from 'sermones novae prophetiae'.[25] The claim by O'Malley that 'Tertullian has taken a long step towards making Scripture irrelevant'[26] is too strong, and suggests wrongly that Tertullian endows the Paraclete with a far greater authority over doctrine than his evident concern elsewhere for the safeguarding of the authenticity of doctrine as apostolic would allow. For Tertullian the Montanists were the true 'heirs' of the primitive community.[27]

[21] See ibid., p. 212, note 224.
[22] J. Pelikan, 'Montanism and its trinitarian significance', *CH* 25 (1956), pp. 105 and 104.
[23] J. F. Jansen, 'Tertullian and the New Testament', *Second Century* 2 (1982), p. 202.
[24] R.F. Evans, *One and holy: the Church in Latin patristic thought* (London, 1972), p. 30.
[25] *Adv. Praxean* 30,5.
[26] O'Malley, *Tertullian and the Bible*, p. 132, claims that Tertullian does so by 'limiting inconvenient texts to the peculiar conditions of the earthly preaching of Christ'.
[27] Monceaux, *Histoire littéraire*, p.185.

And in their capacity as heirs the New Prophets hold an advantage over the church of the 'Psychici' as the legitimate interpreters and, if necessary (see John 14) supplementers, through the Spirit of Truth, of the apostolic witness to the Gospel. Yet it is wrong to claim that the real threat of Montanism was to the traditional status of the Scriptures.[28] Tertullian would probably have had some sympathy for the notion of George Fox that 'it is not the Scripture, it is the Holy Spirit by which men of old gave forth the Scripture, by which religions... are to be tried',[29] but this would in no way suggest any diminution of the pivotal role of the Scriptures in his thought. The claim that Tertullian, under the influence of the Phrygian movement, subordinated the Scriptures to the oracles and writings of Montanus is manifestly untrue. The claim that Tertullian moved towards making the Scriptures irrelevant and that the Montanist movement posed a very real threat to those same Scriptures are both distortions of the actual development of Tertullian's thought. Tertullian simply acknowledged that since the Scriptures were open to abuse by opponents of orthodoxy, some more 'certain' process of interpretation was desirable. Even in his early period he had denied the Scriptures to the Gnostics for fear of their misuse by them.[30] The fact that even the original Montanists themselves drew less inspiration from special New Prophecy sources than they did from prophetic and apostolic ones – Tertullian himself refers to Montanist oracles on only six occasions in his entire extant corpus[31] – should not be ignored. Perhaps *De Ecstasi* – Tertullian's lost treatise – might give us a different picture,[32] but this can only be speculation. We have already seen Tertullian's claim at *De Monogamia* 3,9 that the New Prophecy adds nothing to apostolic witness. At *De Ieiunio* 1,3 Tertullian asserts that the New Prophecies are rejected (recusantur) by the 'Psychici', not

[28] See Powell, 'Tertullianists', p. 52.
[29] Quoted from R. Barclay, *Inner life of the religious societies of the Commonwealth*, p. 210 in R. A. Knox, *Enthusiasm: a chapter in the history of religion* (Oxford, 1950), p. 152.
[30] *De Praescriptione* 15,3.
[31] *De Pudicitia* 21,7; *De Fuga* 9,4 (twice); *De Resurrectione Carnis* 11,2; *De Exhortatione Castitatis* 10,5; *Adv.Praxean* 8.
[32] A.F. Walls, 'The Montanist 'Catholic epistle' and its New Testament prototype', *SE* 3 (1964), p. 443.

because of any doctrinal deviation, heterodoxy or innovation, but on account of their more rigorous disciplinary demands. At *De Resurrectione* 63,9, after arguing that the Holy Scriptures need fresh illumination in order to expose the heretics' distortions of them, Tertullian claims that this can be done 'aperta atque perspicua totius sacramenti praedicatione... per novam prophetiam de paraclito inundantem' (by an open and clear proclamation of the whole mystery... through the New Prophecy overflowing from the Paraclete).

The New Prophecy for Tertullian did not seek to replace the Scriptures; it sought rather only to illuminate and support them by removing the dangers presented by those ambiguities which are regularly and wilfully seized upon by the heretics. The original Montanists – and Tertullian himself – saw themselves here as even more faithful to the sacred texts of the Apostles than the Catholics; these for their part seem prepared, in Tertullian's view, wilfully to expose them to these dangers unprotected.

Under the management (administratio) of the Paraclete is not only the direction of discipline (disciplina dirigitur), but also the 'uncovering' of the Scriptures (scripturae revelantur). The uniqueness of the apostolic witness is by no means undermined, but rather reinforced. An important example is Tertullian's validation of the status, work and authority of the Spirit by reference to the so-called 'Paraclete' passages from John 14-16. With only a few insignificant exceptions, all of these occur in Tertullian's later 'Montanist' writings.[33]

In the later part of his career Tertullian's chief opponents were those whom he named the 'Psychici', a term which, found first in Paul, was common in Montanist circles. The term, however, did not necessarily equate with 'Catholic'.[34] Despite the implications of such passages as *De Ieiunio* 11,1 that the great

---

[33] John 14,16.17 is cited at *Adv. Prax.* 9,3 and 25,1; John 15,25 at *De Praescriptione* 28,1, *Adv. Prax.* 4,1, *De Monogamia* 2,4 and 3,10, *De Pudicitia* 21,8; John 16,7 at *Adv. Prax.* 2,1 and *De Virginibus Velandis* 1,4; John 16,13 at *De Corona* 4,6, *De Fuga* 1,1 and 14,3, *De Ieiunio* 10,6, *De Virginibus Velandis* 1,7, *De Praescriptione* 22,9, *Adv. Prax.* 30,5 and *De Resurrectionis Carnis* 63,9.

[34] Teeuwen, 'Sprachlicher Bedeutungswandel', p. 36, note 2; see also my discussion of this term in note 4 of the Introduction.

bulk of Catholics were 'carnal', Tertullian can also speak of 'spiritual' bishops who are also Catholics.[35] By 'Psychici', then, are meant certain elements within the Catholic hierarchy; elements with whom Tertullian is constantly in conflict – and as much over the validity of ecstatic experience as anything else.[36] And regardless of their precise identity, it is their failure properly to recognise the Paraclete, as much as their subsequent preoccupation with what Tertullian regards as matters unspiritual, that identifies them as 'Psychici'. The New Prophets (nos), by 'recognition of spiritual gifts' (agnitio spiritualium charismatum), deserve to be called 'the spiritual ones'.[37] The others, not accepting the Spirit (non recipientibus spiritum), deserve only the label 'Carnally minded'.[38] The attack on this alleged lack of an authentic spirituality reaches its climax in *De Ieiunio*, where the vitriol bears comparison with Tertullian's earlier attacks on heretics and pagans. At *De Pudicitia* 12,1, where Tertullian speaks of the failure of the 'Psychici' to recognise 'alium Paracletum in prophetis propriis' (another Paraclete in his special prophets) he comes very close to repudiating outright the apostolicity of the Catholic church.

Alongside his assertion that Tertullian's 'Montanism' brings to the fore a sectarian 'exclusivity' over against a Catholic 'inclusiveness', Burleigh also claims that in his later period Tertullian 'never seriously modifies the teaching on the question of authority [sc. found] in *Prescriptions*'.[39] Von Campenhausen argues, however, that only in Tertullian's 'Montanist' period do we find the thought that bishops can err,[40] and O'Malley that there is 'a non-rational source of certitude in Montanism' for Tertullian.[41] Pelikan points out that while Tertullian himself saw a decisive influence coming from the side of the New Prophecy over his doctrine of the Trinity, he sees only a 'modest contribution' by Montanism to Tertullian's trinitarian thought.[42] Poschmann sees in Tertullian's Montanism (v. the oracle at *De*

[35] *De Ieiunio* 16,3
[36] *Adv. Marcionem* IV,22,5.   [37] *De Monogamia* 1,2.   [38] Ibid. 1,3.
[39] J. H .S. Burleigh, 'The Holy Spirit in the Latin Fathers', *Scot.J. Th.* 7 (1954), pp. 117 and 120.   [40] Von Campenhausen, *Ecclesiastical authority*, p. 175.
[41] O'Malley, *Tertullian and the Bible*, p. 133.
[42] Pelikan, 'Montanism', pp. 104 and 107.

Pudicitia 21,7) a 'revolutionary element...undermining the Catholic concept of the Church'.[43] Speigl, however, correctly sees the Montanism of Tertullian moving him not to a greater freedom, but rather to 'mehr Bindung'.[44] Bender makes two interesting suggestions; these are that in Tertullian's Montanist period the Holy Spirit is spoken of for the first time as a 'Person'; and that the influence of the New Prophecy on Tertullian, with respect to the concept of the Holy Spirit, is restricted to three matters: (1) the advent of a 'new era' with the coming of the Paraclete, (2) the understanding of 'ekstase' as 'amentia', and (3) 'die Vergeistigung des Kirchenbegriffes'.[45] De Labriolle contends that Tertullian preferred the term 'Paraclete' to 'Holy Spirit' because the former more clearly designated its role in this last great manifestation, and that Tertullian's eschatology was confirmed, but not determined, by the New Prophecy.[46] This supports our earlier conclusion that Tertullian was not so much influenced by the New Prophecy, as found there a congenial 'home' for his rigorous views. De Labriolle points out further that Tertullian's adherence to Montanism – whatever its formal status – drove him away from his first line of defence against the heretics,[47] namely the accusation of innovation. And thus it happened that the charge of 'novelty', frequently used by Tertullian against heretics in his early period, was turned so enthusiastically back on him later. Van Beneden sees in Tertullian a tendency, as a result of his Montanism, towards minimising the appropriate character of the priesthood in favour 'du sacerdoce universel des baptisés'. This fails, however, to give due weight to Tertullian's consistent and firm adherence to the appropriateness of clerical prerogatives even into his later period (see *De Exhortatione Castitatis* 7).[48]

Two further comments can also be made before concluding this section; one, if true, an intriguing possibility, and the other

---

[43] Poschmann, *Penance*, p. 36.
[44] J. Speigl, 'Herkommen und Fortschritt im Christentum nach Tertullian', in *Pietas*, ed. E. Dassmann (1980), p.177.
[45] W. Bender, *Die Lehre über den Heiligen Geist* (Munich, 1961), pp. 168ff.
[46] De Labriolle, *Le crise montaniste*, pp. 324 and 331.
[47] Ibid., p.xxxi.
[48] Van Beneden, 'Ordo', p. 163. See discussion on priesthood in Part III.

testimony to the nonsense that can result from an inadequate understanding of the true nature of the Montanist movement! De Labriolle points out that Augustine, on the basis of Tertullian's alleged, though now universally disputed authorship of the treatise *Adv. Omnes Haereses*, claimed that Tertullian had, early in his career, been one of the chief opponents of Montanism in North Africa.[49] The second is that Tertullian himself provides evidence of the self-identification of Montanus with the Paraclete.[50] This latter viewpoint, notwithstanding the prophet's apparent idiosyncrasies, was a later slur against his character, and one now dismissed out of hand by most informed scholarship.

De Labriolle also suggests that Tertullian was the editor of the Montanist-like *Passio Perpetuae et Felicitatis*.[51] Barnes, however, while acknowledging some similarities in style and theology between the *Passio* and the known writings of Tertullian, doubts, on the basis of Tertullian's alleged misrepresentation of part of the work at *De Anima* 55,4, that he is so.[52] It has, in any case, been elsewhere conclusively demonstrated by Braun that Tertullian cannot be connected with the *Passio* account, either on linguistic or on stylistic grounds.[53]

[49] De Labriolle, *Le crise montaniste*, p. cxiii.
[50] E. Leske, 'Montanism', *Lutheran Theological Journal* 15 (1981), p. 81.
[51] P. de Labriolle, 'Tertullien, auteur de prologue et de la conclusion de la passion de Perpétue et de Félicité', *Bulletin d'ancienne littérature et d'archéologie chrétiennes* 3 (1913), p. 129.
[52] Barnes, *Tertullian*, pp. 79 and 265.
[53] R. Braun, 'Nouvelles observations linguistiques sur le rédacteur de la "Passio Perpetuae"', *VC* 33 (1979), p.116.

PART II

Tertullian's doctrine of the church

Introduction

While it is true that Christ did not leave behind a formally constituted church, it is equally true that in calling together the first group of disciples he laid the foundation for that institution known as his Body. The New Testament has much to say about the nature and role of this church which Christ called into being. Minear's identification of around a hundred images which the writers of the New Testament employ for the church – some of which are somewhat peripheral and tenuous – provides a useful introduction to the New Testament presentation of the church.[1] He also identifies four 'Master Images' in the New Testament: the church as (1) the People of God, (2) the New Creation, (3) the Fellowship in Faith, and (4) the Body of Christ.[2]

Within the New Testament a number of images offer a comprehensive, if not always consistent, picture of the church. At 1 Peter 3,20f. the church is depicted as like the ark of Noah in that it carries the elect of God through the waters of eschatological crisis.[3] This is, however, only a marginal image.[4] The church is depicted as a 'camp' at Revelation 20,9, but this is, like 'ark', at most marginal. The depiction of the church as 'mother' is generally believed not to be present in the New Testament. Marcion maintained, however (and Tertullian approved his exegesis), that the 'heavenly Jerusalem' described as the 'mother of us all' at Galatians 4,26 was to be identified with the church. The woman giving birth at Revelation 12,1f. is likewise sometimes identified with the church, while 2 John 1,1 and 1,4 carry

---

[1] P. S. Minear, *Images of the church in the New Testament* (London, 1960).
[2] Ibid. pp. 240f.   [3] Ibid. p. 34.   [4] Ibid.

references to the church and its membership as the 'elect lady and her children'. Through the image of the church as 'mother' the church is given a 'persona' (unlike the impersonal images of ship, ark, boat and so on) distinct from her members. She becomes then more than her constituent membership. The church as the 'bride' of Christ, while in Minear's view a 'minor image',[5] is one found in both Pauline and Johannine writings. At 2 Corinthians 11,2f. the image is implied, while at Ephesians 5, 22-31 there is more explicitly represented the church-bride's role of subjection and obedience to her bridegroom Jesus. At Luke 5,34f. the image is again implied, but adds little to our discussion. At Revelation 21,2f. the church-bride as the New Jerusalem is contrasted with the harlot Babylon.[6] The uniting of his bride with Christ to become one body links this image with that of the church as Christ's body. According to Minear, the image of the church as the Messiah's bride (reflecting OT influences – see, e.g., Songs of Solomon 4,8) coalesces easily into other images as disparate as 'nation', 'city', 'temple' and 'body'.[7] It is by itself neither decisive nor determinative within the whole range of NT images. Along with 'virgin' and 'mother' it represents faithfulness to Christ. Welch maintains that in the New Testament (unlike in the OT) the marriage of the Divinity and the faithful bride is not yet completed.[8] The church remains until the End the betrothed. She is to become, at that point only, what she is now in hope and promise. The depiction of the church as 'virgin' (usually as the virgin bride) can be found at 2 Corinthians 11,2, where it represents obedience and fidelity to Christ. At Ephesians 5, 26f. it is clearly implied. At Revelation 14,1f. it is likewise represented by clear implication in the choir of the holy redeemed who surround the Lamb. The image of the church obedient to Christ's covenant is the determinative influence here.[9] It denotes in the Old Testament that singleness of mind with which the bride Israel obeyed her husband God amidst a world awash with harlotry.[10] It signifies perfect obedience and humility before God.

---

[5] Ibid. p. 54.   [6] Ibid.   [7] Ibid. p. 56.
[8] C. Welch, *The reality of the church* (New York, 1958), p. 133, note 2.
[9] Minear, *Images*, p.59.   [10] Ibid.

The most decisive image for the church in the New Testament
is that of the 'body (of Christ)'; see, for example, 1 Corinthians
12, Ephesians. 1,23 and 4,4f, Colossians 1,18-20; 2,19 and
Romans 12. In the New Testament this image points, according
to Welch, always inward, and never outward to the world.[11]
For Minear, it offers both historical particularity and cosmic
inclusiveness.[12] A high ecclesiology results from an emphasis
on the ontological realism of the image, a low one where its
metaphorical character is stressed.[13] For Newbigin, the church
in the New Testament is that real, visible human fellowship in
which Christ is alive in his members;[14] the latter are to grow
up into him who is their Head.[15] There is a real incorporation
of men in the life of the Risen Christ;[16] yet they are no literal
extension of the Incarnation.[17] To say that would be to
confuse 'sarx' with 'soma'.[18] The church is the body of Christ
where the Holy Spirit's presence is experienced as real.[19] In
the New Testament there is no dissociation of the Spirit of
Christ from the Body of Christ.[20] The church as the Body of
Christ is where the Holy Spirit is recognisably present with
power.[21] Yet for Ellis, 'both in its familial and its christological
expression the corporate body represents no mere metaphor
but a reality no less ontological than the individual body . . . As
"body of Christ" it represents the "outward" expression of an
even more frequent "inward" Pauline idiom, existence "in

---

[11] Welch, *Reality*, p.150.
[12] Minear, *Images*, p.217.
[13] Ibid. p. 240.
[14] L.Newbigin, *The household of God* (London, 1957), p. 79.
[15] Ibid.; C .W. Williams, *The church* (London, 1969), p. 62; Colossians 1,18-20 et al.
[16] Newbigin, *Household of God*, p. 80.
[17] Ibid.; Williams, *The church*, p. 62.
[18] Newbigin, *Household of God*, p .80; B. Daines, 'Paul's use of the analogy of the Body of
Christ – with special reference to 1 Cor. 12', *The Evangelical Quarterly* 50 (1978), pp.
74f. implicitly agrees with Newbigin with respect to 1 Corinthians, arguing that the
image is 'best understood as carrying just a metaphorical sense', but acknowledges
also that its use in Ephesians 4 may be 'as more than an analogy or metaphor,
although still only in a limited sense'. Yet, he continues, 'it would be an exaggeration
to see it as a mystical or metaphorical concept'. See also D. J. Harrington, *God's people
in Christ* (Fortress, 1980) and G. S. Worgul, 'People of God, Body of Christ: Pauline
Ecclesiological Contrasts', *Biblical Theology Bulletin* 12 (1982) pp. 24-8.
[19] Newbigin, *Household of God*, p. 92.   [20] Ibid., p.93.   [21] Ibid., p.87.

Christ".'[22] For Robinson, that which stamps the church as the eschatological community (of Christ) is its common possession of the Spirit.[23] For Kasemann, 'neither Judaism's "corporate personality"nor the Middle Stoa's "cosmic organism"' – both of which are commonly accepted as providing the background for Paul's employment of the image of the 'body of Christ' – 'was a mere image which could be set over against reality in the modern manner . . . The exalted Christ really has an earthly body, and believers with their whole being are actually incorporated into it and have therefore to behave accordingly.'[24]

In the New Testament a consistent emphasis is placed upon the necessary unity of the church. It is present in Jesus' prayer for the disciples at John 17,21f., in Paul's call for an end to faction at 1 Corinthians 11,17f., and in the stress on the oneness of the church's proclamation at Ephesians 4,4-6. Yet it is not unity for the sake of itself alone which is critical. In John the unity of the disciples stems from the unity of Father and Son; in 1 Corinthians from the integrity of the Gospel; in Ephesians from the confession of the one Spirit, the one hope, the one Lord, the one faith, the one baptism, the one God and Father of all. Behind much of this is the image of the body; to divide the body (of Christ) is to divide Christ himself. 'The unity of the church of God is a perpetual fact; our task is not to create it but to exhibit it.'[25]

Holiness is also an essential attribute in the New Testament view of the authentic church. At 1 Corinthians 5,1-5, Ephesians 5,7, 2 Thessalonians 3,6 and 1 Timothy 5,22 the congregations are urged to separate from sinners for the sake of the integrity of the Gospel. At Ephesians 5,26f. the image of the church as the

---

[22] E .E. Ellis, 'Soma in First Corinthians', *Interpretation* 44 (1990) p.138; see also E. Schweizer, art. 'Soma' in *The New Exegetical Dictionary of the New Testament*, vol. III, pp.324f.; see also J. A. T. Robinson, *The body: a study in Pauline theology* (London, 1952), p. 51, for whom the image is not a metaphor. Christians are in literal fact the risen organism of Christ's person in all its concrete reality. According to Bellarmine, *Myst. Corpor. Christi* 51, in J. Moltmann, *The church in the power of the Spirit* (London, 1977),p. 72, Christ upholds his church and lives in the church so that she may be said to be another Christ (alteris Christi persona).

[23] Robinson, *The body*, p. 72.

[24] E. Kasemann, 'The theological problem presented by the motif of the Body of Christ' in *Perspectives on Paul* (London, 1971).

[25] W. Temple in D. Kirkpatrick, *The doctrine of the church* (London, 1964), p. 187.

virgin bride of Christ is to the fore. At 2 Thessalonians 1,11 the
faithful are prayed for so that God might make them worthy of
the life to which they are called. This is, of course, part of what it
is for the church to be the eschatological community. It is holy
because it is that community;[26] as Christians must grow into
their Head, Christ, so, too, they must grow into the life of
holiness.[27] 'The holiness of the church places demands on the
church; thus sharing, in the Spirit, the holiness of God, the
church must be presented, on the Day, as a holy sacrifice.'[28] To
be a saint is to become what God through the Spirit has already
made you. The company of the sanctified is bound now to lead
the life of the Kingdom of God to come.[29] But here, of course, is
the rub. As Moltmann properly points out, the church has never
existed in a historically demonstrable ideal, in a form in which
faith and experience coincide.[30] Both Williams and Welch speak
of the ecclesial reality or the dual paradox of the church as 'simul
iustus et peccator'; the latter points also to the church as an
unequivocally creaturely, historical community, marked by the
limitations of all human existence.[31] Where the analogy between
the church and the person of Christ is dominant (rather than the
parallel between the being of the church and the life of a believer
(v. 'simul iustus et peccator')) the stress is placed on the
perfection of the church, perhaps as an extension of the
Incarnation, and the abiding of the Spirit in the church (rather
than upon the fragility of the church, its sin, and the lordship of
Christ over it).[32] This is crucial for understanding Tertullian's
ecclesiology. Catholicity is not a major feature of New Testament
ecclesiology, save for the Great Commission at Matthew 28,19-20
and the various sendings forth of the disciples by Jesus. Apostolicity
as an explicit factor in New Testament ecclesiology is present
truly only in the *Pastorals*.

Tertullian presents no extensive or systematic theology of the
church. While it may be proper to speak of Tertullian's

---

[26] Moltmann, *The church*, p. 339.   [27] Williams, *The church*, p. 65.
[28] Minear, *Images*, p. 133.
[29] R. F. Evans, *One and holy: the church in Latin patristic thought* (London, 1972), pp. 8f.
[30] *The church*, p.21.
[31] Williams, *The church*, p .25; Welch, *Reality*, pp. 21f. and 217.
[32] Welch, *Reality*, p .29.

'constitutionalist' view of the church and of the prominence of his 'theology of Church' in, for example, *De Spectaculis*, he has left no trace of any writing which could bear the title *De Ecclesia*.[33] Nor did any of his Catholic contemporaries offer any such systematic treatment. Further, the nature and purpose of Tertullian's extant writings neither allow, nor call for such. Yet Tertullian does offer a discernible view of the nature of the church that is both innovative and orthodox. Notwithstanding the absence of a treatise 'de ecclesia', certain of Tertullian's extant works devote significant attention to the ecclesiological question. These include the *Apologeticum* (particularly chapter 39) and *De Praescriptione* (particularly chapters 20, 21, 32 and 36), both from his early period, and *De Pudicitia* (particularly chapters 1, 7, 8, 13, 21 and 22) from his later period.

The *Apologeticum* is, as the title suggests, a robust defence of the Christian faith. It is an 'open letter' formally addressed to the 'magistrates (antistites) of the Roman empire' generally and to the Proconsul of Africa particularly; it is written against the background of the vigorous prosecution of Christians in that province. It is written in a spirit of defiance and of bitter satire rather than in one of gentle and persuasive pleading.[34] Tertullian seeks in this treatise to highlight the arbitrary, discriminatory and irrational treatment meted out to Christians in the law courts of the empire; this treatment is, he contends, inconsistent with the normal practices and standards of Roman justice. He draws some parallels between the status and treatment of the various philosophical schools and that of the Christian 'secta' (3,6); he examines the processes employed against the Christians, and those imperial enactments which should afford them some protection (4-6). He discusses some of the specific allegations laid against the church fellowship (7). He offers, among other things, an acerbic view of some of the unwholesome practices of certain pagan cults (9) and a series of sarcastic commentaries on the nature and origins of many Roman deities (10f.). At the same time he points to the naturalness and reasonableness of the Christian religion (17). Taking up the Romans' appreciation of

[33] Von Campenhausen, *Ecclesiastical authority*, p.174; R. Sider, 'Tertullian, on the shows:an analysis', JTS ns 24 (1973) p. 364.
[34] H. M. Gwatkin, *Early church history to AD 313* (London, 1909), vol.I, p.210.

antiquity as a criterion for favourably evaluating any religious system, he draws attention to the considerable longevity of the Jewish religion (19f.) and to the continuity, in some respects, of Christianity with this; he writes at length, too, on particular aspects of Christian teaching, proclaiming without restraint the superiority and sovereignty of the Christian God over the pagan deities (21f.). The Christians, far from being a seditious sect, pray for the very safety of the Emperors (30f.).

In chapter 39 he seeks to explain some misunderstood Christian practices. Depicting the church as both a 'factio' (although later he repudiates this label) and a 'corpus' (association) (1), he describes its worship and community life – prayers, readings, teachings and disciplinary processes employed against erring members (2-3) – and the nature and quality of its leadership (4). He describes the system of voluntary offerings (5) and the practical use of these (6); he writes of the Christians' sharing of property (11-12) and of the common meal – the agape – regularly enjoyed by the community (14-19). These descriptions are accompanied by sharp attacks on the immoral and unsavoury nature of parallel pagan practices. He concludes the chapter by stressing the essentially peaceful and law-abiding nature of Christian gatherings, describing the church as more a chaste 'curia' than a riotous 'factio'(21)! The remaining twelve chapters form a conclusion to this lengthy apologetic.

De Praescriptione is an attack on certain Christian heresies which flourished in Tertullian's time, 'praescriptio' being a legal term meaning 'demurrer' or 'formal objection'. In the opening chapters Tertullian introduces his subject, drawing special attention to the predictions in the Scriptures of the rise of heresy. He suggests that the origin of many heresies lies in the preoccupation of most heretics with the teachings of the various philosophical schools (7). In chapter 13 he introduces the Rule of Faith as an appropriate standard for belief, though the precise status of this Rule is even to this day the subject of considerable debate.[35] This Rule, he says, is sufficient for the Christian and

[35] See L. W. M. Countryman, 'Tertullian and the Regula Fidei', *Second Century* 2 (1982) pp.208-27 and E.F. Osborn, 'Reason and the rule of faith in the second century AD' in *The Making of Orthodoxy*, ed. R. Williams (1989), pp. 40-61.

there should be no curious seeking beyond it. He denies the use
of the Scriptures to the heretics to whom they do not belong;
these writings belong only to those who have the Rule (15). In
chapters 20 and 21 he demonstrates the purity and authenticity
of the teaching of the orthodox churches by tracing the
foundations of these back to the apostles; these latter handed on
through the churches the teaching entrusted them first by
Christ. He later rejects the proposition that the apostles held
back some of Christ's teachings for transmission only to selected
groups, from which groups the heretical communities might
claim descent (25-6). In chapters 32 and 36 he offers the
registers of bishops' names, lists reaching back to the first bishops
appointed by apostles or disciples of the apostles, as a guarantee
of the transmission of unadulterated apostolic teaching. In
chapter 41 he compares the order and discipline of the Catholic
churches with the disorder and indiscipline of heretical
groups.

The writing of *De Pudicitia* was occasioned by the decision of
an unnamed bishop (probably of Carthage) to allow the
readmission to communion of penitent adulterers. Tertullian
was outraged that such an edict ('edictum') should be published
in a 'virgin' church, the 'bride (of Christ)', 'true, chaste, holy
and untainted', and bitterly attacks the perpetrator of this
outrage. In the chapters following he argues that God is just as
well as merciful (2) – his opponents basing their argument upon
the latter attribute alone – and that adultery and fornication are
indistinguishable in nature (4). He examines the testimony of
the Decalogue (5) and other passages from the Old Testament(6);
he discusses the application of the parables of the Lost Sheep and
the Lost Coin (7) and that of the Prodigal Son (8) to the
question. He looks at principles of parabolic interpretation (9)
and condemns the *Shepherd* of Hermas for its compromising
stance towards the reconciliation of adulterers (10). He discusses
the questions of Christian discipline and of Catholic penitential
practice (11-15). He argues that the Apostle (Paul) is consistently
on the side of a more rigorous approach to discipline, contending
that the offender for whom Paul pleads reconciliation in
2 Corinthians is not the same person consigned to perdition in

1 Corinthians (16-17). He pleads for the maintenance of a pure church uncontaminated by grievous sinners (18).

In chapter 21 Tertullian asserts the difference between the exercise of discipline, which he allows to ecclesiastical leaders-qua-leaders, and that of a 'potestas' to remit sin which properly belongs to God alone.[36] He demands proofs from the Catholics of their possession of this apostolic and prophetic power. He acknowledges the authority (as he has previously) of the church to remit lesser sins, but accuses it of 'usurping' an authority with respect to those more serious ones which are the province of God alone. The claim by the bishops of their link to Peter (and to his power of the keys) is invalid since this power (of the keys) was granted to Peter personally and is not transmissible. Again, he acknowledges the right of the church to remit sin, but contends now that it must be a church of the Spirit which exercises this prerogative, a church in which spiritual power is demonstrated, a church comprised of spiritual men, and not one constituted solely by an episcopal structure. In chapter 22 he repudiates the practice whereby confessors claim the right to remit the sin of penitents. A martyr may earn remission for his own sins, but not for those of another. Again Tertullian demands proofs from the confessors of that same 'potestas' which indwelt Christ, the apostles and the prophets.

The varied imagery, which he employs in his understanding of the church, has its roots in the Scriptures, in the writings of earlier Fathers, and in his struggles with the Marcionite churches and the pagan cult of Mithras. Much of his imagery went on to influence Cyprian and others who followed him. The later 'exiled' Tertullian is rarely named, however, even by those on whom he exercised such influence in the matters, for example, of ecclesial imagery and trinitarian language.

[36] In a paper delivered in April 1987 to the Senior Patristics Seminar in the School of Divinity, Cambridge, England, I argued that Tertullian's use of the word 'potestas' (he uses it some 267 times in his extant writings) demonstrates clearly that he regarded 'potestas' as essentially and principally an attribute of God alone. Any possession or exercise of 'potestas' by any other person or thing – be it an emperor, bishop or the devil himself – is essentially derivative and subordinate. They might exercise such 'potestas' but in no way which denies or usurps the primary possession or prerogative of God.

In the second part of this book, the question of Tertullian's ecclesiology will be dealt with in two chapters. First I will consider the ecclesial images employed by Tertullian, 'ark', 'ship', 'camp', 'Christ', 'Spirit', 'Trinity', 'Body', 'Mother', 'school', 'sect', 'bride', and 'virgin'. I will then examine the background of these images in the Scriptures and the Fathers and their special significance for Tertullian's doctrine of church, along with crucial texts from Tertullian's writings. I will also discuss the significance of his use of each image for the 'one, holy, catholic and apostolic' credal formula proclaimed of the Great Church, and any changes in Tertullian's thought from the early to the later period will be investigated. Second, I will consider, in turn, the questions of apostolicity, holiness (including a consideration of Tertullian's eschatology), and unity (including a consideration of the question of catholicity). Under these headings I will examine the background of these concepts in the Scriptures and in the other early Fathers, the crucial texts in Tertullian's writings, and finally, the special significance for Tertullian's ecclesiology of each of these aspects. There will also be a brief discussion of the extent to which, if at all, Tertullian incorporates features of later (Reformed and modern) ecclesiological 'notes' in his treatment of the nature of the authentic church. Third, I will present a summary of findings, giving special attention to Tertullian's employment of particular scriptural texts.

CHAPTER 4

Tertullian's ecclesiological images

THE CHURCH AS AN 'ARK'

There are twenty-two separate references to 'arca' in Tertullian's extant writings.[1] Six – two of which appear in the passages from *De Baptismo* and *De Idololatria* discussed below – refer to Noah's Ark, nine to the Old Testament Ark of the Covenant, four have the common meaning of 'coffer' or 'chest'[2] and two, those discussed below, refer to the Ark as a figure for the church.

At 1 Peter 3, 20-21 there is a reference to the saving, through water, of Noah and his seven companions in the Ark; this water corresponds to the saving laver in the sacrament of baptism. Minear comments that the Ark is, for the author of 1 Peter, a prefigurement of the church, which, like the Ark itself, carries the elect through the waters of eschatological crisis.[3] It is, however, only a 'marginal' analogy in the New Testament. That Tertullian was influenced by this passage, particularly in *De Baptismo* 8, is possible, but is nowhere acknowledged explicitly by him. Among the Fathers before Tertullian, Clement of Rome makes reference to Noah's Ark, but only with respect to the faithfulness and obedience of Noah. His near-contemporary, Hippolytus of Rome, comments unfavourably on Pope Callistus' alleged assertion that as Noah's Ark received animals both clean and unclean, so should the church also learn to live in this present age with sinners in its midst.[4] Thus, even if the Ark in

---

[1] Claesson, *Index Tertullianeus*.
[2] At *Ad Martyras* 4,6 'arca' is used of the container in which the brave and virtuous Regulus was tortured to death by the Carthaginians.
[3] Minear, *Images*, p. 34
[4] *1 Clement* 9,4; *Elenchos* ix,12,22f.

1 Peter 3 is not intended as a prefigurement of the church, its employment as such may pre-date Tertullian.

As in the New Testament this image is at most marginal for Tertullian's ecclesiological thought; it does reflect, however, as employed in at least two passages, a view of the church as a holy, exclusivist 'vessel' of salvation from which all taint of impurity must be removed.

At *De Baptismo* 8,4 Tertullian recalls how after the great Flood a dove had been sent out from the Ark and had returned bearing an olive branch to announce the cessation of God's anger. For Tertullian this event represents the bringing by the Holy Spirit – represented here by the dove – of God's peace from the heavenly realm where the typified Ark, the church, is to be found. That the church was in heaven before it was on earth was a belief embraced from earliest times.[5] In Tertullian the term 'figura' 'regularly also carries a sense of objective reality, or even of tangible shape'.[6] Whether this 'ecclesia in caelis' is identifiable with that 'on earth', or is rather a Platonic 'ideal', of which the earthly one is but an imperfect 'copy', is not, however, clear. While the influence of 1 Peter 3 is certain, the use of this image here is a value-free one for Tertullian; the church is represented as a 'vessel' – that is, the setting – in which salvation is not only announced, but made effective for the believer.

At *De Idololatria* 24,4 the image of the ark is employed to convey an exclusivist, perfectionist view of the church from which all taint of impurity must be excluded. Declaring that the ark is a 'type' (for the church), Tertullian argues that since no animal taken into the Ark was fashioned as an idolater, that which was not in the ark has no legitimate place in the church. The image resembles those of 'sponsa Christi' and 'virgo', images employed particularly in Tertullian's later period when concerns of discipline had replaced those of doctrine in his ecclesiological thought.

[5] E. Evans, *Tertullian's Homily on Baptism. Text, translation and commentary* (London, 1964), p.74.
[6] Ibid., p.75.

THE CHURCH AS A 'SHIP'

The probable background for this image for the church is the 'little boat' of Matthew 8,23f. and 14,22f. and the life of maritime Carthage. With respect to the 'boat' image in the New Testament the implications are, in Minear's view, hard to fathom.[7] Most of Tertullian's references to ships are to real ones, with no theological overtones, although he does refer once to the human body as the 'corporis navis' (*De Anima* 52,4). The Pauline account at 1 Timothy 1,19f. of Hymenaeus and Alexander making 'shipwreck of the faith' – to which passage Tertullian himself frequently refers (*De Pudicitia* 13,15.20.21.; *De Fuga* 2,7; *De Praescriptione* 3,11) – also probably placed this image before him. This minor image clearly reflects in Tertullian a view of the church as 'holy', a church from which grievous sinners are to be excluded. The church is, however, like the 'little boat' of Matthew 8, not itself the source, but rather the context or setting in which Christ makes effective his saving grace.

At *De Baptismo* 12,6f. Tertullian explores the notion that the disciples underwent a type of 'baptism' when caught in the storm on the lake (Matthew 8,23f.). He concludes, however, that the whole concept is 'too forced'. He sees in the boat on which the disciples were buffeted by the elements a figure of the church. Again we are reminded that Tertullian often uses the term 'figura' (here 'figura ecclesiae') in the sense of an objective reality. However even this concept is placed within the context of the all-sufficiency of the person of Christ for the believer. The 'ship' is, again, not itself the source of salvation, but only the setting in which the saving grace of Christ is made effective.

At *De Pudicitia* 13,20 Tertullian deals with the exclusion of grievous sinners from the church on the basis of the incestuous adulterer excluded by Paul at 1 Corinthians 5,1ff. and of the blasphemers Hymenaeus and Alexander at 1 Timothy 1,19f. Those who have made 'shipwreck of the faith', he declares, have excluded themselves from the consolation of the 'ship', that is, the church, and thus from its 'protection'.

[7] Minear, *Images.*, p.33.

THE CHURCH AS A 'CAMP'

A number of 'military' images are employed by New Testament writers (e.g. 2 Timothy 2,3). There is, however, only one New Testament reference to the church as a 'camp'. At Revelation 20,9 the author speaks, in the context of the Millennium, of the 'camp (parembole) of the saints'. Tertullian's use of this particular image for the church may also be influenced by the 'camps' of the Israelites in the Wilderness. Yet neither these nor the Revelation passage cited are acknowledged when Tertullian speaks of the church as a 'camp'. While some of the early Fathers – Clement of Rome and Ignatius, for example – employ 'military' images, only one, Irenaeus of Lyons, uses this image for the church.[8] Tertullian's employment of the image probably reflects, for the most part, the increasing militarisation of Roman provincial society under Severus and Tertullian's own partiality for 'military' images, rather than a particular scriptural influence. Military images were a classic Stoic topos, and Tertullian's indebtedness to Stoic thought is well documented.[9]

Cicero, who exercised a considerable influence on Tertullian, employed the image of the 'camp' to denote both political parties and philosophical schools. At *Pro A. Caecina Oratio* 29,83 he informs a political opponent who he believes is supporting his (i.e. Cicero's) own argument, that 'in meis castris praesidiisque versaris' (you belong in my camp and station). At *Epistula ad Familiares* 9,20,1 – written to Paetus and replete with military images – he describes a personal shift in philosophical position thus: 'In Epicuri nos adversarii nostri castra coniecimus' (We have driven into the camp of our enemy Epicurus).

In his early period Tertullian was more likely to apply the image of the 'camp' to the enemies of the church than to the church itself. Only one of his ecclesiologically directed references, *De Oratione* 19,5, belongs to that particular period. At *De Spectaculis* 24,3 Tertullian asserts that 'nemo in castra hostium transit' (Noone goes over into the camp of the enemy) unless he

---

[8] *Haer.* IV, 20,12, the church as 'the camp of the righteous'.

[9] J. Fuellenbach, *Ecclesiastical office and the primacy of Rome: an evaluation of recent theological discussion of First Clement* (Washington, 1990), p. 19.

breaks first his oath of allegiance to Christ, and at *De Praescriptione* 41,7, that 'nusquam facilius proficitur quam in castris rebellium ubi ipsum esse illic promereri est' (Nowhere is promotion easier than in the camp of the rebels, where being there itself is to deserve merit). In the first passage the 'enemy' is the devil; in the second Tertullian is about to draw a contrast between the discipline, dignity and integrity of the Catholics and the indiscipline and irregularity of the heretics. Later, at *De Corona* 15,3, Tertullian refers to the cult of Mithras as the 'castra tenebrarum' (the camp of darkness). In Tertullian's application of the image of 'camp' to the church we see his desire both to draw a powerful wedge between it and the ominous threat of the cult of Mithras and – as is evident in both his early and later periods – to portray the church as ideally holy and thus free from sinful contamination.

One of the two 'early' references to the church as a 'camp' in Tertullian – at *De Oratione* 19,5 – is of no special significance for our appreciation of his doctrine of the church, since it merely serves as a backdrop for Tertullian's comments on the significance of 'stations' for Christian discipline. At *De Idololatria* 19,2, however, Tertullian begins to draw his later commonplace comparison between the 'camp' of the church and that of her enemies. Though it is likely that the references to the 'camps' of 'light' and of 'darkness' in *De Idololatria* are more general[10] than those of the later *De Corona* (see below), Tertullian may have also had in mind here the militarily popular cult of Mithras. It is generally accepted, however, that the involvement of Christians in military service was not yet the major problem it was to become for Christian apologists a decade later at the time of the writing of *De Corona*.[11] At *De Corona* 11,4, however, the image of the 'camp' bears a greater significance for Tertullian's ecclesiological thought. The increasing militarisation of the imperial provinces meant a growing pressure on Christians to make deliberate choices between the 'camp' of the world and that of the Christian faith. This brought into play considerations which

---

[10] There is, for example, no explicit reference to the cult of Mithras in the treatise.
[11] See, for example, W. Rordorf, 'Tertullians Beurteilung des Soldatenstandes', *VC* 23 (1969), p.118.

were simply not at issue, or at least not to the same extent, in Tertullian's early period. Now Tertullian draws a clear line between the church as the 'camp of light' and its opponents as the 'camp of darkness'. And further, it is clear that in *De Corona* Tertullian has a particular enemy in mind. The whole treatise is set against the background of Roman military life, and the reference to 'camps' is not employed merely as a backdrop as in *De Oratione*. At 15,3 this 'camp of darkness' is explicitly identified with the cult of Mithras. Two issues bring into sharp focus the considerable threat posed to Christian solidarity by this cult. First, there are the similarities in form, to which Tertullian himself draws attention at *De Praescriptione* 40,4, between some cultic practices of the church and those of Mithraism. Second, there is the suggestion that the Christian soldier in *De Corona*, far from being simply the uncompromising 'soldier of Christ' portrayed by Tertullian, was actually seeking for Christian soldiers the same exemption from wearing triumphal laurels as that enjoyed by the followers of Mithras.[12] In *De Corona* at least, the reference to the church as a 'camp of light' promotes the cause of the Christian faith against the claims of one of its chief rivals amongst the pagan sects; and in so doing Tertullian sets the conflict within the context of the life-and-death struggle in which the church is engaged.

The reference at *De Pudicitia* 14,17 to the church as a 'camp' is clearly a reference to an 'exclusive' fellowship. It reflects the concerns of the 'later' Tertullian with the exercise of a rigorous discipline in the life the church. This is demonstrated by its use by Tertullian, against the background of the exclusion by Paul of the incestuous adulterer at 1 Corinthians 5, to support his concept of the true church as one holy and free from contamination by grievous sinners.

THE CHURCH AS THE 'BODY OF CHRIST'

When Tertullian chooses to employ the best known of the biblical images for the church – that of the Body of Christ – he

---

[12] Harnack, *Militia Christi*, p. 83.

describes the church variously as 'corpus', 'Christus' and 'trinitas'. Central to his understanding and consequent employment of these images are the well-known references to the church as the Body of Christ in 1 Corinthians 12, Ephesians 1 and 4, Romans 12 and Colossians 1 and 2 (see Introduction). Of the Fathers before Tertullian, Hermas, Irenaeus and Clement of Alexandria cite some of these passages, though without great significance, while Clement of Rome is much influenced by passages from 1 Corinthians 12 and Ephesians 4 in his condemnation of schism and faction in the congregation at Corinth.[13] Although the Body of Christ is perhaps the most significant ecclesiological image in the New Testament, it is employed infrequently in Tertullian's extant writings. Yet it clearly plays a more significant part in his thought than it does in the Fathers who preceded him; for these, with the exception of Clement of Rome, it appears formally and incidentally.

When Tertullian employs 'corpus' as an image for the church he does so in a variety of ways and settings. At *Apologeticum* 39,1, addressing a non-Christian audience, he uses it in the sense of a 'society' or 'corporation', a sense not found in the Bible. Here employment of the word owes more to Stoicism than to Christianity. He seeks to explain the nature of the church to a pagan audience. Although Tertullian alludes to Ephesians 4,4, he employs the term 'corpus' to portray the church in a manner suited to pagan understanding. This and other analogical images drawn from secular life – 'factio' and 'curia', for example – Tertullian builds upon by proceeding to explain the inner workings of this Christian 'association' (39,2f.). Notwithstanding his non-Christian audience, however, Tertullian did have the Pauline image in mind when he speaks here of the church as a 'body'. At *De Baptismo* 6,2 Tertullian may also seem at first not to reflect the Pauline understanding of the word, but the trinitarian context would suggest otherwise. Tertullian alludes both to the requirements of Deuteronomy 19,15, where it is laid

---

[13] Hermas, *Sim.* IX,13,5 (Ephesians 4,4); IX,13,7 (Ephesians 4,4); Irenaeus, *Haer.*IV, 32,1 (Ephesians 4,16); V,18,2 (Ephesians 4,16); IV,32,1 (Colossians 2,19); V,14,4 (Colossians 2,19); Clement, *Paed.* 1,16 (1 Corinthians 12,13); *Strom.* 1,1 (Ephesians 4,12); *1 Clement* 37,5; 38,1.

down that two or three witnesses be present for a 'criminal' charge to be sustained, and also to both Matthew 18,16 and 2 Corinthians 13,1 where the Old Testament injunction is applied to the refusal of an erring brother to repent. Thus, through the benediction uttered at a person's baptism, the three divine Persons are represented by Tertullian as being witnesses and guarantors of both an orthodox faith and the gift of salvation. And alongside of these three divine Persons is the church which is declared, by way of allusion to Matthew 18,20, to be a 'body of three'. While the crucial image is here, however, not that of the 'body', but rather the 'Three', the Pauline image of the church as the Body of Christ cannot be far from Tertullian's mind. He seeks to link the church in its 'three-ness' with the triune Godhead. Here 'the three divine persons are the guarantors of the solid reality of the church'.[14] The guarantee of the salvation signified in the sacrament of baptism, and offered through the agency of the church, is provided by the 'witness' of the triune God. A passage from *Adversus Marcionem* v,8,9 reflects, in common with normal early patristic usage, a formal employment of 1 Corinthians 12. It is used to underscore the essential unity of the Old and New Testaments as manifested by the harmony of the Isaianic and Pauline lists of spiritual gifts and derived from the Lordship of the one Creator God. Tertullian continues his demonstration of the identification of the God of the Old Testament with that of the New by comparing the lists of spiritual gifts as given under the two dispensations, those at Isaiah 11,1-3 and at 1 Corinthians 12. Tertullian sees the Apostle's affirmation of the unity of the Body of Christ (in his members) as manifesting the unity of the Godhead. Everything points to the identity of the Creator God of the Old Testament with the Father of Jesus Christ in the New. At *Adversus Marcionem* v,19,6 Tertullian begins by seeking to affirm, on the one hand, the priority and thus the validity of the orthodox rule of faith, and, on the other, the lateness and consequent invalidity of heresy. Priority evidences apostolicity. Tertullian asserts the absurdity of the Marcionite distinction between the Creator

---

[14] Bévenot, 'Tertullian's thoughts', p.133.

God of the Old Testament and the strange god of the New, arguing that sinful humanity can be reconciled only to its own Creator. Conciliation can be had with a strange god, perhaps, but not reconciliation. He then affirms that such reconciliation has taken place through the death of Jesus, the Christ of the Creator God, and not of some strange, later one. Tertullian reinforces his earlier rather routine and unimaginative deployments of the image through the implication that references to the church as the Body of Christ are normally to be understood figuratively. Yet this particular relegation of the image to the realm of the metaphorical is necessitated here by the need to affirm both the reality of the flesh of Christ (against a Marcionite docetism) and the confession that through the death in that flesh alone has come the reconciliation of fallen creation to its own God, 'non propterea et in totum mentionem corporis transferens a substantia' (but not on this account to interpret every mention of the body (of Christ) as only a metaphor and not as real flesh). It is important to acknowledge this, for elsewhere (see below) Tertullian appears to suggest both that the image bears a more concrete and less metaphorical meaning, and that there can be a real sense in which the true church (that of the Spirit) is an extension of the Incarnation and thus identifiable with the Risen Christ.

In two passages from *De Paenitentia* there is a close identification between the person of Christ and the church as his Body, though this may be no more than the acknowledgement of the church as Christ's agent or vicar which acts in his name (see the Petrine commission in Matthew 16). At *De Paenitentia* 10,5 Tertullian encourages those who hesitate to undergo public '*exomologesis*', for fear of personal and public humiliation, to reconsider their position. He refers to Ephesians 4,4f. as he depicts a church drawn together by a shared joy and suffering and by a shared hope and the common worship of the one Lord and Father. He depicts a fellowship in which the penitent sinner will surely find support and understanding, since fellow members will automatically share in his suffering in a tangible way. Drawing also on the imagery of 1 Corinthians 12,21f, he describes the church fellowship as a body obliged to aid an afflicted 'part'.

At 10,6, having established the benefits for the reluctant penitent of allowing his church brethren, who are members of the one body, to support him, Tertullian goes on to explain that whatever the church fellowship does on behalf of the penitent is in fact done by Christ. For example, if the congregation prays for the penitent sinner, it is Christ who intercedes for him; if they weep, it is Christ who weeps. The church – the allusion is to Matthew 18,20 – is partially constituted by her human membership, but that can only ever be her earthly reality; the true church is indeed more than that. She is, in her heavenly fulfilment, identifiable with Christ, or at the very least, acts as his vicar, a deputy authorised and empowered to act in his name. The suggestion that in this passage Tertullian intends to introduce no abstraction, that 'diese Gleichung [ist] sehr konkret'[15] that the church is an extension of the Incarnation, may overstate the case; there is evidence, however, to support the view that this is the message which Tertullian means to convey. The presence of such a 'high' view of the church in one of Tertullian's early writings would explain, in part, his later desire to make more stringent the conditions under which the 'power' and the 'authority' due to the church as the 'successor' to Christ might properly be exercised.

THE CHURCH AS A 'TRINITY'

The scriptural background to the image of the church as 'trinity' is provided by a fusing of Deuteronomy 19,1, Matthew 18,16 and 2 Corinthians 13,1 with Matthew 18,20. The first three contain the requirement that there be at least two or three witnesses to testify either to the commission of a 'divine' offence or – in the case of the second passage cited – to the refusal of an erring brother to repent. The last cited contains the dominical prescription that 'where two or three are gathered in my name, there am I in the midst of them'. Tertullian speaks elsewhere of this church of 'threes' at *De Fuga* 14,1, 'Non potes discurrere per singulos, si tibi est in tribus ecclesia' (You cannot run about

---

[15] E. Altendorf, *Einheit und Heiligkeit der Kirche* (Leipzig, 1932) p. 20.

singly, if the church is for you in threes), and at *De Exhortatione Castitatis* 7,3, 'scilicet ubi tres, ecclesia est, licet laici' (where there are three, there is the church, notwithstanding they be laypersons). In neither of these, however, is the church represented as the 'trinity'. Tertullian refers also to the requirement of 'two or three witnesses' elsewhere (see, for example, at *De Praescriptione* 16,2), but again without any 'trinitarian' signification.

'Trinitarian' emphases in both *De Baptismo* and *De Pudicitia* – writings from both periods of Tertullian's career – suggest, however, and without apparent equivocation, a concretised identification, an authentic extension of the Incarnation in the church, and represent one of the 'highest' points of Tertullian's ecclesiology. At *De Baptismo* 6,2 Tertullian alludes to Matthew 18,20 when he declares that where there are the three – that is, Father, Son and Holy Spirit – there is the church which is a 'body of three'. At *De Pudicitia* 21,16, 'Nam et ipsa ecclesia proprie et principaliter ipse est spiritus, in quo trinitas unius divinitatis, Pater et Filius et Spiritus sanctus. Illam ecclesiam congregat quam Dominus in tribus posuit' (For the church is itself properly and principally the Spirit itself, in whom is the Trinity of the one Divinity – Father, Son and Holy Spirit. [The Spirit] brings together that church which the Lord has set down in three). Tertullian reinforces this theme, but does so with a greater emphasis on the active role of the Spirit as the manifestation, in the church, of the will and the power of the triune God. It may be, of course, an overstatement to suggest seriously an absolute identification by Tertullian of the church with either the Spirit or the triune Godhead. See, for example, the extravagant assertion of D'Alès that for Tertullian 'l'Eglise, c'est la trinité'.[16] Rather, as we shall see below, Tertullian seems to suggest that the authentic church is ultimately constituted by the presence within its life of that Spirit in whom is present the Trinity, 'the body of three' of *De Baptismo* 6,2. Such a view would tend to bear out the contention of Welch that where the dominant ecclesiological emphasis is on the analogy between the church and the person of Christ (rather than that between

[16] D'Alès, *La théologie de Tertullien*, p. 326.

the church and the justified yet sinful believer) we find the stress placed on the perfection (holiness) of the church;[17] and that of Minear that a high ecclesiology, such as is evident in Tertullian, derives from an emphasis on the ontological realism of the depiction of the Body of Christ.[18] Nothing in these passages suggests that the historical church becomes, in Tertullian's mind, divine in any absolute sense; rather, through the empowering by, and the direction of, the divine Spirit, it represents the reality of the divine will and purpose to the world. The church – as a 'body of three' – is witness to the reality of the involvement of the triune God in the world. The presence of such a view in a 'Montanist' treatise like *De Pudicitia* provides further proof that Tertullian's 'high' view of the church remained intact even after his transition to the New Prophecy.

From such a high ecclesiological view comes, in part then, Tertullian's emphasis on the necessary unity, holiness and apostolicity of the authentic church. A church which is the true Body of Christ cannot be divided lest Christ himself be divided. A church which is the true Body of Christ must become now what it is to be in the future and in promise; this leaves no room for sin or other taint of impurity in the present. A church which is the true Body of Christ must have received its form, if not its essential nature (which is Christ's), from those whom Christ himself commissioned to go out into the world. However concretely Tertullian identified the true church with the Risen Body of Christ, he certainly surpassed even the New Testament in the valuation he gave to the employment of the image of the 'body'. He thereby assisted the development of the progression towards Cyprian's view of the church and other, later 'high' ecclesiologies.

Such passages lead us now to a fuller consideration of the church as 'Spirit'; for Tertullian only that church which exhibits the Spirit in its life shows thereby that it is the authentic Body of Christ. Where is the true church? Where the Holy Spirit is recognisably present in power.[19] How is the church the authentic Body of Christ? It is, insofar as it has the Spirit in its midst.

[17] Welch, *The church*, p.29.   [18] Minear, *Images*, p.240.
[19] Newbigin, *Household of God*, p.87.

THE CHURCH AS 'SPIRIT'

Robinson declares that 'that which stamps the church as the eschatological community is its common possession of the Spirit'.[20] Newbigin points out that in the New Testament there is no dissociation of the Spirit of Christ from the Body of Christ and that it is the presence of the Holy Spirit within its midst which constitutes the church.[21] Any evaluation of Tertullian's employment of this image must also acknowledge his later involvement in the New Prophecy movement and his commitment to the concept of a pure, 'primitive' church; and, further, his desire to limit the damage done to the church's integrity by what he perceives as debilitating compromises over penitential discipline.[22]

We have seen how at *De Pudicitia* 21,16 Tertullian declares explicitly that the 'church is properly and principally the Spirit'. Yet an actual identification of the church with the Holy Spirit – as with the Trinity – is utterly foreign to Tertullian's thought. Tertullian is speaking here about a church whose authenticity is guaranteed, both by the presence of the Spirit within, and by its conformity to the demands of the Spirit as 'representative' of the Triune Godhead. The 'divine' power which such a church will exercise is validated only by the direction of the power-giving, life-giving Spirit. The authentic church is that which is constituted by the Spirit. At 21,17 Tertullian clarifies his meaning in the earlier passage. The model of apostolic verification has changed, in Tertullian's mind, from a test of doctrinal orthodoxy to one of the validated exercise of 'power' through the administration of right discipline. It is God who, initially through dominical and apostolic foundation and now through extraordinary spiritual confirmation, constitutes his church, and not the assembly or the decisions of human appointees. Tertullian does not reject tradition or the church hierarchy; he simply puts each in its proper place! Evans correctly perceives a shift in Tertullian's

---

[20] Robinson, *The body*, p.72.

[21] Newbigin, *Household of God*, pp.93 and 90.

[22] There is little evidence to suggest that Tertullian's position is the result of '[le] orgueil blessé' as D'Alès, *La théologie de Tertullien*, p. 490, claims.

thought from the concept of a church proved by historical-empirical continuity to one authenticated by the presence of the Spirit; a new criterion, the witness of the Spirit, has replaced that of episcopal succession. But this is so only to the extent that Tertullian is speaking about a criterion for demonstrating both the mark of apostolicity and the church as the authentic Body of Christ.[23] There is also evidence for the concept of an 'ecclesia spiritus' in Tertullian's 'Catholic' period.[24] Tertullian finds himself enmeshed in the dilemma that the realities of the visible, historical church and the demands of the Spirit, as he understands them, simply do not coincide. Again we glimpse something of Tertullian's 'high' view of the church; a view which, in the context now of his repeated clashes over ecclesial discipline, he had constantly and consistently to review and restate. However, his use of the image of the Spirit for the church should not be misunderstood nor given more prominence than certain other images and concepts which are equally as important for his ecclesiology. It was the presence of the Spirit within its midst which, according to Robinson, stamped the church as the authentic eschatological community, that community of those Last Days in which the millenarian Tertullian believed himself to live. As in the New Testament, the experienced presence of the Spirit within a church proves that church to be authentically the Body of Christ.[25]

THE CHURCH AS 'MOTHER'

At *Scorpiace* 7,1 Tertullian quotes a passage from Proverbs 9,2, 'Sophia. . .iugulavit filios suos' (Wisdom has murdered her sons).The Septuagint version reads '*Sophia esphaxe ta eautes thumata*' (Wisdom has slaughtered her own victims). Subsequently, at 7,3, Tertullian refers to Sophia as the 'bona mater'. Though one would be reluctant to read too much into this, it is possible that Tertullian may have perceived here an identification between the divine Wisdom and the pre-existent church. At 2 John 1 the author refers to the church congregation

---

[23] Evans, *One and holy*, p. 29.
[24] Altendorf, *Einheit*, p. 23.   [25] Newbigin, *Household of God*, p.92.

addressed by him as *'eklektei kuriai kai tois teknois autes'* (the elect lady and her children), thus representing the church as a 'mother'. Other scriptural passages which may have informed Tertullian's employment of this image include Galatians 4,21-31, or at least Marcion's reconstruction of it,[26] and Revelation 12,1f., though Tertullian's extant writings bear no explicit reference to this latter text.

Irenaeus declares in *Adv. Haereses* that 'those therefore who do not partake of him [sc. the Spirit of Truth] are neither nourished into life from the mother's breasts [a mamillis matris], nor do they enjoy that most limpid fountain issuing from the body of Christ' (III,24,1) (A-NCL alt.). This allusion to the church suggests the Body of Christ as a mother suckling her young. Earlier, at 1,8,4, Irenaeus had claimed that the Valentinians explain the Parable of the Lost Sheep by having the lost sheep signify 'their mother, by whom they represent the church as having been shown'. Eusebius records a letter which was sent by Irenaeus' church at Lyons at the time of the persecutions in the late second century. This letter speaks of those who first apostatised under torture, but later summoned the courage to confess anew their faith.

But the intervening time was not idle nor fruitless for them but through their endurance was manifested the immeasurable mercy of Christ, for through the living the dead were being quickened and martyrs gave grace to those who denied. And there was great joy to the virgin Mother [tei parthenoi metri] who had miscarried with them as though dead, and was receiving them back alive. (*Ecclesiastical History* V,1,45)

Again, the reference to 'mother' is clearly an allusion to the church. Clement of Alexandria frequently refers to the church as 'mother' in the *Paedogogus*. At 1, 21,1, alluding to Isaiah 66,12f., he declares that 'the mother comforts her children, and we seek our mother, the church'. At 1,42,1, treating of the unity of the Father and the Spirit, he again represents the church as the 'virgin mother' who 'calls her children to her and nurses them with holy milk, with the Word for childhood'.

---

[26] See above in the Introduction to Part II.

Tertullian was not then the first to apply the title 'mother' to the church,[27] although he uses it more conclusively and with particular emphasis for his own 'high' view of the church. In these early Fathers the church, given the image of 'mother', is granted for the first time a living identity distinct from her members. She becomes more than the sum of her membership. The image is connected also to that of the Body of Christ. In the Fathers before Tertullian the image of the church as 'mother' usually bears the sense of one who nourishes and comforts her children. It is never employed to maintain a 'high' ecclesiology; it only ever depicts the church as a major source of teaching and comfort. In Tertullian, however, the image begins – particularly as linked to that of God as 'Father' – to represent a more elevated view of the church. Only at *Ad Martyras* 1,1 does Tertullian employ the image specifically to portray the church as a 'nursing' mother; such usage could be said to reflect a New Testament influence. The reference recalls Irenaeus and Clement of Alexandria and the 'Lady Mother' image of 2 John 1. The image of the church-as-mother is here of one who will provide for the faithful both spiritually and materially. At *De Praescriptione* 42,10, *De Baptismo* 20,5, *De Monogamia* 16,4, *Adversus Marcionem* v,4,8 and *De Pudicitia* 5,14 Tertullian again employs the image in an uncommitted way, though *De Baptismo* 20,5 and *De Monogamia* 16,4 probably reflect, though indirectly, the mother/church–father/God association (see below). At *De Praescriptione* 42,10 Tertullian compares the irregular and undisciplined fellowship of the heretics with the more disciplined and discriminating Catholic practice. The heretics' lack of an authentic 'mother' puts them outside of the true church, for it separates them from the source of 'divine' life, from an access to God. They are illegitimate. It is perhaps only a small step from here to Cyprian's absolutist, uncompromising position enunciated

---

[27] Quasten, *Patrology II*, p. 330. I regret that I have not had access to J. C. Plumpe, *An Inquiry into the Concept of the Church as Mother in Early Christianity* (Catholic University of America, 1943). In a chapter 'The Mater Ecclesia of Tertullian', pp. 45-62, Plumpe apparently makes the correct assumption that an understanding of the church as 'mother' was already in place before Tertullian.

in *De Ecclesiae Unitate*.[28] At *Adversus Marcionem* v,4,8 Tertullian quotes with approval Marcion's re-construction of Galatians 4,26 which transfers the identification of the 'mother' embracing true believers from 'Jerusalem above' to the 'holy church'. This introduces another possible influence on Tertullian's employment of ecclesiological images. He was perhaps not prepared to allow the arch-heretic Marcion – whose followers, in Tertullian's view, were influential far and wide in his own time[29] – to hold a more elevated view of that church than he. As some commentators have pointed out, the employment by Tertullian of his opponent's language is normal for him.[30]. In the same way as he was influenced by those philosophers whom he claimed to despise, he was possibly also influenced by some heterodox Christians.

At *De Baptismo* 20,5 we have the first explicit connection made by Tertullian between the 'motherhood' of the church and the 'fatherhood' of God. With it comes the possibility that the church does not become 'mother' to the believer – and even that God may not become 'father' – until the catechumen has been baptised. We are moving closer to a point when the acknowledgement of the church as 'mother' becomes a pre-requisite for that of God as 'father', and acceptance by the latter becomes somewhat dependent on that by the former. *De Monogamia* 16,4 supports the assertion that the intimate relationship of church members – that is, their status as 'brethren', as 'sons' of the same 'parent' – derives as much at least from the 'motherhood' of the church as from the 'fatherhood' of God. This is confirmed by reference above to *De Baptismo* 20. (See also *De Pudicitia* 5,14.) At *De Oratione* 2,6 and *De Monogamia* 7,9, however – each coming from different periods of Tertullian's career – his use of the image of the church-as-mother in connection with that of God-as-father clearly does reflect a 'high' ecclesiology. Tertullian was certainly not the first to call the church 'mother'; but he was the first to connect this image

---

[28] Cyprian, *De Ecclesiae Unitate* 6, 'He cannot have God as father who does not have the Church as Mother.' See also *De Lapsis* 9: 'They (i.e. heretics) have denied to us the church as a Mother; they have denied God as a Father', and Tertullian's *De Oratione* 2,6.

[29] *Adversus Marcionem* v,19,2.

[30] See O'Malley, *Tertullian and the Bible*, p. 2 and van der Geest, *Le Christ et l'ancien Testament*, p. 57.

to that of the 'fatherhood' of God, and to make such 'motherhood' a virtual article of faith.

Except for the *Adversus Marcionem* passage addressed above,
where 'sancta' is affixed to 'mater', Tertullian does not appear
explicitly to link the 'motherhood' of the church to her holiness.
Unlike the church at Lyons and Clement of Alexandria,
Tertullian never explicitly associates the images of the church as
'mother' and as 'virgin'. Further, one might ask whether there is
in Tertullian's ecclesiological thought at all the image of the
eschatological/messianic community as a mother (reflecting
Revelation 12?) bearing and nurturing children? It seems then
that part at least of Tertullian's hostility towards the Catholics
in his later period was aroused not by a low, but rather by an
elevated view of the church. This hostility was not then directed
at the church, but at those who by their indifference threatened
her integrity. 'Ne mater quidem Ecclesia praeteritur, siquidem
in filio et patre mater recogniscitur, de qua constat et patris et
filii nomen' (Nor indeed is our mother the Church overlooked,
since the mother is recognised in the son and the father, and
from her the name of both father and son is established)(*De
Oratione* 2,6). Tertullian is dealing here with the first clause of the
Lord's Prayer. The proposition that here Tertullian 'conceives
of the Motherhood of the Church as corresponding upon earth
to the Fatherhood of God in heaven, as though without the
agency of the Church we could not have the Fatherhood of God.
It is through the Church that we become sons of God' is an
overstatement.[31] Such an elevated view of the church was
certainly that of Cyprian, but can we attribute it to Tertullian?
It is elsewhere claimed that such a concept of the 'motherhood'
of the church was evidently known to Tertullian's audience;
that Tertullian probably didn't intend to imply here that the
relation between God as father and God as son introduces the
church as mother, but rather that in calling upon God as father,
we acknowledge the church as mother.[32] While the latter
construction or interpretation is more accommodating to a

---

[31] R. W. Muncey, *'De Oratione' of Tertullian* (London, 1926), p. 27; J.F. Bethune-Baker,
An introduction to the early history of Christian doctrine to the time of the Council of Chalcedon
(London, 1933), p. 361   [32] Muncey, *'De Oratione'*, p. 45f.

'lower' view of the church, it does not accord with the simple meaning of Tertullian's words which seem to conform to the 'higher' view.

What emerges from the pen of Tertullian here is a concept which comes close to the later Cyprianic view and which suggests that only those who actually recognise the one, catholic and apostolic church of God as 'mother' can truly be said to acknowledge properly the 'fatherhood' of God. It is perhaps the most elevated height to which Tertullian carries his understanding of church. A reading of *De Monogamia* 7,9 demonstrates clearly that this 'high' view of the church was not abandoned in his later period. The association of the church-as-mother with God-as-father remained a constant in his thought.

THE CHURCH AS A 'BRIDE'

The scriptural precedents for this image can be found at Psalm 19, 5.6, The Song of Solomon 4,8, Luke 5,34-35 (the Parable of the Bridegroom), Ephesians 5,22ff. and 2 Corinthians 11,1f. According to Ephraem Syrus, the Marcionites also called the church 'sponsa', as did the African Novatian.[33] Tertullian's employment of this image – closely associated as it is with that of the church-as-virgin – is tied up with a demand for submission and obedience by the church to Christ, with the idea of perfectionism and the church's essential unity. It is noteworthy that he does not use it, while he does that of the church-as-virgin, in his earlier writings. The scriptural precedents for the image are clear and serve to underline the necessity of preserving the church untainted by grievous sinners and of maintaining its integrity undivided. Exclusions do not themselves make the church 'holy', but the essential 'holiness' of the true 'spouse' of Christ renders such exclusions necessary. Similarly Cyprian regarded the church as 'holy', neither because its members had achieved great sanctity nor because the unholy had been expelled from it, but rather because it was the Bride of Christ.[34] The church is the Bride – although the actual wedding does not

---

[33] *Contra Haereses* 47,3; *De Trinitate* 29.
[34] S. L. Greenslade, *Schism in the early church* (London, 1953), p.170.

take place until the End[35] – and she must become in the present that which she will be at that End, cleansed and pure. The image of the church as the Bride of Christ also has as its correlative figure that of the Body of Christ. For in the union of Christ and his church is one body formed, as it was in their prefigurement in Adam and Eve;[36] to sunder this union would be to sunder Christ himself.

Tertullian underpins the concern evident at both *De Monogamia* 5,7 and 11,2 to defend the validity of monogamy by reference to the spiritual 'monogamy' in which Christ and his church are joined. He employs the 'bride' image to emphasise the essential 'oneness' of the church; in the first passage by reference to the monogamous relationship of Adam and Eve, and in the second by associating the image with that of the church as a 'virgin', a virgin whose very honour is compromised by the dishonourable actions of some clergy. The church is the virgin bride whose obedience and faithfulness contrasts so nobly with the disobedience and faithlessness of her clergy.

Tertullian's double trilogy at *Adversus Marcionem* v,18,9:

At enim Christus amavit et carnem sicut ecclesiam. Nemo non diliget imaginem quoque sponsae, immo et servabit illam et honorabit et coronabit. Habet similitudo cum veritate honoris consortium. Laborabo ego nunc eundem deum probare masculi et Christi, mulieris et ecclesiae, carnis et spiritus. . .

(But surely Christ loved the flesh as he did the Church. For no person will love a picture of his wife, without that he will serve, honour and crown her. The likeness partakes with the reality in the fellowship of honour. I will strive to prove that the same God is that of both man and Christ, of wife and of church, of the flesh and the spirit. . .)

represents an exceptionally 'high' view of the church. The man is almost certainly Adam (Christ being the second perfect Adam) and the woman Eve (the church being the second perfect Eve). In the much celebrated passage from *De Pudicitia* 1,8 the image of the church as 'bride' is associated again with

---

[35] Welch, *The church*, p.133, note 2.
[36] *Genesis* 2,24. F. F. Bruce, *The Epistles to the Colossians, to Philemon and to the Ephesians* (NIC) (Grand Rapids, 1984), p. 395, 'The formation of Eve to be Adam's companion is seen to prefigure the creation of the church to be the bride of Christ.'

that of 'virgin' – the influence of Ephesians 5,32ff. is evident – and is employed to underline the essential 'holiness' of the church. It serves also to underscore the assertion made elsewhere that Tertullian's disagreement in his later period is not with the church as such – for he retains throughout a 'high' ecclesiology – but rather with those who threaten her dignity and integrity. (See also *De Corona* 14,3; *De Fuga* 14,2; *Adversus Marcionem* 4,11,8; 5,12,6; *De Pudicitia* 18,11.)

THE CHURCH AS A 'VIRGIN'

Unlike its companion image of the church-as-bride, this does not have many scriptural precedents with direct reference to the church. At 2 Corinthians 11,2, Paul refers – in terms similar to Ephesians 5,26f. – to the church as a 'pure virgin' offered to Christ. Ephesians 5 itself applies this image only implicitly to the church.

Patristic precedents are, however, not so difficult to find. Clement of Alexandria, in his *Paedagogus*, describes the church as both 'mother' and 'virgin'.[37] At 1, 42,1 he speaks of the 'virgin mother' nourishing her children with 'holy milk'. In a letter sent out by the persecuted church at Lyons in the time of Irenaeus the church is alluded to as the 'virgin mother', and in such a way as to indicate clearly that the recipients of the letter readily understood the allusion.[38] Hegesippus is also reported to have claimed that the church was a 'virgin' until the time of the emperor Trajan.[39] And yet, notwithstanding the numerous patristic precedents available for this image, it is clear that, even without them, Tertullian, given his determination to present the church as essentially holy, would probably have invented it.

Tertullian, for whom 'castus' and 'sanctus' are correlatives,[40] employed the image of the church-as-virgin consistently throughout his writings to represent the authentic church as 'holy' and free from contamination. The transition from 'Catholic' to 'Montanist' involves, however, a change in the manner in which

[37] 1,42.   [38] Eusebius, *Ecclesiastical History* 5,1,45.   [39] Ibid., 3,32,7.
[40] G. Bray, *Holiness and the will of God: perspectives on the theology of Tertullian* (London, 1979), p.137.

the term 'virgin' is understood and employed by him. This transformation reflects a change in the focus of Tertullian's thought from doctrine to discipline.

At *De Praescriptione* 44,2 Tertullian speaks of the church as a virgin, 'besmirched through heretical doctrine'.[41] It is the church's doctrinal 'virginity' which is here at stake. In condemning the apparently widespread practice of wealthy Christians bribing their way out of persecution, the church (and its discipline) is depicted at *De Fuga* 14,2 – from one of Tertullian's later writings – as a 'virgin' who should not be bought or sold, as it were, on the open market. At *De Monogamia* 11,2, and at *De Pudicitia* 1,8 and 18,11 the authentic church is represented as a 'virgin' untouched by irregular discipline. In those passages the image is closely linked to that of the church-as-bride and the allusions to Ephesians 5,26f. and to 2 Corinthians 11,2 are obvious, even if not explicit.

This image serves to underline Tertullian's perfectionist view of the church and, especially in those passages taken from his later period, conforms with Tertullian's basic eschatological outlook and his appreciation of the demands of sanctification. The church is to become what she is already, the spotless, pure virgin bride, to be presented to Christ as such on the Day. As individual Christians, sanctified by Christ, are bound now to lead lives worthy of the Kingdom to come, so, too, must the church. The image expresses, in complete conformity with regular New Testament usage, that complete singleness of mind with which the bride Israel obeyed her husband, and along with the images of the church as bride and mother, denotes the faithfulness and humility of the authentic church in the presence of Christ.

THE CHURCH AS A 'SCHOOL'

Precedents for this image can be found in the secular world of philosophy and education. Tertullian makes at least five references in his writings, apart from the three to the Christian 'schola', to

---

[41] K. Adam, *Der Kirchenbegriff Tertullians* (Paderborn, 1907), p. 35.

secular 'scholae' – the secondary schools of antiquity – at least seven to philosophical 'scholae' – most to the Epicurean – others to a gladiatorial 'schola', two to 'scholae' within the Valentinian sect, and one to the 'schola' of Ptolemy, a disciple of Valentinus.[42] This image is employed by Tertullian to explain the Christian faith and church in terms immediately recognisable to his pagan neighbours. His purpose is not only, however, to find a sympathetic ear for his exposition of Christian teaching, but also to demonstrate the clear superiority of Christian 'scholarship'. Tertullian also employs this image to represent the church as the authentic successor to the first apostles of Christ.

In chapter 8 of his *Scorpiace* Tertullian discusses whether martyrdom is part of the divine imperative. He seeks to combat those heretics – called by him 'scorpions', hence the title – who cast doubt on the authenticity of this divine command to undergo martyrdom. Tertullian recalls the examples of the Old Testament prophets Elias, Jeremiah, Isaiah, Zacharias and Daniel, who were all summoned by God to accept suffering for their refusal to render homage to pagan idols. At 9,1 he sarcastically asks whether it should be any different for the followers of Christ; to this question he himself answers clearly in the negative. The 'schola' of the Christians is seen as providing a continuity with that of these Old Testament prophets.

At *Scorpiace* 12,1 Tertullian again attacks those heretics who deny the dominical and apostolic pronouncements on the inevitability of persecution for true believers; he seeks confirmation of this from the teachings of the apostles. He depicts the original disciples as being formed by Christ into a 'schola' of his own. This 'schola' did not die out with those first apostles; it continues in the life of the 'apostolic' church which exists in direct succession to that original 'school'. This concept of 'schola' is analogous to that of the pagan schools and their understanding of 'succession'.

At *De Anima* 1,6 Tertullian again compares the 'schola' of Christ – the 'schola caeli' – with the schools of pagan philosophy, particularly with those who revere the memory of Socrates.

[42] The reference at *Adv. Valentinianos* 11,2 is to a division over some aspect of Valentinian doctrine; ibid., 33, 1.

Tertullian compares this Christian 'wisdom' more than favourably with that claimed to be possessed by the pagan philosophies. Such Christian wisdom has the sanction of heaven, unlike that of the pagan philosophies which are essentially human creations.

THE CHURCH AS A 'SECT'

The background for this image is – as it was for 'schola' – the philosophical schools of antiquity. References to some of these groups can be found at *Apologeticum* 3, passim, *De Praescriptione* 7,8, *Ad Nationes* 1,4,2, *De Resurrectione* 2,1, *De Fuga* 12,9, as well as some to heretical Christian sects at *Scorpiace* 1,7 and *De Idololatria* 9,6 (that of Simon Magus). Tertullian is again seeking (as a good apologist) to present the Christian faith in a way immediately intelligible to pagans, but also (as a good controversialist) in such a way as will demonstrate the intellectual superiority of the Christian school over the pagan. Other uses of the word 'secta' by Tertullian worthy of comment include: *De Pudicitia* 14,27, where he refers to the 'apostoli secta', by which he means the 'character of the Apostle' (i.e. Paul); *De Monogamia* 11,1, where he refers to the 'secta' (i.e. order) of widows in the church; and *Adv. Marcionem* IV, 23,11 and 27,5, where 'secta Creatoris' means the '[doctrinal] rule of the Creator'.

As with 'schola', Tertullian employs 'secta' to depict the church and its teaching tradition in a manner recognisable to pagan audiences. He does this notwithstanding the dangers posed by this approach to the unique nature of the Christian faith. And yet, while claiming for the Christian 'sect' the same consideration under the law as that afforded to other 'tolerated associations' in Roman society, he is also at pains to demonstrate the clear moral and intellectual superiority of the Christian faith. It was an approach involving great risk, but Tertullian employed both it and the image itself consistently throughout his career. In one passage – *Apologeticum* 47,9 – Tertullian employs the image to emphasise the essential 'oneness' of the Christian church. In a number of others – by implicit comparison with the pagan schools and their succession of teachers reaching back to an original founder or founders – Tertullian employs it to underline the essential apostolicity of the church. Only some of the many passages in which the image of a 'sect' is employed will be discussed, since many make similar points. For those passages not discussed in detail references will be given.

At *Apologeticum* 3,6 and 7 Tertullian's defence of the Christian 'school/sect' is based upon the accepted process of the founding and naming of pagan philosophical schools. Tertullian's argument is that the church is treated most unfairly in comparison with these other schools. He argues that an equal consideration would at least present the Christian faith in a more reasonable light. He appeals to the Romans' sense of justice, asking that they put to one side their innate prejudices against sects of this type. Tertullian links the Christian 'sect' with Judaism at *Apologeticum* 21,1 in an attempt to credit the church with a continuous teaching tradition stretching back into antiquity. This is similar to his use of 'schola' in *Scorpiace* 9,1 above. This was important when addressing the claims of the Christian faith to Romans, for whom patriality and longevity were important criteria for determining religious authenticity, and which attributes were commonly believed to be lacking in Christianity.

At *Apologeticum* 39,6 Tertullian claims for the church the same toleration and privileges as enjoyed by some non-Christian groups on the basis that it – like some other social institutions in the empire – supports its destitute members. He argues for the 'law-abiding' nature and 'propriety' of the Christians who pose no threat to the general community. At 43,2 Tertullian presents the Christians as a 'community service' organisation, offering society invaluable (divine) 'protection'. At 46,2 he laments that the pagans, some of whom do recognise the Christians as a valid 'school', unfortunately do not acknowledge the divine sanction which underpins it. At 47,9 Tertullian may even be suggesting that some heretical groups might belong to the Christian 'sect' when he speaks of the many varieties of approach within the Christian faith. He is aware, as were other Christian apologists, that many pagans did not fully appreciate the subtleties of orthodox-heterodox differences. It is more likely, however, that he means simply to indicate here the different approaches to some aspects of the Christian faith within orthodoxy itself.

Tertullian's reference at *Ad Scapulam* 1,1 to the 'pactum' on which membership of the Christian 'sect' is based – again he seeks to represent Christianity in secular terms recognisable to pagans – recalls his reference at *De Pudicitia* 12,9 to the 'pactum' which exists between the Paraclete and the New Prophets. His reference at *De Pallio* 6,2 to the philosopher's cloak and its 'fellowship' with the 'school' of the Christians is designed to draw an analogy between the church – as an institution propagating and handing on a body of tradition through a succession of teachers – and the better known philosophical 'schools'. (See also *Apologeticum* 1,1; 5,3; 21,27; 37,3; 38,1; 40.7; 50,13; *De Spectaculis* 2,3; *Ad Scapulam* 3,4; 4,6.7; 5,4; *De Fuga* 12,8.9; *De Idololatria* 9,6; *De Corona* 7,2; *Ad Nationes* 1,4,1.2.)

CHAPTER 5

The church as 'one, holy, catholic and apostolic'?

INTRODUCTION

The great affirmation of the church as 'one, holy, catholic and apostolic' was not formulated precisely or stated explicitly until the promulgation of the Niceno-Constantinopolitan Creed in 381. Yet the seeds of this declaration of the essential notes of the true church were sown well before this time.

UNITY as a note of the true church has its scriptural basis in passages such as the prayer of Jesus for the unity of his disciples at John 17,21f., Paul's condemnation of division in the congregation at 1 Corinthians 11,17f., and at Ephesians 4,4-6, where the author ties the unity of the church to that of the Godhead. Among the Fathers before Tertullian, Clement of Rome, Hermas and Irenaeus of Lyons all place emphasis on the necessary unity of the church and frequently either cite or allude to Ephesians 4,4-6 to make their point.[1]

HOLINESS as a note of the true church was very early linked to the question of discipline. The assertion that the church is the virgin Bride of Christ at Ephesians 5,26f., the case of the man living with his father's wife at 1 Corinthians 5,1-5, the treachery of Hymenaeus and Alexander at 1 Timothy 1,19f., and the warnings to separate from an erring brother and other immoral persons at 2 Thessalonians 3,6, Ephesians 5,7f, and 1 Timothy 5,22 all confirm the necessary holiness of the church; this is usually accompanied by a call for a rigorous discipline which will lead to a church fellowship untainted by grievous sinners.

---

[1] *1 Clement*,46,5.6 (LCL). Clement constantly condemns schism and division in the church; Hermas, *Sim* ix,xiii,5.7; *Haer.* I,10,2; III,24,1.

CATHOLICITY as a note of the true church has its origin in both the Great Commission of Jesus at Matthew 28,19-20 and the account in Acts of the regular and controlled spread of the Gospel message throughout the Roman world and the accompanying establishment of new churches. The word '*katholike*' does not appear in the New Testament in this context; where it does appear, for example, at *Acts* 4,18, it is used in the adverbial form with the meaning of 'at all' or 'completely'.

APOSTOLICITY as a note of the true church is not as explicitly addressed in the Scriptures as are the others, but is implied in both the *Pastorals* and in the attribution to various of the apostles (especially Paul) of particular New Testament writings.

It is immediately obvious that Tertullian does not, any more than any Father before him, explicitly affirm the true church as that which is essentially 'one, holy, catholic and apostolic'. That he does, however, come much closer by implication to the credal affirmation of the Great Church than any before him is clear. Our discussion of Tertullian's ecclesial images has shown conclusively how an exclusivist-perfectionist (holiness) view of the church dominates Tertullian's thought in both major periods of his career (see 'arca', 'navis', 'castra', 'mater', 'sponsa' and 'virgo'). Further, images such as 'secta' and 'schola' highlight the equally crucial significance to his thought of the notion of apostolicity. The attribute of unity as a note of the true church is demonstrated by an image such as 'corpus'.

These notes of the true church (catholicity being discussed alongside unity) – and their significance for Tertullian's overall ecclesiological thought – will be discussed with reference both to those images employed by Tertullian which implicitly represent them and to those passages which deal with them explicitly.

PERFECTIONISM AND ESCHATOLOGY – THE CHURCH AS HOLY

The background to Tertullian's thought on the 'holiness' of the church is found both in his eschatology and in scriptural texts such as Ephesians 5,7f. and 5,26f., 1 Corinthians 5,1-5, 2 Thessalonians 3,6, 1 Timothy 1,19.20, and 1 Timothy

5,22.[2] The Parable of the Tares at Matthew 13,24-30, 36-43 is referred to a number of times by Tertullian, but only in relation to the 'tares' planted by Praxeas and the Devil.[3] The Fathers before Tertullian said little explicitly on this question, though this should not imply that the holiness of the church did not concern them. Irenaeus quotes Ephesians 5,7 but not especially so as to address the ecclesiological question.[4] He also alludes to Ephesians 5,26f. within the context of a general discussion of the question of sanctification.[5] None of Tertullian's predecessors – Clement of Rome, Justin and Irenaeus, for example – cite 1 Corinthians 5,1-5, 1 Timothy 1,19f. or 5,22. Irenaeus quotes Galatians 4,26, but does so with the conventional textual reading rather than that used by Marcion (and approved by Tertullian).[6] Polycarp also cites the passage, asserting, however, that 'the mother of us all' is the faith built upon the foundation of Paul's teaching.[7]

It has long been taken for granted among scholars that Tertullian, at least in his later period, had a narrow 'perfectionist' view of the church; that he had an 'exclusive sectarian concept of Church' which was 'a society of the morally righteous... uncontaminated by the presence of sinners'.[8] For Tertullian, 'la sainte Eglise est le terme final de toute la discipline';[9] an essential characteristic of his concept of the church is its 'Heiligkeit', and such a church cannot long endure sinners in its midst.[10] Tertullian, in contrast to Clement of Alexandria and Origen for whom the church 'on earth' is but an incomplete image of the 'heavenly' ideal, sees the Church on earth as identical to that 'in caelis'.[11] The assertion that this 'later' Tertullian had a perfectionist view of the church is well supported by his writings, especially by

---

[2] *De Pudicitia* 18,9 (Ephesians 5,7); ibid. 18,11 (Ephesians 5,26; 1 Corinthians 5,1-5; 2 Thessalonians 3,6); ibid. 13,15.20.21 (1 Timothy 1,19,20); ibid.18,9; *De Baptismo* 18,1 (1 Timothy 5,22). Note, however, that 1 Timothy 5,22 relates more to personal than to ecclesial holiness.

[3] *Adv. Praxean* 1,6.7;*De Praescriptione* 31,1; *De Anima* 16,7.

[4] *Haer.* IV,27,4.   [5] Ibid.IV,20,12;   [6] See *Adv. Marcionem* v,4,8.   [7] *Phil.* 3,3.

[8] G. W. H. Lampe, 'Christian theology in the patristic period', in *A history of Christian doctrine*, ed. J. Cunliffe-Jones (Edinburgh, 1978), p. 61.

[9] V. Morel, 'Le développement de la 'disciplina' sous l'action du Saint Esprit chez Tertullien', *RHE* 35 (1939), p. 260.

[10] Altendorf, *Einheit*, p. 27.   [11] Ibid.

De Pudicitia. That such a view of the church was not held by the 'earlier' Tertullian – the notion of a Catholic inclusiveness against a 'later' Montanist exclusiveness – is less easy to defend.[12]

Tertullian clearly demonstrates a perfectionist ecclesiology as much before as after his transition to the New Prophecy.[13] Minor differences only exist between his eschatological outlook as found in his Catholic works such as the *Apologeticum, De Praescriptione* and *De Baptismo*, for example, and that represented by the later *De Pudicitia*. For Tertullian – both Catholic and New Prophet – the church was ever to be regarded as 'holy' and maintained free from 'contamination' by the unworthy.

At *Apologeticum* 2,18 and 39,4 Tertullian addresses the practice of exclusion from the fellowship of the church. In the second passage Tertullian acknowledges with approval that church members may be 'banished' (relegetur) from the congregation with no suggestion of a later readmission. This 'exile' he sees as a significant foretaste of the coming judgement. 'Relegare' usually bears the sense of a permanent rather than a temporary status, and was also used in antiquity with the meaning 'to bequeath (property) back to its original owner'.[14] At *Apologeticum* 44,3 Tertullian contends that any Christian who finds himself in the gladiatorial arena on any charge other than that of being a believer immediately forfeits the name of Christian and thereby, by implication, is excommunicate. When Tertullian contends at *Apologeticum* 46,17 that those who 'withdraw from the rule of [Christian] teaching...cease to be counted [as] Christians among us', it is possible that he is simply stating the obvious; that those who cease to believe, cease to belong. It could also be, however, that he is speaking of those Christians who desert the orthodox 'camp' for that of the heretics. This would be evidence of perfectionism in the area of doctrine, reminiscent of 2 Thessalonians 3,6 where Paul recommends separation from those brethren who reject orthodox teaching.

---

[12] As implied by Lampe in n. 8 above, and by Burleigh, 'The Holy Spirit in the Latin Fathers', p.117, though the latter does not explicitly confine Tertullian's perfectionism (as does Lampe) to his later period.

[13] R. F. Evans, 'On the problem of Church and empire in Tertullian's Apologeticum', *SP* 14 (1976), p. 29.   [14] Iunius Mauricianus, *Digest* 33.2.23.

Tertullian's refusal at *De Praescriptione* 3,6 to accord the status of 'Christian' – and hence the right to enjoy the fellowship of the church – to those who, for whatever reason, are unable to hold out indefinitely against the threat of persecution is undeniably perfectionist. In thus excluding those guilty of apostasy from the church, Tertullian stands unquestionably in the tradition of the primitive church. The expression 'communicatio deliberata' at *De Praescriptione* 43,5 does not necessarily require the conclusion of an 'exclusive' fellowship. Yet it does suggest that certain 'exclusivist' ethical requirements are laid upon those admitted to the sacramental life of that fellowship. While the consignment to the 'fire' of one who returns to his sinful ways after baptism and admission to the church spoken of at *De Baptismo* 8,5 does not necessarily preclude readmission to the fellowship, the sense of the passage suggests a permanent status.

Tertullian argues at length at *De Pudicitia* 13,25 that the adulterer condemned and ejected from the congregation by Paul in 1 Corinthians 5,5 is not to be identified with the offender whose reconciliation to the church Paul seeks in 2 Corinthians 2,5-11. The former, he maintains, Paul had intended to be excluded from the congregation forever. To argue otherwise, he maintains, would be seriously to compromise the holiness of the church. And thus, he asserts, Paul's demand in 1 Corinthians and his later treatment of the blasphemers Hymenaeus and Alexander in 1 Timothy 1,19-20, support his own campaign for a 'holy', exclusive church free from contamination by grievous sinners. Tertullian argues again at *De Pudicitia* 18,11 for the permanent exclusion from the church of grievous sinners. Here he makes extensive use of the Scriptures, citing passages from both the Old Testament – from Proverbs 6,32-34 and Psalms 1,17,25 and 49 – and the New – from 1 Corinthians 5 (again), 1 Timothy 5,22, Ephesians 5,7f. and 2 Thessalonians 3,6. Tertullian alludes here to Ephesians 5,26f. and the image of the church as the Bride of Christ. The concept of the church evoked is undeniably perfectionist, of a fellowship untainted by the presence in its midst of grievous sinners. At 2 Thessalonians 3,6 Paul also urges separation from brethren who reject orthodox doctrine, but Tertullian here, unlike at *Apologeticum* 46,17, gives no hint of this type of discipline. At *De Pudicitia* 19,25 Tertullian lists those sins for which there can be no pardon, 'quae veniam non capiant...' (those which do not receive pardon) – murder, idolatry, fraud, apostasy, blasphemy, adultery and fornication. For these, he asserts at 19,26, 'Christ will no longer plead'. The commission of one of these offences results in the automatic exclusion of the perpetrator – and forever – from the ranks of those privileged to be the sons of God. Exclusion from the 'family' of God means here exclusion from the 'holy' fellowship, the authentic church of God. Cyprian's view, which he upheld against Novatian, that the church is holy not because its members have achieved eminent sanctity nor because the unholy have been expelled from its midst, but rather because the church *is* the holy 'bride' of Christ,[15] would have struck a sympathetic chord in the Tertullian of both periods.

Tertullian views the church in a 'thoroughly eschatological way'.[16] His demand for ecclesial holiness, for example, rests on Paul's view of Christ presenting his 'virgin bride', the church, spotless and unblemished at the last. Nothing Tertullian says on second marriage, on flight from persecution, and so on, makes sense unless we understand that he is speaking from such a stand-point. Paul's exhortation to the Thessalonians to become worthy of the life to which God has called them (2 Thessalonians 1,11) is reflected in Tertullian's explicit challenge to the church to become that which the Spirit has already made it by stamping it as the eschatological community. The latter's exhortation to Christian women at *De Cultu Feminarum* ii,7,3, with respect to the question of personal appearances, 'hodie vos tales deus videat, quales tunc videbit' (Today let God see you such as he will then), has an even broader application. His refusal of the title of 'martyr' to the Catholic confessor Pristinus, an alleged glutton, reflects his view that even martyrs, whatever their actual fate, must be morally worthy of martyrdom.[17] For Tertullian chastity and fasting are both manifestations of Christian holiness; their absence is indicative of the contrary. Orthodox belief leads to moral purity (and probably vice versa); heresy, wrong

[15] Greenslade, *Schism*, p. 170.
[16] Evans, *One and holy*, p. 8.   [17] *De Ieiunio* 12,3; Bray, *Holiness*, p. 53.

belief, leads to immorality and indiscipline (*De M*

The imminence of the parousia requires in Te total and immediate sanctification.[18] Welch's con future of the church (eschatology) defines its p. (ontology) would have found ready agreement from Tertullian. So, too, would that of Moltmann that the holiness of the church is inseparably linked to the eschatological question in so far as the church is the 'community of the last days'.[20] When, however, Williams speaks of the 'ecclesial reality' and Welch of the 'paradoxical nature' of the church as 'simul iustus et peccator', and the latter also of the church 'as an unequivocally creaturely, historical community, marked by the limitations and antiquity of all human existence' the African would only protest.[21] The immediate demands of sanctification and the imminence of the End leave no room for error, no place for human weakness. Such are, for Tertullian, not worthy of the church of the apostles.

ESCHATOLOGY – TERTULLIAN, A 'MAN OF THE END'

Tertullian was a 'man of the End'.[22] Eschatological reflection profoundly influences everything he says. In his ecclesiological thought Tertullian sees perfectionism as the sole solution to the crucial demands of sanctification.[23] Tertullian's eschatology leads to his 'indifférence sociale', and his horror of compromise hastened him to safeguard the integrity of 'l'absolu chrétien'.[24] It is suggested, too, that the influence on Tertullian of his eschatology is more pronounced in his later period than earlier – a Montanist 'not yet' against a Catholic 'realised' eschatology.[25] His eschatology, for example, is clearly a major influence on the

---

[18] Bray, *Holiness*, p.150. [19] Welch, *The church*, p.140.

[20] Moltmann, *The church*, p.339.

[21] Williams, *The church*, p.25; Welch, *The church*, pp.21f. and 217.

[22] J. Klein, *Tertullian: Christliche Bewußtein und sittliche Forderungen: ein Beitrag zur Geschichte der Moral und ihrer Systembildung* (Düsseldorf, 1940), p. 197.

[23] Bray, *Holiness*, p. 155.

[24] Guignebert, *Tertullien*, p.376; M. Spanneut, *Tertullien et les premiers moralistes africaines* (Paris, 1969), p. 55.

[25] J. Pelikan, 'The eschatology of Tertullian', *CH* 21 (1952), p.118, who maintains that Tertullian's eschatological emphases changed in his later period because he perceived that the church was concentrating increasingly on the 'already'.

ɔpening section of *De Pudicitia*. The sentence 'sed ut mala magis vincunt, quod ultimum temporum ratio est...' (but evil is increasingly in the ascendancy, which is a sign of the last times...)(1,2) is no mere rhetorical flourish.

Nevertheless, this does not require the conclusion that Tertullian's eschatology is a salient feature of his 'Montanist' period alone. For though the nature of his expectations may have been reinforced by his association with the New Prophecy – for example, the embracing of millenarianism – passages such as *De Oratione* 5,1 and *Apologeticum* 39,2 suggest that eschatology played a significant part in his theological formation from the very beginning. In *De Oratione* he speaks of the 'regnum Dei, quod... adveniat oramus, ad consummationem saeculi tendat ...' (the Kingdom of God, which we pray may come, tends towards the consummation of the age...); in the *Apologeticum* he speaks, too, of Christians praying 'pro mora finis...' (for the delay of the end...), which 'postponement' they seek for the sake of the empire's security. Again, these are no mere rhetorical flourishes, but examples of an earnest conviction which is evident even in his Catholic period. R. F. Evans speaks of Tertullian as viewing the Christians of his time as 'people set apart awaiting the end', and the church as a 'shadow Empire', as a 'colony', as an 'outpost of the heavenly kingdom to come'; he does not believe, however, that Tertullian identifies the earthly church with the Kingdom of God.[26] One need here only be reminded of Tertullian's scripture-based assertion that the 'citizenship of the Christian is in heaven'.[27]

THE CHURCH AS APOSTOLIC

The scriptural basis for Tertullian's understanding of the apostolic nature of the church is found in both the Great Commission of Jesus in Matthew 28, as a witness to the historical reality of the church's origins in the sending forth of the apostles, and the account in Acts of the spectacular growth of the young church.
Among the Fathers before Tertullian only Irenaeus explicitly

[26] Evans, *One and holy*, pp. 12, 19, 24 and 9.
[27] See *De Corona* 13,4 and *Ad Martyras* 3,3, both echoing *Philippians* 3,20.

declares apostolicity to be an essential attribute of the true
church. This can be seen in some of those passages cited above
with respect to catholicity.[28] He witnesses also to the foundation
of the various churches by apostles and to an apostolic succession
evidenced by formal episcopal lists, in particular that of the
church at Rome.[29] This latter list is probably that identified by
Eusebius as compiled by Hegesippus from information which
the latter obtained at Rome.[30]

At *De Praescriptione* 37,5 Tertullian declares, 'Ego sum heres
apostolorum' (I am an heir of the apostles). Thus did he regard
himself as standing in that tradition of the Catholic church
reaching back to the apostles appointed by Christ. This was no
less true in his later period than earlier. For the New Prophet as
much as for the Catholic Tertullian the mark of an authentic
apostolicity is fundamental to his ecclesiology.[31] It is clear from
the evidence of passages such as *De Praescriptione* 20, 6-7 and 21,7
that, in his early period at least, Tertullian regarded apostolic
foundation or consistency with apostolic teaching as critical
marks of the true church. *De Praescriptione* 21,4 confirms this
notion that continuity and/or conformity with apostolic doctrine
and teaching is part of that which for Tertullian marks the
church out as authentic. It is important to point out, however,
that in this passage the origin of correct doctrine is traced not
only back to the apostles, but beyond them to God himself.
Moltmann's comment that faithfulness to the beginning is
faithfulness to the origin, that only as the church is that of Christ
is it truly apostolic,[32] is pertinent to a proper understanding of
Tertullian's thought. At *De Praescriptione* 32,1-2 Tertullian
suggests a method for such apostolic 'tracing back', while at 32,6
he asserts that it is conformity with apostolic doctrine and not
exclusively a 'physical' link with the apostles which constitutes a
particular fellowship as authentically apostolic. This is a foretaste
of the subtle change in emphasis regarding the criteria for

---

[28] See especially *Haer.* I,10,I and 24,I.   [29] *Haer.* III,3,4.
[30] *EH* IV,22,2.3. Von Campenhausen, *Ecclesiastical authority*, p.165, note 90, argues on
grammatical grounds for this identification in that Irenaeus changes tense when he
inserts his own incidental comments on the list.
[31] D'Alès, *La théologie de Tertullien*, p. 214; Harnack, *History of dogma*, p. 74.
[32] Moltmann, *The church*, p. 312.

authentic apostolicity which can be seen in Tertullian's transition
to the New Prophecy. Nevertheless the criterion of 'physical'
continuity remains valid for Tertullian. His claim at *De
Praescriptione* 36,1 that the very 'seats' of the apostles themselves
(cathedrae apostolorum) are found in those churches of direct
apostolic foundation testifies to this. And yet it is still faithfulness
to apostolic teaching and tradition rather than any 'physical'
pedigree which is of the greater importance in Tertullian's
ecclesiological thought.

At *Adversus Marcionem* 1,21,4-5 – from his later period –
Tertullian appears, in agreement with the earlier writings, to
place equal emphasis upon the facts both of apostolic continuity
or 'succession' and that of conformity with apostolic teaching.
Such 'apostolic' churches can do no other than hand on the
apostolic teaching, as witness his reference to an orthodox faith
in the Creator (4). Those churches which are undoubtedly of
apostolic foundation will of necessity demonstrate those undeniable
criteria by which claims of apostolicity, especially the teaching
of the apostolic tradition, are to be authenticated.

At *Adversus Marcionem* IV,5 Tertullian seeks to demonstrate the
authenticity of the orthodox Gospel against that proclaimed by
Marcion by application of the formula 'verius quod prius',
which axiom was later to trouble him as a propagandist for the
New Prophecy. Again he has recourse to the argument that the
orthodox churches were established by Christ's chosen apostles.
At IV,5,1 he speaks of a visible continuity which exists between
those apostles and the orthodox churches of apostolic foundation,
which continuity has preserved authentic apostolic teaching. At
IV,5,2 he makes mention of those churches which can trace their
precise origins back to the Apostle John and at IV,5,3 of the
heretics' failure, alongside overwhelming proof of their 'apostasy',
to evidence such 'apostolicity' in themselves. At IV,5,7 we find
the application of a rather convoluted argument similar to that
found at 1,21,4. The churches which are authenticated by their
apostolic orthodoxy become, in turn, by virtue of this, those
churches which lend a measure of authenticity to such doctrine
by virtue of being apostolic! The existence of such passages
supporting the notion of an essential doctrinal apostolicity in his

later thought demonstrates that it is not exclusive to the Catholic Tertullian.[33]

The claim that Tertullian replaced historical apostolicity as a basis for his understanding of the nature of the true church with a more 'spiritual' concept is based on the erroneous assumption that for him the two are incompatible. What does change in the course of his own transition from Catholic to New Prophet is the way in which this apostolicity is to be demonstrated. The 'early' Tertullian discusses the church from the standpoint primarily, though not exclusively, of doctrine and its authentication; the 'later' Tertullian does so from the standpoint of discipline and the exercise of 'potestas'.[34] For the Tertullian of both periods the basic formula is straightforward: God sent Christ, Christ appointed and sent out the apostles, the apostles established the church. Tertullian would have had little difficulty in affirming Newbigin's assertion that 'it is as anointed with his (sc. Christ's) Spirit that the apostles are bearers of his commission and in no other way'.[35] For Tertullian, any church in the present age which claims such apostolicity must likewise demonstrate such anointing. And yet this apostolic foundation also takes on a more concrete and historical connotation in Tertullian than in any previous Christian thinker.[36] The assertion that there is no tension in Tertullian's thought between the concept of a Spirit-filled church and that of the apostolic tradition is also undoubtedly correct.[37] Likewise, the acknowledgement of another source of tension, that between the demands of the Spirit and the claimed endowments of ecclesial office in the early centuries of the Christian era, so marvellously laid out by von Campenhausen, should never lead to the conclusion that the two are somehow mutually exclusive.[38] They certainly need not have been so for Tertullian, though such tension is clearly present, especially in *De Pudicitia*. At *De Pudicitia* 21,6 it is by 'proof' of a form of 'descent' from either the apostles or the prophets – though not

[33] By general agreement, books IV and V at least of *Adversus Marcionem* belong to Tertullian's later period.
[34] R.E. Roberts, *The theology of Tertullian* (London, 1924) p. 186.
[35] Newbigin, *Household of God*, p. 95.
[36] E. Flessmann-van Leer, *Tradition and scripture in the early church* (Assen, 1954), p. 151.
[37] Ibid., p. 156.   [38] *Ecclesiastical authority*.

by way of physical succession alone – that one is acknowledged to possess the requisite authority to forgive sin. At 21,16 it is 'descent' from 'spiritual men' such as the apostles (but not only them) who, represented in the person of Peter, are indisputably indwelt by the Spirit; this, in turn, authenticates their claim to the power (potestas) to remit sin. At 22,8 it is by a demonstration of proofs (probationes) of power similar to those exhibited by Christ (and, by implication, by the apostles) that one is able validly to claim the authentic exercise of such power (potestas). That church is indeed the true church which exhibits – and acknowledges – the indwelling of the same Spirit which indwelt the apostles and the prophets.

For the church 'in terris' to correspond at all with that 'in caelis', it must demonstrate a continuing 'apostolic' character; there can be no automatic presumptions of apostolicity (in the sense of apostolic authority) for the Catholic episcopate. In the early period, this was done by way of historical proofs through the evidence of episcopal lists and a continuity and community of teaching and tradition. The relevant question was the relatively uncomplicated: 'Who then are the witnesses?' The question of the essential nature of the church itself was simply not important nor posed in such stark terms. What was crucial was rather: 'Who teaches rightly and faithfully?' With the rise of the penitential-discipline question, however, the matter of 'right' teaching was, in a very real sense, pushed into the background; the key question now became: 'Who holds or exercises the power?' As the Body of Christ, and as the apparent successors to the possessor of the 'power of the keys', the Catholic church and episcopate laid claim – though over a considerable period of time and development – to such power and authority. For Tertullian, and for those who thought as he did, there could be no suggestion that such 'power' did not properly belong to the church. But for them there also arose the crucial question: 'Who or what is the authentic church?' It was not so much that the answers were altered, as that the questions themselves were transformed. And so, the question of the nature of the true church comes now to the fore. The question 'To whom has Christ, through his chosen apostles, given his teaching?', receded into the background of Tertullian's thought. An alternative, 'To whom did he give the power?', becomes the critical question. And the answer, for Tertullian at least, is simple. Christ has evidently given his power to whoever demonstrates the presence of that same Spirit which indwelt him and which he in turn passed on to the apostles. As the common teaching of the 'apostolic' churches had given valid witness to those origins which initially guaranteed its authenticity, so the apostolic Spirit bears witness to their origins as authentic churches. The mark of apostolicity remains crucial for Tertullian's ecclesiology; yet it is transformed, as Tertullian himself makes the transformation from Catholic to New Prophet, from one witnessed to by the possession of 'right' teaching and tradition, to one evidenced by the abiding presence of the Spirit. And thus, the apostolicity of the true church is no longer proved by its possession of an apostolically founded episcopal order which itself continues to guarantee by its ordered succession the 'rightness' of its doctrines. This is done rather by the presence within it of the Spirit of God who guarantees all.

THE CHURCH AS ONE

The key scriptural texts for the unity of the church are John 17, 21, 1 Corinthians 11,17f. and 12,12f., Romans 12,4f. and Ephesians 4,4-6, the last three concerning the church as the Body of Christ. Tertullian makes explicit use of the passages from 1 Corinthians and Ephesians, but none whatever of material from John or Romans.

Clement of Rome repeatedly condemns the divisions in the church at Corinth, and makes an impassioned plea for unity by way of clear allusion to Ephesians 4,4-6. That he also makes considerable use of 1 Corinthians would suggest that he had also 1 Corinthians 11,17f. in mind, though he does not refer explicitly to these particular texts. Hermas also emphasises the necessary unity of the church and at least twice quotes Ephesians 4, to underline this.[39] Irenaeus quotes Ephesians 4,5-6 when

[39] *Sim.* IX,13,5.7.

addressing the necessary unity of the church, though elsewhere, when pointing to the consistency of the church's teaching, employs no particular biblical text to underline his argument.[40]

In the late second century, catholicity, to the extent that it was seen as an attribute of the authentic church, was normally linked to that of unity (and in some places to that of apostolicity). Its scriptural bases are found in both the Great Commission (Matthew 28) and the account in Acts of the growth of the infant church. Ignatius of Antioch speaks of the *'katholike ekklesia'* at *Smyrnaeans* 8,2, by which expression he means the whole church rather than the local episcopally governed congregations; it may also mean little more than the sum total of these local communities. The account of Polycarp's martyrdom is addressed to *'pasais tais kata panta topon tes hagias kai katholikes ekklesias paroikiais'*,[41] and at 19,2 there is a reference to the *'oikoumene katholike ekklesia'*. This latter reference in particular gives recognition to 'the increasingly apparent reality of a whole Church, within which the individual Churches are bound up together, a general and all-embracing Church.[42] Irenaeus speaks of the uniformity and consistency of the teaching of the churches, though they are spread far and wide, and also of their unity-in-catholicity.[43] The attribute of catholicity here does not, however, achieve the importance it was to have later for the Great Church. At the end of the second century it is still linked closely to that of unity.

No passage can better demonstrate than *De Virginibus Velandis* 2,2 that Tertullian's commitment to the 'unity' of the true church transcended his transition from faithful Catholic to factious New Prophet. Here we have the clearest indication from one of his later writings that Tertullian is no schismatic. Tertullian reaffirms his belief in the unity of the orthodox church, from which church he will not exclude the Catholics/Psychici as he has the heretics. The community of belief between New Prophet and Catholic in the one God, the one Christ, the one body of tradition, the one hope and a common sacramental practice (Ephesians 4,4-6 is again undoubtedly the text he has in

[40] *Haer.* IV,32,1; I,10,2; III,24,1.
[41] See the introduction to the account.
[42] H. Kung, *The church* (London, 1968), p.297.   [43] *Haer.* I,10,2; III,24,1.

mind) leads Tertullian inescapably to the conclusion of the 'one' church to which both New Prophet and Catholic belong. 'We are one church' (una ecclesia sumus). Right belief requires confession of 'one' church. Even when he could no longer countenance the authority of certain Catholic bishops, believing that they had lost contact with their apostolic origins, he could not deny that they were part of the 'one' church of Christ. To put them outside of the 'one' church would be mistakenly to place them with the heretics who possess no authentic church at all. Despite their differences, both Catholics and New Prophets still belonged to the 'una ecclesia in caelis' (*De Baptismo* 15,1). Much of Tertullian's understanding of the necessary unity of the true church stems from his understanding of the indivisibility of the Body of Christ. As Moltmann asserts, our doctrine of the church must evolve both from our Christology and our eschatology.[44] The unity of the church is not some future ideal, but a present reality. 'The unity of the church of God is a perpetual fact; our task is not to create it, but to exhibit it.'[45]

At *De Praescriptione* 5,4 Tertullian recalls with obvious approval Paul's condemnation of schism, dissension and heresy in the latter's plea for the unity of the congregation at 1 Corinthians 11,17f. Cyprian of Carthage is generally credited with being the first Christian theologian to equate schism with heresy. Tertullian comes close to such an equation here when he declares that 'haereses vero non minus ab unitate divellunt quam scismata et dissensiones. Sine dubio et haereses in ea condicione reprehensionis constituit in qua et scismata et dissensiones' (heresies certainly no less than schisms and dissensions sever [men] from unity. Without question he [sc. Paul] classes heresies under the same head of censure as he does schisms and dissensions). We are reminded here of *De Praescriptione* 20,6ff. where Tertullian established the criteria of verifiable source and historical and doctrinal continuity as bases for the recognition of the one authentic, apostolic church by tracing the establishment of the various orthodox churches back to the apostles. Thus, for Tertullian, though there are many 'branches' of this one church,

---

[44] Moltmann, *The church*, p. 20.
[45] W. Temple (1937) in Kirkpatrick, *Doctrine*, p. 187.

some of which can claim a considerable dignity and power in their own right, they are all, being derived and sprung from the one 'root', of the one 'tree'. The evidence for this community of nature and thereby the authentication of apostolic origin is their community of fellowship and mutual recognition. For Tertullian sees the 'pax' between individual churches as being a mark of the true church, much as the 'pax' within a local congregation in part authenticates that Christian fellowship.[46] It is above all, at least in Tertullian's earlier period, their community or consistency of doctrine, that is, their catholicity of belief, which merits this. At 21,7 Tertullian states, 'Communicamus cum ecclesiis apostolicis quod nulla doctrina diversa' (We join with these apostolic churches because there is no divergence [between us] in doctrine) by which he makes a similar point. At 28,3 Tertullian reaffirms that that which might properly be called the unity-in-catholicity of the true church is defined by the commonly acknowledged 'traditum'; that is, by that which has been 'handed down' from apostolic times, and by a verifiable process, to each of the many churches within the one church. At 32,8 Tertullian confirms that the reverse of this proposition is also true; namely, that it is the heretics' diversity of doctrine, which excludes them from the fellowship of orthodox churches, which denies to them the necessary marks of apostolicity and catholicity, and thereby any claim to be part of the one, authentic church. At 43,5 Tertullian condemns the indiscipline of the heretics as compared with the ordered behaviour of the Catholics. He links the former's alleged association with magicians and astrologers to their not fearing God. Where God is not feared, he is not; where he is not, there truth is not; where truth is not, there is no discipline. On the Catholic side, however, there is acceptance that 'the fear of God is the beginning of wisdom' (Proverbs 1,7; 9,10; Psalms 110,10). Such faithfulness and discipline promotes an 'ecclesia unita' which is itself a mark of God's favour. Activity directed towards the maintenance of unity in the church reflects right thinking and right behaviour; that towards disunity is indicative of heterodoxy and faithless indiscipline.

_____

[46] *Haer.* 1,10,1.2; III,24,1.

At *De Baptismo* 15,1 Tertullian adds a gloss to the text of Ephesians 4, 4-6, 'et una ecclesia in caelis'. This is appropriate – though not perhaps in the best textual tradition – as consistent with the spirit of the biblical text. Clement of Rome, who also cites this text, provides no such gloss, but implies a similar thought.[47] Tertullian maintains that belief in one Lord and one God, and the maintenance of a unified faith and sacramental discipline, necessarily imply the affirmation of 'one church' as a corollary.

At *De Monogamia* 5,7 – from his later period – Tertullian maintains that monogamy is an integral part of the natural and proper order of things which can be traced back to the very beginnings of humankind. It is beyond doubt that both the first Adam, at least 'ante exilium' (5,5), and the last Adam (Christ) were 'entirely unwedded' (innuptus in totum). Tertullian asserts, however, that if a Christian is not capable of such perfection – that is, of celibacy – then Christ can offer even there, by way of example, his monogamous 'marriage' to his spouse, the church. But this church must be the sole spouse 'wedded' to Christ; Christ cannot have polygamous relationships with a number of such ecclesial 'brides'. The ideal for the monogamous state is to be found in the spiritual union of Christ and his single spouse-church. No other 'church' can have Christ as its head or husband; thus, no other 'church' can authentically be a church at all. The image of the church as the Body of Christ is also very much in the background of Tertullian's thought here. Tertullian displays outrage at 11,2 at the presumption of those who request a second marriage in the precincts of the church at the hands of the clergy. It is even a greater presumption, even if it should be 'in the Lord' – and thus in accordance with the Law and the teaching of the Apostle (i.e. Paul) – when it is sought from persons for whom second marriages are forbidden. And further, what is even more distasteful again in Tertullian's eyes is the apparent ease with which some clergy will celebrate such marriages 'in a virgin church, the one spouse of the one Christ'.

Tertullian's view of the church as catholic is founded, then,

[47] *1 Clement* 46,6.

more upon his perception of its history, its growth and the nature of its present reality than upon a particular scripture-based understanding. There is no doubt that Irenaeus was, with regard to the unity-in-catholicity of the church, a major influence on Tertullian's thought. Though the catholicity of the church is by no means a major feature of Tertullian's ecclesiology – it is present explicitly only in *De Praescriptione* – its apparent absence from explicit consideration in his later writings does not mean that it was excluded from his thought. For Tertullian to argue from the catholicity of the church when there was such a considerable gulf between much Catholic and New Prophecy practice – if not in doctrine – would have been very awkward. The catholicity of the church is, for Tertullian, intimately connected to the question of its unity, as it was for many of the Fathers before him, and to a lesser extent to that of apostolicity. But to what extent unity or catholicity can be said to be essential marks of the church in Tertullian's thought is not easy of determination.[48]

COMMENT ON OTHER ECCLESIOLOGICAL 'NOTES' IN TERTULLIAN

While Tertullian clearly presents an ecclesiology which conforms quite closely to the early credal confession of the church as 'one, holy, catholic and apostolic' he also reflects aspects of later ecclesiological confessions. A consistent Reformed ecclesiology would normally include reference to the true church as being that in which (1) the Word is preached truly, (2) the sacraments are administered rightly, and (3) a godly discipline is maintained.[49] Tertullian was undoubtedly concerned with the proper handing on of authentic apostolic doctrine, at least in his early period, though he does not give significant attention to the preaching ministry of the church. He does not make it clear, for example, who is responsible for preaching; we can assume that it was at the very least the task principally of the bishop. This maintenance of orthodox teaching, the handing down of the Gospel of Jesus

---

[48] D'Alès, *La théologie de Tertullien*, p. 214, contends that its catholicity is such a note, at least in *De Praescriptione*.　　[49] Williams, *The church*, pp. 27f. and 101.

Christ preserved pure and inviolate, is a major feature of his early writings and certainly no small concern of the later ones. This concern corresponds quite closely to the Reformed 'note' of preaching the Word truly. Tertullian was also concerned, as we will see more clearly in our discussion of his doctrine of Christian office and ministry, with the proper administration of the sacraments. This is a major feature of his thought in both *De Baptismo* (from his earlier period) and *De Exhortatione Castitatis* (from the later). Although he would allow administration of the sacraments by both the lower clergy and the laity – in the former case under the authority of the bishop and in the latter in case of necessity – it was normally the prerogative of the bishop alone to preside at the sacraments. This concern for the proper and ordered administration of the sacraments held true in both periods of Tertullian's career and corresponds closely to the second Reformed 'note'. His deep concern for the maintenance of a rigorous discipline in the life of the church hardly needs restating here. This was the major concern of the later period of his career and contributed greatly to his demand for an authentically holy church; yet such was not lacking in the ecclesiological considerations of his earlier period. In that early period it was not for Tertullian only the heretics' preoccupation with heterodox doctrines which stamped them as lacking authenticity, but also, as stated in *De Praescriptione* 41,7, the alleged irregularity of their disciplinary life. This corresponds neatly with the third Reformed 'note'.

The preoccupation of some modern theologians with a supposed ecclesiological dichotomy between the church as 'institution' and as 'event'[50] has little relevance to Tertullian's thought. Tertullian might appear to stand with those who affirm the 'event' character of the church, in line with his requirement of an openness to the movement and demands of the Spirit; and yet it can properly be said that Tertullian was concerned not so much to minimise the question of the form of the church as institution, but rather to determine just what particular form it might properly take. Few, if any, of Dulles'

[50] Moltmann, *The church*, p.333 ; Williams, *The church*, pp. 27f.

five ecclesiological categories, the church as Institution, Mystical Communion, Sacrament, Herald, and Servant[51] would appear to conform or correspond very neatly to Tertullian's ecclesiological thought-forms. And, yet, his concern for the proper ordering of the church might possibly correspond to the view of the church as Institution, his concern for the correct transmission of apostolic teaching to that of the church as Herald (of the kerygma), and the priority given in his ecclesiological thought to the church as the Body of Christ to that of the church as a Mystical Communion.

[51] A. Dulles, *Models of the church* (Dublin, 1976), pp. 31, 43, 58, 71 and 83.

Conclusions: the church according to Tertullian

Occasional references to an 'ecclesia in caelis' can be found in Tertullian's writings. Yet, for the most part, Tertullian sees the true church as an historical, empirical reality the authentication for which can be found at least partly in the present age. This reality is partly determined by the nature and the circumstances of the church's foundation by the apostles, and partly by its Spirit-driven activity in the present time, but, above all, by its present nature, consistent with its promise as the eschatological community, as both the Body of Christ and the Bride of Christ.[1] This church in the power of the Spirit, which power enables it to become now what it is in promise, is not yet the Kingdom of God, but its anticipation in history.[2] In this Tertullian differs from both Origen and Clement of Alexandria, for example, for whom the present reality is but an imperfect shadow of some heavenly, as yet unrealised ideal. Tertullian is consistent in his understanding of the historical and empirical nature of this church, and, in this sense, no significant difference is discernible in his ecclesiology in the transition from Catholic to New Prophet. What do change, however, are the criteria by which for him the reality and the authentication of the true church are evaluated; that is, what it is for this church to be faithful to its essential and authentic nature.

Some of the images employed by Tertullian to depict the church are drawn from secular life, though most do have biblical and other Christian connections. 'Castra', though reflecting the influence of both the Old Testament and the book of Revelation,

---

[1] Moltmann, *The church*, p. 20.   [2] Ibid,. p. 196.

was an obvious image for those who lived in the increasingly militarised world of the Severans. The employment of 'navis', though it might reflect the influence of the Gospels – the 'little boat' on which the first disciples experienced some of their most significant encounters with the power of Jesus – would also be an obvious one in a province dependent on the sea for its contact with the rest of the Roman world. 'Schola' and 'secta' are the images most obviously reflecting a non-biblical milieu. Drawn from the world of pagan philosophy and education, they were employed by Tertullian both to provide useful points of recognition for pagans and to proclaim the moral and ideological superiority of Christianity over its pagan rivals. Tertullian's depiction of the church-as-mother – used consistently throughout his career – though not original with him, is given such a new treatment in his ecclesiology that it yet lays claim as a quasi-original 'Tertullianism'! Noone before him had so decisively employed the image as one which established the church as possessing a personalised identity separate from her members. In nothing else, save perhaps in his trinitarian language and his emphasis on the essential holiness of the church, was Tertullian to exercise such a lasting influence on later Christian thought.

Tertullian's presentation of the church as the Body of Christ is reflected in his employment of the images 'corpus', 'Christus', 'Spiritus' and 'trinity'. While he could use the first mentioned in the secular sense of an 'association' and at times in a particularly formal and routine manner, his use of all four images suggests most strongly that he understood the image of the church as the Body of Christ in a more than metaphorical sense. There is with him an unmistakable identification between the true church and the person of Christ which comes perilously close to seeing the church as an extension of the Incarnation itself. And yet such an identification would be by no means absolute for Tertullian and is possible only where the Spirit is demonstrably present in the midst of the church. The use of the image of the Body of Christ reinforces Tertullian's emphasis on the necessary unity of the church, which church, being the Body of Christ, cannot be divided against itself and can only be that which in reality it is called to be. Tertullian employs the images of 'virgin' and 'Bride of Christ' – and often together – in a manner which corresponds very closely to New Testament and early patristic usage. These images emphasise the necessary holiness of the church and in a thoroughly eschatological way. The church is not to become at the End the virgin Bride of Christ; she is that in the present-time, and can be none other now than that which she is to be at the End. The images are not unconnected, as we saw above, to that of the church as the Body of Christ.

Had Tertullian lived to see the development of the now familiar ecclesiological formularies, he would almost certainly have approved of the affirmation of the church as 'one, holy, catholic and apostolic'. Throughout both major periods of his Christian life he constantly stressed the necessary unity of the church, from the communion of the various congregations spread throughout the known world, to that 'oneness' and 'peace' within a single congregation.[3] For Tertullian the scriptural bases for this essential unity are found at Ephesians 4,4-6 and in Paul's criticism of division in 1 Corinthians, passim. The images which are employed by him most often to illustrate this 'unity' – particularly at the local congregational level – are those related to that of the Body of Christ; though at least one of these, as already pointed out, could also be employed by Tertullian in a more secular sense. Whether this unity was essential to the authentication of the true church, or was merely a useful though non-essential indicator, is not clear.

The catholicity of the church, which at this time was an attribute primarily associated with that of its unity, was also very important, at least in Tertullian's early thought; it receives no explicit mention later on. Given the widespread suspicion of the New Prophecy movement, even in his own day, it may not have been prudent for Tertullian to lay too much stress on this aspect of his ecclesiology. None of the particular images employed by him speak directly to it, though he undoubtedly understood its scriptural bases to lie both in the Great Commission at Matthew 28,19f. and in Acts. Catholicity seems for him not to have been essential to the authenticity of the true church, but

---

[3] *De Baptismo* 17.

rather a useful indicator of that church's unity and apostolicity.

The holiness of the church in Tertullian's thought is, however, another matter. It is crucial to his understanding of the essential nature of the authentic church; this is particularly so in the later period, though it is far from absent earlier; it is an attribute without which the church cannot be the true church, and is surpassed in importance in this regard possibly only by that of apostolicity. Its scriptural bases are found in 1 Corinthians 5, 1 Timothy 1,19f., Ephesians 5 and 2 Corinthians 11. Tertullian's understanding of this holiness is also profoundly influenced by the eschatological framework of his thought, by his consequent understanding of the demands of sanctification and of 'holiness' generally, and by the natural rigour of his own personality. At least four of the major images employed by Tertullian represent this particular aspect of his ecclesiology – those of 'ark', 'camp', 'bride (of Christ)', and 'virgin'. Three of these – the first, the third and the fourth – draw their inspiration from the Bible. The second is drawn principally from the secular world. This particular attribute of the true church is given most emphasis in his later writings, but is also present in the earlier period when concern for the purity and exclusiveness of doctrine is found in the foreground of his thought. It denotes for him one of the crucial aspects of the 'primitive' church, which church should be the model for his own time. The holiness of the church, however, lies not in the process of its historical development, nor in some ideal to be sought though perhaps never achieved, but in what it is by the grace of God. A less than holy church is, for Tertullian, not logically possible. Anything less than holy cannot authentically be the church. It is not that the church should be or could be holy; it is holy. It is already, in the present-time, the virgin Bride of Christ. It can seek only to conform to its own inherent nature.

It is the attribute of apostolicity which denotes for Tertullian the second plank of the essential nature of the one, true church. It is not only because thereby – in the Stoic sense – it can be 'traced back' to its (earthly) origins, but rather because it can thereby be traced back to a divine authentication. God sent his Christ, Christ anointed and sent out his apostles, and they in turn founded the church. This is what sets the church above and apart from all other human institutions. In theory those others could well be united, catholic, perhaps even holy (though probably not), but they could never trace their origins back to the apostles appointed by Christ. Apostolicity remained for Tertullian the key to the nature of the true church; it was only the manner in which this attribute was to be demonstrated which was to change in his transition from Catholic to New Prophet.

At *De Pudicitia* 21,1 Tertullian seeks to distinguish between 'doctrinam apostolorum et potestatem'. Both were important to his concept of the church and Tertullian never denied oversight of the former to the bishops. Yet when he was faced with the administration of penitential discipline, with the forgiveness of grievous sinners and their possible readmission to communion, and with the question of who possessed the authority to 'act' in the name of God, the question of 'power' (potestas) became of primary importance. While doctrinal orthodoxy can be traced by way of episcopal succession back to the tradition established by the apostles themselves, disciplinary 'power' had to be authenticated in the contemporary church by proven possession of that same Spirit which had indwelt Christ, his apostles and the prophets.

Schweizer comments that 'God's Spirit marks out in freedom the pattern that church order afterwards recognises; it is therefore functional, regulative, serving, but not constitutive, and that is what is decisive'.[4] Tertullian's observation in *De Pudicitia* 21,17 that the true church is that of the Spirit, and not that which is constituted by a number of bishops, reflects this same sentiment. And yet Moltmann's assertion that 'the church has never existed in a historically demonstrable ideal, a form in which faith and experience coincided'[5] is one to which Tertullian could not give assent if it meant agreeing that such coincidence is never possible in the present age. Tertullian was an 'heir of the Apostles' and the church was truly both the 'Body of Christ' and the 'virgin Bride of Christ'. In these particular aspects of Tertullian's thought lie the answers to many of the questions

concerning his 'high' ecclesiology – his apparent identification
of the visible church with that 'in caelis', for example – and his
understanding of what constituted the essential attributes or
notes of the one, authentic church founded by the apostles of
Christ.

PART III

Tertullian's doctrine of ministry and office

Introduction

As with his doctrine of church, Tertullian offers no systematised
theology of ministry. His writings, however, provide indicators
to prevailing ecclesiastical structures and practices, as well as
evidence of his own preferences and prejudices. Tertullian offers
a view of what had by then become the normative three-tier
structure of ecclesiastical office – bishop, presbyters and deacons;
this structure he never repudiated, notwithstanding the seemingly
endless conflict in which he became engaged with some members
of the Catholic hierarchy. Throughout his career, and despite
the perennial tension between himself and some Catholic
leaders, Tertullian consistently reaffirmed this structure. By
'office' I mean not to convey the rather broad sense of the Latin
'officium', which can bear a varied range of meanings,[1] but
rather the narrower sense of a formally (institutionally) recognised
function, position or rank within an organisation bearing some
measure of administrative oversight, duty or authority.

Apart from the three traditional offices, Tertullian also
provides useful information on the existence and function of at
least six others – widow, virgin, doctor, lector, prophet and
martyr. The extent to which any or all of these – particularly
with regard to the last two listed – were considered, either by
Tertullian or by the church, as 'offices' in any formal sense is not
clear. Over against his recognition of an 'official' Christian
ministry, we can sense Tertullian's personal leaning towards
prophetic 'charismata' and 'men of the Spirit'. This is especially

---

[1] From a 'favour' or 'courtesy' through an 'obligation' or a 'part' to an 'official duty' or
'employment'.

discernible in his days as a New Prophet, though by no means exclusively so.

The perennial tension between the claims of 'office' and the demands of the Spirit[2] is reflected in Tertullian. Other questions also need attention in any discussion of Tertullian's understanding of ministry. Does this understanding undergo any substantial change in his transition from Catholic to New Prophet? Second, does such a transition necessitate the conclusion of schism? It will be argued that the answer to both questions should be in the negative; that any major transformation was undergone by the Catholic church itself; that Tertullian's own positional shifts were essentially reactions to those changes which were at that time occurring in the circumstances, discipline and outlook of the church.

Von Campenhausen sees in the period between the late New Testament and the sub-apostolic eras the emergence of three distinctive models for ministry. These mirrored the tripartite aspects of Jesus' ministry – those of prophet, priest and king – and also largely determined the later patterns evident in the three great confessional traditions, Roman, Orthodox and Reformed.[3] Von Campenhausen sees in the Pastoral Epistles the model of the Christian minister as prophet in the emphasis given to the exclusive teaching function of the bishop-presbyters. Herein lie the seeds of the later Reformed emphasis on the minister as teacher and preacher. He sees in *1 Clement* the model of the minister as priest in the emphasis laid upon the role of the bishop as cultic official of the congregation. Such reflects the later Roman emphasis on the minister as priest. In the letters of Ignatius of Antioch von Campenhausen sees the kingly aspect in the emphasis given to the bishop as sacral focus of the congregation. In this lies the later Eastern Orthodox model. Our purpose will be in part to determine whether Tertullian's presentation of Christian ministry reflects these particular aspects and whether one or other model or pattern dominates his thought.

In chapter 6 I will discuss, first, Tertullian's understanding of ministry as 'service', with particular reference to his employment

---

[2] Von Campenhausen, *Ecclesiastical authority*, passim.
[3] Ibid. p.120f.

of terms such as 'ministerium' and 'charismata'. I will then explore his understanding of ministry as 'office', acknowledging both his clear discrimination between clergy and laity and his concept of clerical office itself, with particular reference to terms such as 'ordo', 'senatus' and 'seniores'. In chapter 7 I will discuss the offices of the church. I will consider the major offices of bishop, presbyter and deacon as they appear in his writings, with particular reference to the origins of these and their specific functions – leadership, pastoral and cultic; I will also consider the minor offices of lector and doctor. In chapter 8 I will explore Tertullian's understanding of the role of women in ministry with specific reference to the 'orders' of widows and virgins. In chapter 9 I will discuss other ministries like those of martyr/ confessor and prophet. And, finally, in chapter 10 I will examine the methods of appointment to the various ranks within the church with specific reference to terms such as 'adlectio', 'eligere' and 'promotio'.

CHAPTER 6

Ministry as 'service' and as 'office'

MINISTRY AS 'SERVICE'

Tertullian rarely speaks of ministry in the sense of a general 'service'. There are very few references in his extant writings to any such service in the sense of the Greek *'diakonia'*. When he wants to refer to ministry in such terms, however, he normally employs 'ministerium', 'virtutes' or 'charismata', or even 'officium' (though this latter term can also be used of 'office' proper).

'Ministerium'

'Ministerium' is an obvious Latin translation for the Greek words *'diakonia'* – though not to be confused with the formal, diaconal order – *'leitourgia'* and *'latreia'*. Yet only once, at *De Oratione* 15,1, does Tertullian directly quote a New Testament passage in which one such 'service-ministry' expression is found. Tertullian here translates the Greek *'latreia'*, from Romans 15,1, as 'officium' with its alternative and (here) appropriate meaning of a 'ceremonial observance'.

There are no obvious patristic precedents by which to appreciate better Tertullian's employment of the word 'ministerium'. He employs it with a wide variety of meanings, though usually with reference to non-ecclesiastical matters. He employs it to mean 'implements' at *Adv. Marcionem* II,16,2, a 'fellow culprit' at *De Anima* 40,4, an 'agency (of persecution)' at *De Fuga* 2,1, the *'exousiai'* (rulers) mentioned at Romans 13,1, 'ministers (of God)' at *Scorpiace* 14,1 (again as part of a translation of Romans 13), and the organs of the human body at *De Corona* 5,2. Tertullian also calls *'exomologesis'* a 'ministerium' (handmaid) of repentance at *De Paenitentia* 12,8 and refers to the 'sacrificial services' of Numa Pompilius as 'ministeria' at *De Praescriptione* 40,6. He speaks of the 'ministerium' (as service) of idolatry at *De Pudicitia* 7,15 and of the tongue as the 'ministerium' (instrument) of confession at *Ad Nationes* 1,18,4. At *De Anima* 40,2 he speaks (three times) of the flesh as a 'ministerium', as an instrument of agency with no independent capacity for action, much as a cup may minister to a thirsty man. At *Apologeticum* 11,4 he speaks of the 'ministeria' or 'services' of those through whom a great God might perform or exercise his divine functions, and at 39,2 of the officials of the Emperor as his 'ministri'. At *De Exhortatione Castitatis* 10,5 he employs a Montanist oracle which states that 'sanctus minister sanctimoniam noverit ministrare' (the holy minister knows how to serve holiness). While a number of commentators assume that this reference is to a human 'minister' and that the tendency of the passage is towards a Cyprianic perfectionism, the 'sanctus minister' is in fact the Holy Spirit, or, more correctly, the spirit of the pray-er.[1] At *De Idololatria* 11,1 Tertullian refers to mendacity as the 'minister' of covetousness in the sense of a 'promoter'.

Perhaps two of the most important texts in which Tertullian employs 'ministerium' with the meaning of 'ministry-as-service' are found at *De Idololatria* 18,6 where Tertullian refers to the ministry rendered by Jesus to the disciples when he washed their feet (John 13), and at *Ad Nationes* II,16,3 where it is employed to signify religious service due the Creator in acknowledgement of a debt of honour. 'Ministerium' is a term employed by Tertullian to denote any form of agency, instrument or general service. In the setting of the church he employs it to denote Christian ministry in general, much as the New Testament employs 'diakonia'. Neither – not 'diakonia' in the New Testament, nor 'ministerium' in Tertullian – has a specific application. It might also be said, however, in light of his employment of 'ministerium' in secular and impersonal settings, that it denotes Christian 'ministry' as operating without independent authority and thus normally as an agency or

[1] De Labriolle, *Le crise montaniste*, p. 80. 'Cette hostia est d'autant plus parfaite que le spiritus qui l'offre est plus intègre et mieux épurée . . .'

instrument through which God seeks to effect his divine purposes.

At *De Praescriptione* 29,3 Tertullian attacks with facetious irony those heretics (Marcionites and Valentinians) who claim that they have set truth free from Catholic error. 'Ministeria' is listed by Tertullian along with a number of other both general and specific 'ministry' terms, viz., 'virtutes', 'charismata', and 'sacerdotia'. It refers to general 'ministries' or 'services' performed in and through the church. Tertullian is not specific. It has no obvious sacerdotal significance. A reference at *De Pudicitia* 21,6 to Catholic clergy 'ruling' not with power (imperio), but in service (ministerio) is a barbed reminder to the clergy that their leadership is a humble service exercised under God's gracious sovereignty, and not a 'power' exercised by them in his stead. Tertullian does not repudiate the important functions allotted the clergy, but he seeks to restrain what he perceives as a presumptuous foray beyond their legitimate jurisdiction.

'Charismata'

Tertullian's use of this Greek loan-word is well supported in biblical and patristic literature. The major inspiration for Tertullian's use of it can be found in Paul's description of the spiritual gifts in 1 Corinthians 12. Apart from this use of the term to denote 'gifts' for ministry and service, Tertullian also employs it in other, though not unrelated, settings. At *De Ieiunio* 10,5 he speaks of that 'caelesta charisma' which might compensate for the lack of scriptural authority behind Catholic fasting practices, and at 16,8 he condemns those allegedly gluttonous 'Psychici' who he alleges treat their cooking condiments as 'charismata'. At *De Anima* 58,8 Tertullian speaks of 'charismata' as 'spiritual disclosures' promised through the witness and instrument of the Paraclete when he alludes to the Paraclete passages in John 14-16.

Although Tertullian was willing to acknowledge the existence and the importance of 'charismata' in his early 'Catholic' period,[2] it was during his time as a New Prophet that his appreciation and promotion of them as demonstrations of divine

---

[2] See both *De Baptismo* 20,5 and *De Praescriptione* 29,3.

approbation and inspiration came especially to the fore. In this later period Tertullian asserts that it is their recognition of the 'charismata' bestowed by God, among other things, that separates adherents of the New Prophecy from the 'Psychici'.[3] Tertullian's defence of the 'charismata' arises from his desire both to distinguish the New Prophecy from 'carnal' Christianity, and to promote the gift of prophecy as an authentic ministry. Despite his dependence on a scriptural passage such as 1 Corinthians 12 – and, to a lesser extent, on Isaiah 11,1-3 – he makes no explicit mention of any particular 'charisma' except that of prophecy. His references to 'charismata' in his early period are general in nature, while those from the later are almost exclusively concerned with both the validation of prophecy, particularly that exercised by the New Prophets, and the enforcement of a rigorous discipline in the church.

The 'charismata' referred to by Tertullian at *De Baptismo* 20,5 are those about which Paul speaks in 1 Corinthians and which are given to all baptised Christians. Tertullian does not specify the nature of these gifts, and later, as witness *De Ieiunio* 8,4, he became convinced that prior baptism was unnecessary for their reception. At *De Praescriptione* 29,3 Tertullian makes a general reference to the Pauline 'gifts' along with other 'ministry-service' words such as 'virtutes', 'sacerdotia' and 'ministeria'. He does not specify the precise nature of these gifts when he rejects the suggestion of both Marcionites and Valentinians that these 'gifts', inter alia, have been wrongly used by the orthodox. And although Tertullian speaks at *De Anima* 9,4 generally about the 'spiritual gifts' bestowed by God, it is within the context of the particular gift of prophecy. Tertullian there tells of the experience of a Montanist 'sister' who experiences visions during worship and later recalls them for consideration and evaluation by her brethren.

At *De Anima* 9,3 Tertullian claims for followers of the New Prophecy the gift of prophecy; this gift, he maintains, and contrary to general opinion, did not cease with John the Baptist. The possession of this gift is made dependent on the acknowledgement of 'gifts' generally, which the 'Psychici' are assumed

---

[3] *Adv. Prax.* 1,7 and *De Monogamia* 1,2.

not to do (see *De Monogamia* 1,2f.). At *Adversus Praxeam* 1,4
Tertullian accuses 'Praxeas' of having neutralised the effective
exercise of these divine gifts and asserts that this action is
grounded in his not having the love of God within him. At
Adversus Praxean 1,5 Tertullian laments that the bishop of Rome
had been on the verge of 'recognising' officially the charismatic
ministry of Montanus and his associates, but had been convinced
otherwise by 'Praxeas'. At *De Ieiunio* 8,4 Tertullian recalls the
experience of Cornelius at Acts 10,4f. who was given the general
gift of the Holy Spirit, and the specific one of prophecy, even
before his baptism. This, in Tertullian's eyes, confirmed the
priority of God's activity over man's. At *De Monogamia* 1,2
Tertullian names that which separates the New Prophets from
the 'Psychici'; it is 'our' acknowledgement of the reality of the
spiritual gifts which the latter do not make. Thus, Tertullian
makes an exalted claim for the New Prophets on the basis of
their openness to spiritual 'gifts'. This countered claims on the
Catholic side to 'official' charismata based on the holding of
particular offices. (See also *Adv. Praxean* 28,12; *De Ieiunio* 11,6.
Adv. Valentinianos 4,4; and *Adv. Marcionem* v,8,4.)

MINISTRY AS 'OFFICE'

Clergy and laity

It is obvious both from the historical context in which Tertullian
writes and the terminology he employs that he draws a clear
distinction between clergy and laity in terms of appointment,
dignity, authority and function. Such a distinction is already
partially present in some New Testament writings and an
official ordering of the church into clergy and laity is present in
the writings of both Clement of Rome and Ignatius of Antioch. I
will here consider the evidence for Tertullian's understanding of
both the nature of this important distinction and its importance
for his doctrine of ministry.

'Minor/maior locus'

There is no obvious precedent in biblical, patristic or other
contemporary writings for Tertullian's use of these expressions.

At *De Baptismo* 17,2 Tertullian states 'Sed *quanto*[4] magis laicis disciplina verecundiae et modestiae incumbit cum ea [quae] maioribus competant, ne sibi adsumant [dicatum] episcopi officium' (But how much more does the discipline of discretion and modesty apply to lay persons – seeing that these prerogatives [sc. of baptising] belong to their superiors – lest they assume to themselves the role of the bishop). 'Maioribus' clearly stands against 'laici' and denotes here the clerical order headed by the bishop. The passage implies that clergy possess a status greater in dignity and authority (in this instance a sacramental one) than lay persons. At *De Fuga* 11,1 Tertullian designates lay persons and the clergy as possessing a 'lesser' and a 'greater' status respectively. Thus, even in his later period the clergy are perceived by him as possessing a superior dignity and authority. We possess here also an additional – though somewhat unrelated – piece of information; that a lay confessor, by virtue of his endurance of suffering under persecution, was regarded as having been 'raised' to a status equivalent to that of the 'higher' Christians, that is, the clergy. What this might mean in practical terms – for example, admission to the sacerdotal order and to sacerdotal prerogatives – is not clear.

'Clerus'

'Clerus' is a Greek loan-word.[5] At Deuteronomy 18,2 the Septuagint reads '*kurios autos kleros autou*' (the Lord is their inheritance). Acts 1,17 speaks of Judas as having '*ton kleron tes diakonias tautes*' (a share in this ministry), and at 1,26 of the '*kleros*' (lot) falling to Matthias to replace Judas. Ignatius of Antioch speaks of his '*kleros*' (lot) (sc. of martyrdom); in like manner the author of the *Martyrdom of Polycarp* writes of that venerable bishop's '*idios kleros*' (appointed lot [sc. of martyrdom]).[6] A letter from the church at Lyons, written late in the second century, carries ideas similar to both the letters of Ignatius and the *Martyrdom of Polycarp*, when it reports that the confessor Vettius Epagathos has joined the '*kleros ton marturon*' (the ranks of the martyrs).[7] Clement of Alexandria, perhaps the first to employ the term with reference to entry into the clerical order, employs the

---

[4] The Cod. Trecensis prefers 'quando' to 'quanto', but the sense is the same.
[5] Teeuwen, *Sprachlicher Bedeutungswandel* p.16.
[6] *Trallians* 12,3; *Martyrdom*,6,2.   [7] *Ecclesiastical History* v,1,10.

expression 'kleroson kleron' with the sense 'to ordain'.[8]

At *De Monogamia* 12,1f. Tertullian employs the same argument as used concerning appointment to the presbyterate in *De Exhortatione Castitatis* 7. If all lay people were to remarry it would be impossible to find candidates for election to the monogamous order of clergy! One of the other interesting aspects of this passage is that Tertullian appears to distinguish between the lower clergy – the presbyters and deacons – and the bishop, something not yet common practice in the Western church, when he refers to 'the bishops and the clergy'. Tertullian's use of this term in this passage and (to a lesser extent) at *De Fuga* 11,2 reflects the terminology of his present opponents.[9] Consistent with this custom of employing his opponents' language, Tertullian probably made use of the term as a concession to them. He does not use it again. It cannot therefore have been a key term for his understanding of ministry, though this need not imply that the New Prophets did not distinguish between clergy and laity. They clearly did. In his infrequent employment of the term he betrays no acquaintance with the Greek loan-word's meaning of 'share' or 'lot'.

'Laicus'

'Laicus' is a loan-word from the Greek, a Latinised version of 'laikos'.[10] In the Septuagint it is used of unconsecrated bread, and as late as Clement of Alexandria it is used with the common meaning of 'ordinary' or 'profane'.[11] Hippolytus of Rome uses it of lay persons in his *Church Order*,[12] as does Clement of Rome, the one major Christian writer whose influence on Tertullian's ecclesiology is obvious. In Clement's epistle to the Corinthians he declares that '*ho laikos anthropos tois laikois prostagmasin dedetai*'[13] (The lay person is bound by the ordinances for the laity).

In Tertullian's use of 'laicus' and in that of those Fathers before him there are echoes of the Greek word's meaning of both

---

[8] *Quis Dives Salvetur?* Ch. 42; Evagrius Ponticus, a fourth-century Libyan monk and mystic, is said at *Ecclesiastical History* 2,8 to have spoken of the 'clerus' as a class of clergy distinct from the bishop, much as Tertullian appears to do at *De Monogamia* 12,1.2.
[9] See above in Part I.   [10] Teeuwen, *Sprachlicher Bedeutungswandel*, p. 16.
[11] 1 Kings 21,4; *Paed* 2,10.   [12] 19,1.   [13] 40,5.5.

'unconsecrated'[14] and 'common'. Given that a possible strain of laicism evident in *De Exhortatione Castitatis* is also probably present even in the earlier *De Baptismo*, the contention that in *De Exhortatione Castitatis* 7 Tertullian allows to the laity what was previously denied them is wrong.[15] At *De Baptismo* 17,2 the laity, distinguished from the three regular, sacerdotal offices, have conceded to them the right to baptise, though only in case of necessity. Tertullian demonstrates that his underlying concern is one of proper order and not sacralism, which view simply reinforces that reflected at *De Praescriptione* 41,8 where he condemns the irregularity and indiscipline of ministerial appointments within some heretical groups. In the *De Baptismo* passage he asserts further that when given this right to baptise – though, for the sake of order, only in necessity – lay persons must accept the obligation to observe a discipline of modesty and reverence. And this is so because, given that the right to baptise (and to preach) normally belongs strictly to the clergy, the laity must not abuse the privilege of baptising so as to be thought to usurp a dignity not theirs by right.

At *De Exhortatione Castitatis* 7,6 Tertullian again clearly distinguishes the laity from the clergy. He argues that the laity must, in the first instance, be monogamous so that there can continue to be a supply of potential presbyters (see *De Monogamia* 12,1.2). Earlier, at 7,5, Tertullian condemns those digamist (twice-married) clergy whose marital status renders them incapable of presiding with due propriety as priests. He concludes from this that digamist lay persons with the right of acting as priests, even with the compulsion of necessity, act in an equally inappropriate and immoral manner. The earlier reference at 7,3 to the 'priesthood' of all Christians – 'Nonne et laici sacerdotes sumus?' (Are we laypersons not also priests?) – an allusion to Revelation 1,6, does not repudiate Tertullian's previously maintained distinction between the laity and the clergy. It is a concept which Tertullian employs not only to concede to lay

---

[14] 1 Kings 21,4.
[15] H. Karpp, *Schrift und Geist bei Tertullian* (Gütersloh, 1955), p. 16; Bévenot, 'Tertullian's thoughts', p. 134. See my arguments in the General Conclusion concerning *De Baptismo* 17 and *De Exhortatione Castitatis* 7.

persons the formal right to celebrate the sacrament but more especially to lay upon them the 'priestly' obligation of monogamy. The inverse translation of this sentence by those who start with the (wrong) assumption that Tertullian was himself a priest is untenable[16]. The allusion to Matthew 18,20 in the same passage supports Tertullian's consistently held view (see *De Pudicitia* 21,17) that the church is not of necessity constituted by the existence of a clerical order. While the demands of order might be met by such in normal times, unusual times, such as persecution, require only a gathering of a faithful few, albeit laypersons, for a validly constituted congregation to have assembled.

Tertullian is a champion, not of the fundamental rights of the laity, but rather of their obligations and responsibilities. His opinion of the 'lay person' as simple and ignorant is well documented. For Tertullian the laity were the 'flock', the 'herd', the 'sheep' who need constant attention and continuous nurture. At *De Fuga* 11,1 Tertullian condemns those clergy who flee in the face of persecution and leave their congregations vulnerable and confused about the appropriate Christian response. Leaderless and perhaps lacking the appropriate material resources they will be forced to face the coming assault without their regular protection. 'Laicus' is contrasted here with 'actor', the latter denoting someone exercising pastoral oversight of the laity.

Tertullian's concession to lay persons of the right to baptise and even to celebrate the Eucharist is simply an outcome of his non-sacralist view of ministry. Yet even he will only allow the lay person to 'act as priest' in the case of necessity, and this is true for both major periods of his career. His concession of the right to exercise the priestly office to the laity in both *De Monogamia* and *De Exhortatione Castitatis* is in part a manoeuvre by which to impose the obligation of monogamy on lay persons as on the clergy! His opposition to the alleged heretical practice of laying priestly responsibilities on lay persons, so eloquently expressed in *De Praescriptione* 41, is determined more by a concern for order than for any sacralist reasons. His sacramental directives in *De*

---

[16] See Part I.

Baptismo and *De Exhortatione Castitatis* are determined as much by commonsense as they are by the strict demands of theological correctness. Tertullian is not a 'proto-Protestant'. His thought here is not ecclesiologically, or liturgically, or sacramentally driven, but always by concern for proper discipline; what is good (or bad) for the priest must also hold for the lay person.

'Plebs'

In the Roman world the term 'plebs' normally designated the ordinary plebeian class and 'ordo' the patrician-senatorial. Within this Roman social system 'plebs' was also often used pejoratively to denote the common people as the 'mob', as the 'masses', and it is in this sense that Tertullian may have employed the term, even in the setting of the church. Tertullian is clearly influenced here by common Roman usage and tradition. 'Plebs' stands in contrast to 'ordo', much as 'laicus' (the unconsecrated) does to 'clerus' (one set apart). Tertullian's pejorative use of the former term probably reflects his own social status and prejudices. In the Fathers before Tertullian the term is never used exclusively of the laity. In the *Passio Perpetuae et Felicitatis* the angels instruct the bishop Optatus to reprove his unruly, fractious congregation: 'Corrige plebem tuam' (Bring your people into order).[17] At *Ad Nationes* 1,10,39 Tertullian employs 'plebs' to denote a 'crowd' of celestial beings, at II,13,20 the 'general body' of pagan gods – both times pejoratively – and at *Apologeticum* 35,6 the 'indigenous people' of the Seven Hills of Rome. At both *De Monogamia* 12,2 and *De Ieiunio* 13,3 'plebs' is used generally of a class of Christians under authority. This is done explicitly in the first, where 'plebs' is contrasted with 'praepositi'; it is no less obvious in the second. It clearly denotes the laity in both cases. There is implicit at *De Anima* 9,4 an image of the 'plebs' as a common class of ordinary Christians who are dismissed quickly at the conclusion of the service so that important matters can be dealt with by the leadership. At *De Exhortatione Castitatis* 7,3 we have for the first time, and explicitly, the Roman-like distinction between the patrician class of the church – the clerical 'ordo' – and the common people, the 'plebs'. Tertullian declares here that 'Differentiam inter ordinem et plebem constituit ecclesiae auctoritas et honor' (the authority and honour of the church determines the difference between the Order and the people). The difference is recognised by Tertullian as essential for the maintenance of peace and order in the life of the church more than to satisfy any sacralist requirement.

'Grex' and 'gregarius'

The Old Testament and the Johannine portions of the New Testament abound with such pastoral images. At *Adv. Marcionem* IV,11,5 Tertullian refers to the followers of Christ – as he does those of the Baptist – as his 'grex'. 'Grex', used either to denote the 'common herd', or the 'lower ranks' in a military formation, is employed by Tertullian in a way which reflects his pessimistic assessment of both the coping skills of ordinary Christians and the pastoral acumen of the 'shepherds' or 'commanders' entrusted with their care. Indirectly it confirms the notion advanced by Tertullian that one of the major responsibilities of the clergy is the pastoral care and protection of their people.

At *De Pudicitia* 7,4 'grex' does not explicitly designate the laity as opposed to the clergy, but rather that whole church of which Christ is the sole shepherd. At *De Fuga* 11,3, on the other hand, 'grex' specifically designates the laity while the clergy are designated as those 'qui gregi praesunt'. The clergy are the 'pastors' whose responsibility is to shepherd the flock of Christ. This ruling aspect of 'shepherding' brings to mind Minear's observations that in both the Old and New Testaments the 'shepherd' image coalesces with that of 'king', and the 'flock' with that of the 'Kingdom', and that the 'kingly' power of Jesus is always congruous with his function as shepherd.[18] At *De Fuga* 11,1 we see the transformation of a basically agricultural image, 'gregarius', which normally means 'of the common herd', into a military one, denoting those from 'the ranks'. The 'duces' (commanders) – the clergy – despite their

---

[18] Minear, *Images of the church*, at p.86.

clear duty to stay with their 'troops' – the laity – flee at the first sign of danger.

'Pecus'
We have at *De Fuga* 11,1f. another description of the way in which Tertullian perceives the Catholic congregations as abandoned by their 'pastors' in time of peril. Although the scriptural image of the congregation as a 'flock' (pecus) is normally a positive one, it indicates, on the part of Tertullian, a rather pessimistic view of the ordinary Christian. For although 'pecus' can be used of a flock of sheep (the more common New Testament image), it seems more often to have been used of cattle! Tertullian seems to prefer to depict the ordinary Christians as in constant need of nurture and guidance, as fundamentally ignorant and incapable of self-maintenance.

Conclusions
Tertullian draws a clear distinction between 'clergy' and 'people'. Only once does a 'people' word ('plebs' at *De Pudicitia* 7,4) include both laity and clergy. Both his terminology and his general tone suggest that Tertullian, even in his later period, regarded the clergy as occupying a position of dignity and authority vastly superior to that of the laity (v. 'maior' and 'minor locus'). And this, despite the fact that in both major periods Tertullian clearly regarded the distinction as based as much on the requirements of a proper order in the life of the church as on any particular demands of sacralism. His rigorous stance with regard to matters of morality and discipline also brought him to the conclusion that the laity were bound by the same ethical standards – for example, the rule of monogamy – as applied to the clergy. He tended, however, to argue for this position on the grounds both that the fundamental right of the layperson to 'act as priest' (in the administration of baptism) – though, for the sake of peace, only in necessity – carried with it the obligation of a 'priestly' discipline, and that the need for a monogamous presbyterate demanded the retention of a monogamous laity from whose ranks presbyters were appointed. He had a generally low regard for the mass of the laity and saw their

relationship with the clergy as one of general subservience, as that between the simple and the learned, the ill-disciplined child and the caring but strict parent. The laity were for the most part a flock in desperate need of shepherding, an ill-informed and easily misled class of persons in need of constant nurture and attention. Apart from his perception that many of the Catholic clergy had failed utterly to uphold proper standards of Christian behaviour and morality in both their own lives and those of their charges, it was their failure properly and faithfully to carry out their duty as shepherds of God's people which most condemned them in his eyes.

Clerical office

The clergy as an 'ordo'

In the writings of the Fathers before Tertullian are found some concepts which may have influenced his understanding and use of the term 'ordo'. Clement of Rome employed the Greek word 'tagma' – which normally signified a military formation or unit – to denote the various 'ranks' within the church, but did so relying on a rather dubious interpretation of 1 Corinthians 15,23.[19] In the Latin version of *1 Clement* 'tagma' is translated as 'ordo'; yet, while the Roman presbyter's influence on Tertullian in many respects is well attested, it is not evident here. Irenaeus, to whom in many matters related to church order Tertullian is clearly indebted, employs 'taxis' – which word signifies the actual battle placements of troops – to denote a priestly rank.[20] Hippolytus of Rome employs 'taxis' to denote the clerical hierarchy of the church,[21] but the extent of Tertullian's acquaintance with his writings is unclear.

In the secular sphere the term 'ordo' could be employed to indicate a line, a row or a series of things, a military formation or any of the various 'orders' – patrician and plebeian – which made up Roman society. It was normally employed, however,

[19] 37,3; 41,1. Paul himself employs 'tagma' in the sense of an 'order of priority' in which first Christ and then the faithful – at the time of his coming – will be raised from the dead.
[20] 1,8,3.
[21] P. van Beneden, *Aux origines d'une terminologie sacramentelle* (Louvain, 1974), p. 44, n. 99.

to distinguish the senatorial 'ordo' or the 'ordo decurionum' –
the town council of the provinces – 'un corps dirigeant', from the
'common' people, the 'plebs'.[22]
Tertullian employs the term 'ordo' with a variety of meanings,
and at times in a way which can only be properly described as
'imprecise'.[23] That he used it ecclesiastically to distinguish the
clergy from the laity is generally true, but even in this regard he
is not always consistent.[24] There is general agreement that
Tertullian borrowed the term primarily from profane Roman
'Amtssprache', though in that context it could be still used of
social classes generally.[25] Although for Tertullian 'ordo' often
signifies the 'sacerdotal order', the order 'par excellence dans
l'Eglise',[26] it was also frequently employed to include non-
sacerdotal offices as well. Only when there is the sense of an
'ordo sacerdotalis', as at *De Exhortatione Castitatis* 7,2, where
Tertullian wants to distinguish those who possess the exclusive
right ordinarily to act as priests, can we be assured that he means
the expression in an exclusive or limited sense. One useful, but
by no means certain, way of ascertaining Tertullian's precise
meaning is whether he employs 'ordo' in the singular or in the
plural. Almost always the singular form designates the sacerdotal
order exclusively, while the plural generally (though not always)
includes all the various offices of the church membership,
sacerdotal and non-sacerdotal alike.

At *De Praescriptione* 32,1 and *Adversus Marcionem* IV,5,2 'ordo'
signifies a 'list' or 'register', much in the sense of the Roman
'fasti', rather than an 'order' or 'class'.[27] Tertullian probably
here had in mind the Roman senatorial (and other similar)
registers, sometimes also called 'ordines'.[28] Another example of
the influence of secular thought on Tertullian is found at *De
Corona* 13,1. A reference to the secular community's social

[22] Ibid., p. 2; I. M. Barton, *Africa in the Roman empire* (Accra, 1972), p. 54.
[23] Van Beneden, *Aux origines*, p. 43.
[24] See *De Exhortatione Castitatis* 7,3; see *De Corona* 13,1. Van Beneden, 'Ordo', p. 166 calls it Tertullian's 'Lieblingswort'.
[25] J. Klein, *Tertullian* (Düsseldorf, 1940), p. 273; see Pliny 37; *De Spectaculis* 17,4 and *De Corona* 13,1.
[26] Van Beneden, *Aux origines*, p. 30.
[27] See also *De Praescriptione* 32,2. These 'fasti' included both official registers of the higher magistracies and also historical annals.   [28] Van Beneden, *Aux origines*, p. 19.

'orders' is paralleled by one to the Christian ones. One may conclude from the references to 'magistrates' that the ecclesially referenced 'ordines' is used inclusively of all Christians, as the secular is probably of all citizens. The 'ordo ecclesiae' referred to at *De Monogamia* 8,4 and 11,4 – implicitly in the first, explicitly in the second – certainly includes the tripartite structure of bishop, presbyters and deacons; it possibly also includes the widows, given the fact that monogamy was expressly laid down as a requirement for admission to that latter body. That 'ordo' is employed in these passages to distinguish the clergy from the laity, whatever the precise composition of either group, is clear. The expression 'ecclesiastici ordines' found at *De Monogamia* 12,2 and *De Exhortatione Castitatis* 13,4 is clearly a reference to the various clerical 'orders' of the church – the episcopate, presbyterate and diaconate – and, with regard possibly to the second passage, to that of the widows (and virgins?). The feminine form 'quantae' in the *De Exhortatione* passage would seem to guarantee this, although the reading 'quae' is the better attested.[29] Though CCL prefers 'quantae', the more widely preferred reading would render the inclusion of the women groundless. 'Ordines' here certainly does not include the 'order' of the laity as it did at *De Corona* 13,1 above.

The distinction drawn by Tertullian between the clerical 'ordo' and the lay 'plebs' at *De Exhortatione Castitatis* 7,3 is influenced by the secular distinction between the senatorial 'ordo' and the common 'plebs'. It may even carry the suggestion of a Christian 'senate' of clergy. The passage highlights that the distinction is one of discipline and proper order and not of essential nature. It nevertheless indicates a clear distinction between the two main categories of church members measured in terms of power, authority and dignity; a distinction, despite a non-sacralist context, above a mere functionalism brought about by the demands of discipline and order. The members of the clerical 'ordo' are the Christian noble class, the 'maiores' ruling the 'minores'. At *De Idololatria* 7,3 Tertullian speaks of an 'order' whose members exercise the normally exclusive right to

---

[29] The Cod. Florent. Magl. and the Edition Beati Rhen. prefer the reading 'Quanti igitur et quae in ecclesiis ordinari in ecclesia solent, qui deo nubere maluerunt.'

preside at the Eucharist. The thrust of the passage is that those who make idols should not touch – and thereby contaminate – the holy elements. Note, too, that in this passage 'ordo' is in the singular, while at *De Exhortatione Castitatis* 13,4 it is in the plural form. This exclusive prerogative of presidency would certainly exclude from this 'ordo' the members of the female orders to whom this was certainly not permitted.

Tertullian's other uses of the word 'ordo'
Elsewhere Tertullian employs 'ordo' with a wide variety of meanings. It is used of the various Roman social classes at *De Corona* 13,1. At *De Monogamia* 12,2 he employs it to denote the 'status' of monogamy, at *De Pudicitia* 9,11 the 'story' of the Prodigal Son, and at 11,3 the 'ordo' of faith, that is, the time of the coming of Christ and the church. At *De Idololatria* 9,3 he employs it to denote the 'order of the dead' (ordo mortuorum), that is, that class of pagan divinities comprising deceased humans now deified. At *De Resurrectione Carnis* 2,7, he uses it of the 'appropriate method' for conducting disputations, at 25,1 for the 'ordo temporum' in Revelation, and at 48,10 to translate the Greek 'tagma' from 1 Corinthians 15,23. Unlike Clement of Rome[30] Tertullian uses it here in its proper context.

Other words etymologically related to 'ordo'
It might also be profitable to look briefly at some words which are etymologically related to 'ordo' and which became so important in the period beyond that of Tertullian, viz. 'ordinare' and 'ordinatio'. At both *Apologeticum* 21,23 and *Scorpiace* 12,1 'ordinare' is used to denote Christ's sending out of the disciples after his Resurrection. At *De Praescriptione* 32,3 it is used to describe the installation of Clement at Rome. This usage of the term casts doubt on the assertion that 'adlegere in ordinem' cannot mean 'ordinare',[31] unless one means to invest the phrase 'to ordain' with all the precise signification of a later age. Tertullian cannot normally be said to have intended by his use

---

[30] See note 19 above.   [31] Van Beneden, *Aux origines*, p. 59.

of 'ordinare' more than the simple meaning of the word, that is, 'to set in order' or 'to regulate'. At *De Praescriptione* 41,6, however, where he condemns the irregular discipline of the heretics, he speaks of 'ordinationes', by which word he clearly means to denote appointments to the clerical order. Yet we do not speak here of 'le caractère indélébile' or even of 'les fonctions sacerdotales', but rather of the requirement of due order in the appointment of ministers within the church.[32]

'Senatus'

The senate was in theory the governing body of the Roman state. By the time of Tertullian, however, its powers had been curtailed by progressive imperial encroachments. The governing councils of the cities and towns of the Empire – the 'ordo decurionum' (see above) – were sometimes also known as 'senates'. Although at *Apologeticum* 39,21 Tertullian refers to the church as a sort of 'curia' when he dismisses allegations that the church is an illicit organisation, nowhere else, with the possible exception of the passage from *De Ieiunio* to be discussed below, does he allude to the church hierarchy in explicitly 'senatorial' terms.[33] There are no biblical or patristic precedents for this, apart from one reference in Ignatius to the presbyterate as the 'synedrion' (council) of God.[34]

The phrase 'senatus consulta' at *De Ieiunio* 13,5 may be a reference not only to decrees of the Roman Senate, but also, by way of allusion, to decisions of the Catholic presbyterate concerning the practice of fasting. Tertullian might be suggesting at least two different but related things; firstly, that the practices of the New Prophets breach the guidelines set down by the Catholic hierarchy with regard to fasts, and secondly, that these practices might also constitute an infringement of government regulations concerning associations. The latter would profoundly concern the Catholic leadership, in that it might further jeopardise already strained relations with the wider Roman

[32] Ibid., p. 57.
[33] Though the term 'ordo' can, as we have seen, designate a senate-like assembly.
[34] *Trall.* 3,1.

community. Given the tenuous nature of this interpretation, however, it would be inappropriate to draw any firm conclusions concerning the presbyterate as a type of 'senate', except that it is an obvious image for that body.

'Seniores'
There is no obvious precedent for the use of this term either in the Bible – in both Greek and Latin the word 'presbyter' is used for 'elder' – or in the Fathers before Tertullian. In the *Passio Perpetuae et Felicitatis* the 'elders' who appear in the vision of Satyros – alluding to those who sat around the throne of God in the book of Revelation – are called 'seniores'.[35] In only one other passage, apart from that discussed below, does Tertullian employ the term 'seniores' to denote an 'office' rather than persons of a certain age-group. At *De Ieiunio* 7,3 he uses it of the 'elders of the priests' (seniores sacerdotum) of the Jewish nation under Hezekiah.

At *Apologeticum* 39,5 Tertullian asserts that 'praesident probati quique seniores, honorem istum non pretio, sed testimonio adepti' (our presidents are elders of proven character, men who have achieved this honour, not for a price, but by character). These 'seniores' oversaw the penitential processes of the church, sitting as a sort of tribunal.[36] Their precise identity, that is, whether they might be identified with a particular ecclesiastical 'order', is not clear. It is possible that they were drawn from a wealthier class of Christians separate from the regular 'orders' and that Tertullian feels it necessary to defend them against the accusation of corruption. That they are, however, to be identified with the presbyterate or with the clergy generally is more than probable. Tertullian's infrequent employment of the term suggests that it was not an official title in his time and that he uses it here rather casually.

Frend contends that a group of persons known as the 'seniores laici' held a traditional ecclesiastical office peculiar to Africa,

---

[35] *Passio* 12,4.
[36] See below at pp. 155f. the use of 'praesidere' as an expression designating a judicial function.

that they are not to be identified with the presbyterate, and that they possessed the power to excommunicate.[37] Monceaux asserts that in the post-Cyprianic age the 'seniores' replaced the unwieldy 'general assembly' of the local congregation, and that in the late fourth century they oversaw matters related to church finance and property on behalf of the bishop.[38] Under Augustine, in the early fifth century, there existed an 'ordo seniorum', also known as the 'senatus'.[39] In a most exhaustive treatment of the whole question Caron argues that the first mention of the 'seniores' – the reference at *Apologeticum* 39,5 is ignored – occurs during the persecution under Diocletian when the sacred objects of the church at Carthage were entrusted to the 'fideles seniores' by the bishop Mensurius.[40] These were 'un collège de notables laïques' who represented the laity of the church and were divided into two distinct classes.[41] The 'seniores ex plebe' possessed a greater dignity than the deacons but one inferior to the presbyters. They were concerned with the 'foreign relations' of the congregation and with disciplinary matters. The 'seniores ecclesiae', a group possessing an even lesser status, were concerned exclusively with property and finance.[42] It is generally agreed that Tertullian's 'seniores', whether they were a separate non-clerical class, or to be identified with the presbyterate, had a special responsibility for the disciplinary processes of the church. Caron also argues that the 'graves viri' referred to by Cyprian as overseers of the disciplinary process in his church were probably forerunners of the later 'seniores', and that the 'seniores' of *Apologeticum* 39,5 were likewise concerned with the exclusion of malefactors from the church.[43] He argues further that these 'seniores' possibly had also a teaching role and maintains the vague possibility that the 'elders' referred to by Hermas were 'teaching elders'.[44] Adam contends, however, that

---

[37] W. H .C. Frend, 'The seniores laici and the origins of the Church in North Africa', *JTS* ns 12 (1961), p. 282.

[38] P. Monceaux, 'Les seniores laici', *Bulletin. Societé Nationale Antiquaires de France* (1903), pp. 283-4.   [39] Ibid., p. 285.

[40] P.G. Caron, 'Les seniores laici de l'Eglise africaine', *Revue Internationale des droits de l'antiquité* 6 (1951), p. 10.   [41] Ibid., p. 13.   [42] Ibid., p. 16.

[43] *Ep.* 38,2; Caron, 'Les Seniores laici', p. 19.

[44] *Vis.* II,4,2; Caron, 'Les seniores laici', p. 20.

the 'seniores' referred to by Tertullian were ordinary clergy and that he used a term easily recognisable to pagan Romans.[45] Bévenot argues that these 'seniores' are bishops.[46] It is also worthy of note that the Montanists in Phrygia had church officers called '*koinonoi*' who, like the later post-Diocletian African 'seniores laici', exercised property and financial oversight on behalf of the congregation.[47]

It is unlikely that the 'seniores' of Tertullian were forerunners of the 'seniores laici' of the fourth and fifth centuries. It is more likely that the term is meant to denote either the Christian clergy in general or at least the presbyterate. The involvement of these 'seniores' in the disciplinary processes referred to in the passage discussed, and mention of the presbyterate as thus involved at both *De Paenitentia* 9,4 and *De Pudicitia* 13,7, would seem to settle the matter. Tertullian's failure to mention elsewhere a separate order of 'seniores' would otherwise be most unusual.

A note on the term 'officium'

For Tertullian 'officium' is largely a neutral term. He virtually never uses it of a formally constituted position in the sense of the English word 'office'. Where it does bear such a designation – e.g. of the officiating angels of God (*De Anima* 37,1; *Adv. Valentinianos* 16,1) and of the officiating agents of a principal actor, the soul (*De Anima* 40,4) – it is used more for its imagery than in any substantive sense. He employs it to designate a formal obligation or function – *De Anima* 12,6; *De Pudicitia* 21,6; *Ad Uxorem* 1,4,3 – a duty – *De Ieiunio* 2,7; 10,2; 11,4; *De Paenitentia* 3,6; 5,14; 6,14; 10,3; 10,13; *De Resurrectione* 16,7; *Ad Uxor.* II,3,4 – a formal service – *De Fuga* 14,1; *De Idololatria* 17,1; *De Ieiunio* 13,2; *De Pudicitia* 7,15; *Ad Scapulam* 4,4 – and of religious observances – *De Ieiunio* 11,1; 11,6; 15,3; 16,4. Where it is used with reference to an ecclesial office as such – 'praesidentis officium' (the official province of the church president) at *De Pudicitia* 14,16, 'episcopi officium' (the function of a bishop) at

---

[45] Adam, *Kirchenbegriff*, p. 60.
[46] Bévenot, 'Tertullian's thoughts', p. 132.
[47] Vokes, 'Montanism and the ministry', p. 308.

De Baptismo 17,2 and 'praerogativa virilis aut gradus aut officium' (any masculine prerogative or rank or office) at *De Virginibus Velandis* 9,1 – it is employed in a largely value-free context, and as such adds little to our understanding of Tertullian's view of Christian ministry.

Conclusions

Office as a formally constituted and recognised rank or position, bearing a function or authority by virtue of such rank, is in Tertullian's thought applied almost exclusively to the clergy, and only rarely to the minor offices of lector, doctor and the two female 'orders'. An office of the laity can properly be said to exist only in the sense in which it is an 'ordo' within the broad definition of that term as applied, for example, to the various classes – patrician and plebeian – within Roman society. In all other respects the laity are not formally constituted as such, nor do they possess any particular function which would distinguish them, save those of submission to authority and of the administration, in case of necessity, of the sacraments. The clergy form, in Tertullian's mind, a sort of de facto priestly caste, a type of Christian senate; to them alone – in those times when the normal, ordered life of the congregation is not rendered impossible – is granted the sacred functions of administering the sacraments.

Within the church according to Tertullian's thought there exist a number of 'orders' – lesser and greater – as there did within the broader Roman society; but, as with the latter, there is in the church only one 'Order' proper. And this is that of the priestly class. Theirs is not the only formal Christian office, but it does set the pattern for all other offices within the broader framework of Christian ministry. To the priestly office do all others owe a measure of submission and respect.

CHAPTER 7

The offices of the church

MAJOR OFFICES: BISHOP, PRESBYTER AND DEACON

It is not my present purpose to attempt a detailed study of the development of the nature and function of Christian ministry from New Testament times to the opening years of the third century as it relates particularly to the three traditional major offices. It will suffice to say that the recognisable Christian offices of bishop, presbyter and deacon make their first tentative appearances at Philippians 1,1 where Paul addresses the bishops and deacons of that congregation and in the Pastorals (1 Timothy 3,1f.; 5,17f.; Titus 1,5f.) where the question of the responsibilities of and the qualities desirable in bishops, presbyters and deacons are addressed. In these latter writings it appears that bishop and presbyter are largely synonymous terms.

In the *Didache* – a work of uncertain dating – the author comments on the poor regard – in comparison to travelling prophets and teachers – in which the local bishops and deacons are held by the local congregation.[1] Clement of Rome cites Isaiah 60,17 as scriptural authority for the validity of the episcopate and diaconate,[2] though his letter suggests that the pattern of church government preferred at Rome, and which for him was established by the apostles, is presbyteral. In the West as represented by Rome (and this is confirmed by Ignatius' epistle to that church) the single, all-powerful bishop had yet to establish himself independent of the presbyteral college.

In the East, however, or at least in that portion of the East

---

[1] para.15.   [2] *1 Clement* 42,5.

represented by the writings of Ignatius, there is evidence in the early years of the second century of a clearly-defined three-tier clerical structure (such as emerged in the late second century in the West) with a single, all-powerful bishop at the head; without this bishop nothing can legitimately be done.[3] This (single) bishop presides in the place of God, the presbyters in that of the apostles and the deacons are entrusted with the ministry of Jesus Christ.[4] Polycarp also affirms the monarchical episcopate.[5] In the West, however, the background of the Rome-based *Shepherd* of Hermas is clearly a presbyteral church government, while in Irenaeus' writings the monarchical episcopate has begun to assert itself; yet even this bishop can still regard himself as essentially a co-presbyter within the college. He is certainly 'primus inter pares', but the Cyprianic episcopate is not yet in evidence. Hegesippus and Irenaeus have, however, already begun to compile succession lists of bishops running back to primitive times. These lists include the names of some who, while not monarchical bishops in their own time, have been regarded as such by later generations. For Tertullian these succession lists and the historical fictions inherent in them provide a given historical reality. In this section we shall look firstly at the origins of the major offices and then at the roles and functions allowed them by him, specifically the leadership, the pastoral and the priestly.

Origins of Christian office

The origins of Christian office, for the author of the *Pastorals*, and for Clement of Rome, Ignatius, Hermas and Irenaeus, lay in its establishment by the original apostles. Pious fiction or not, this was the generally accepted view and, as we shall see, exercised no small influence on Tertullian's own perceptions. Tertullian never repudiated the authenticity of the apostolic foundation of the Catholic ministry, not even in his most virulent anti-clerical moments. At no point, however, not even

---

[3] *Philad.* 7.   [4] *Magnes.* 6.   [5] *Philippians*, passim.

as a Catholic apologist, did his understanding advance beyond
that of seeing the bishops – or at least their line of succession –
as guarantors of the transmission of unadulterated apostolic
doctrine. Tertullian himself would indeed applaud the following
paraphrase of his own position on apostolicity and the episcopate. It is contended that, in his thought, 'der Geist selbst
spricht durch die Apostel';[6] but he would limit the apostolic
nature of the episcopate to the relatively uncontroversial,
faithful handing on of apostolic teaching through the orderly
succession of office by successive generations of the faithful.
The episcopate was for him of authentic apostolic foundation;
but this did not make the bishops the successors of those
apostles with all rights and privileges intact. And Tertullian
makes the further point, as much implicitly as explicitly, that
bishops are actually no more 'apostolic' than ordinary Christians;
for is not he himself an 'heres apostolorum'(*De Praescriptione*
37,5)? Are not all Christians equally 'apostolici seminis fruti-
ces'(*Scorpiace* 9,3)?

Passages from both of Tertullian's periods – for example, *De
Praescriptione* 32,3 and *De Fuga* 13,3 – underline his conviction
that the Catholic episcopate was of apostolic foundation.
Apostolicity was for him an essential mark of the authentic
church and of its ministry. He was unquestionably influenced in
this by both Clement of Rome and Irenaeus, as well as by simple
'historical' observation.[7]

At both *De Praescriptione* 32,1 and *Adversus Marcionem* IV,5,2
Tertullian speaks of an 'ordo' of bishops. Its employment reflects
the influence of Irenaeus on Tertullian, in that the word here
denotes a 'register list' rather than an 'order' in the organisational
sense. In both passages is reflected the Stoic idea of 'tracing'
something back to its origins in order to more fully understand
its true nature. In both passages emphasis is given to the
apostolic foundation of the episcopate, and thus to the continuity
of the late-second- and early-third-century Catholic episcopate

⁶ Bender, *Lehre*, p. 112.   ⁷ 1 Corinthians 42,2; *Haer.* III,3,4.

with that founded by the apostles.[8] Both passages link this continuity to the authentication of apostolic tradition and teaching in the Catholic church – against the heresy of Marcion and others – though Tertullian does not, unlike Irenaeus, explicitly assign a specific teaching function to the episcopate;[9] more important still, while one passage comes from Tertullian's early period, the other comes from the later, demonstrating the consistency of his thought in this matter;[10] The reference to the 'cathedrae apostolorum' at *De Praescriptione* 36,1 is probably to the office of bishop, but only so in the sense of recognising a teaching authority, reflecting the ancient custom whereby the

[8] Blum's assertion that 'die bischöfliche Nachfolge' offers the necessary empirical-historical guarantee of apostolic tradition, 'Der Begriff des Apostolischen im theologischen Denken Tertullians', *KerDo* 9 (1963), p.118, makes a valuable point, while Eno offers some refreshing insights. He maintains, for example, that even in *De Praescriptione* Tertullian's understanding of the episcopate does not reflect an appeal to authoritative office, but rather to a point of historical verification, 'Ecclesia docens; structures of doctrinal authority in Tertullian and Vincent', *Thomist* 40 (1976), p. 105. He maintains further that for the 'early' Tertullian the episcopate is subordinated to the tradition transmitted, ibid., p.107, and that what the episcopate provides is a historically verifiable genealogy, a 'pedigree of doctrine', ibid., p. 114. Adam likewise maintains, correctly, that while the 'Montanist' Tertullian never repudiates the 'apostolicity' of the Catholic episcopate, he was never concerned with apostolic 'Gewalt'; he only ever stressed its value as a historically commended witness to correct tradition and teaching, *Kirchenbegriff*, p. 41; it was always a purely human institution, never, as in Irenaeus, 'der göttliche Beistand', ibid., p. 42. *De Pudicitia* 21 bears this out.

[9] I have no argument with von Campenhausen when he asserts that for Tertullian the teaching office was not a clerical preserve, *Ecclesiastical authority*, p. 228. It might also equally be said, however, that the African's silence on this matter might actually imply an unspoken acceptance of such an identification of bishop and teacher. And, yet, at *De Praescriptione* 3,5 Tertullian appears to distinguish between the two.

[10] Harnack's assertion that the combination of episcopacy and the 'charisma veritatis' did not, in Tertullian's view, invest the episcopate with the apostolic office in its fullest sense, *History of dogma*, p. 70, is of a rather negligible value seeing that Tertullian, unlike Irenaeus, never attributes such a charisma to the bishop's office. I do agree, however, with his assertion that Tertullian questioned neither the bishops' roles as guarantors of Christian (teaching) purity, ibid., nor that their office provided continuity for the handing on of the Rule of Faith, ibid., p. 79. Flessmann-van Leer is correct when she asserts that, again unlike in Irenaeus, the bishops in Tertullian's view only ever play a minor role, that they are of the 'bene esse' and not of the 'esse' of the church, *Tradition and scripture*, p.155; episcopal succession merely 'dates' the tradition, ibid., p. 161. The assertions of Michaelides that the dynamism of the tradition is 'indissociable' from the episcopal succession, *Foi écritures et tradition, ou les 'praescriptions' chez Tertullien* (Paris, 1969), p. 79, and that episcopacy for Tertullian is of the 'esse' of the church because episcopal succession guarantees the transmission of Christ's teaching, ibid., p. 81 are not tenable. They contradict the very words of Tertullian himself (see *De Pudic.*21,17).

learned sat down to teach. At *De Monogamia* 8,7 Tertullian speaks of Christ occupying the 'cathedra Moysi' – that is, the 'office' of teacher of God's people – and placing in his own 'cathedra' those whom he in turn entrusted with that office. The *De Praescriptione* passage may also reflect an explicit trust on the part of Tertullian in the historical fiction that the original apostles physically ministered from the episcopal chairs found in the apostolic churches of his own time.

Yet at *De Pudicitia* 21,5 we see how prepared Tertullian was to restrict the extent of the Catholic claim to apostolicity. The scornful reference to the bishop as 'apostolice' is neither a downgrading of the status of the apostles in favour of the prophets, nor is it a repudiation of the historical apostolic foundation of episcopal office. Tertullian is far too committed to the latter. It is rather a vigorous refutation of Catholic episcopal claims to the authority and prerogatives of the original apostles based solely on a purely historical connection. It is a defensive move against what Tertullian perceives as a presumption of the Catholic hierarchy, here that of a divine 'potestas' to forgive sins granted originally both to the apostles and the prophets.

Tertullian explicitly denies the title of 'antecessor' to the bishops at *De Virginibus Velandis* 1,7. The implication is that it was claimed by or for them. It is a word used by Tertullian at *Adversus Marcionem* 1,10,4 to denote 'He who came first', that is, the Creator God, but most often it is employed by him of the original apostles of Christ. He employs it also twice in *De Virginibus Velandis* with the meaning of 'teachers'. At 2,1 he uses it also of those apostles nominated by the primitive congregations as authorities in the debates over veiling. At *De Praescriptione* 32,1, in a discussion of episcopal 'lists', Tertullian accepts it as axiomatic that for one of the first line of bishops to have been validly appointed he must be able to point to either an apostle or an 'apostolic man' (i.e. someone clearly associated or identified with one of the former) as his 'auctor' (promoter) or 'antecessor'. At *De Oratione* 22,10 Tertullian accepts without question the dictum that 'non putat institutionem unusquisque antecessoris commovendam' (everybody does not think that the institution of his precedessor must be overturned). The A-NCL correctly suggests that by 'unusquisque' is meant each individual bishop or church-president. By 'antecessor' is probably meant the original apostolic 'founder' of the particular bishop's 'cathedra' rather than his immediate predecessor. At *Adv.Valentinianos* 5,1 Tertullian makes reference to those Christian 'teachers' upon whose testimony he relies in refuting the Valentinian heresy. He calls them 'antecessores' and means by this either the apostles themselves or those who stand clearly within the apostolic succession.[11] 'Antecessor' was a title normally reserved by Tertullian for the original apostles of Christ. It appears that some Catholics had begun to apply it to the office of bishop as a means, perhaps, of claiming 'succession' from the apostles and thereby of confirming its apostolic prerogatives. Tertullian could not endorse such a claim and so denied this title to the bishops, reserving it – and exclusively so in the present age – for the Paraclete.

Roles and functions of office

General

At *De Baptismo* 17,2 the expression 'episcopi officium' is the equivalent of 'episcopatus'. It reflects a Clement of Rome-like concern for strict order in the life of the church. As we shall have cause to remark later, *De Baptismo*, of all of Tertullian's writings, most clearly demonstrates the Roman presbyter's influence. And while the sentence 'Episcopatus aemulatio scismatum mater est' (Envy is the mother of all schisms) probably draws inspiration from Paul's condemnation of division in the church in 1 Corinthians, it shows also the influence of Clement. The latter consistently asserts that envy – most specifically envy of the priesthood – is a major cause of division in the church.[12] *Adversus Valentinianos* 4,1 provides an illustration of this. Valentinus' alleged frustration at not being elected to the episcopate is seen – correctly or not – as a major cause of his abandonment of the Catholic church. *De Anima* 16,6 clearly demonstrates how

---

[11] At *De Pudicitia* 5,15 Tertullian refers to the adulterer as 'antecessor' to the murderer, and as 'successor' to the idolater.

[12] 43,2 and 3,2 et al.

Tertullian prefers to argue historically rather than scripturally for the authentic basis of ecclesial office. He quotes 1 Timothy 3,1 – which passage is a key proof-text for episcopal office – but does so only to illustrate an entirely different point, that being the appropriateness of 'desire' on the part of a Christian. *De Praescriptione* 30,2 is significant in that we have here one of the first occasions when the term 'episcopatus' is employed to denote a particular period of time, much as one dates an event by reference to a particular emperor's reign. At *De Monogamia* 11,1 Tertullian confirms that the clergy were required to be monogamous; it also provides a glimpse into a possible 'consecration' rite for appointment to the order practised in Tertullian's time when the candidate apparently took at least an oath of monogamy.

At *De Corona* 9,1, from one of his later writings, Tertullian includes the bishop in a list of Judaeo-Christian leaders running from the patriarchs down through the apostles to the bishops of his own day. The bishop is certainly named last in the list, but this list is determined as much chronologically as in terms of dignity. It demonstrates a high regard for the episcopal office coming from the pen of a New Prophet, placing the episcopate in a succession of sorts from the patriarchs and religious leaders of antiquity! At *De Monogamia* 12,3 Tertullian condemns an unnamed but clearly identifiable North African bishop for pederasty. He does not repudiate the episcopal system as such, but rather a particular bishop who he alleges has behaved as if his position places him above the law – both that of God and man's. He demands only that bishops know their place; they are above neither God nor his law. *De Pudicitia* 21,17 is considered by a number of commentators to contain one of the most potent repudiations of the episcopal system as such; yet for such a negative construction to be put on Tertullian's words is not tenable. Tertullian has finally conceded, in the face of persistent Catholic claims, that the church indeed does possess the power to forgive sins. He adds, however, that it must be the true church, that is, that church which is constituted by the presence of the Spirit, such presence being demonstrated by the active participation in the life of that church of Spirit-filled men. A church, says Tertullian, whose sole claim to exercise the authority to pronounce forgiveness is based upon an episcopal structure, no matter that it can be traced back historically to the original apostles of Christ, will have such a claim rejected outright. Such a succession might – and indeed does – authenticate the correct transmission of unadulterated apostolic teaching; but it cannot provide the mandate to act, in the forgiving of serious sin, in the name of God. Tertullian is here limiting the extent of episcopal prerogatives, something that in his earlier period was probably not deemed necessary. *De Ieiunio* 16,3, with its reference to 'spiritual bishops', provides clear evidence, not only that Tertullian did not consider all bishops to come under the opprobrium of the title 'Psychici', but that there were some who may have been associated with him in his condemnation of Catholic discipline. It is probably some of these same men whom Cyprian has in mind when he refers at *Epistle* 55,21 to bishops of a generation previous to his who would not accept the readmission to communion of grievous sinners. It is a clear demonstration that Tertullian's attacks were in the main directed more at particular bishops and their presumptuous claims than at episcopal office as such.

Leadership and authority (administration)

Tertullian has much to say on the governing role of the clergy, that is, those leadership functions distinct from specific pastoral and cultic (priestly) responsibilities. Apart from some references to specific leadership functions (see 'Other texts' below) Tertullian employs words such as 'actor', 'dux', 'honor', 'praepositi' and 'principes' to represent his understanding of this particular aspect of Christian ministry.

'Actores' (leaders/stewards) or 'auctores' (founders/teachers)

There is no particular biblical, patristic or other background to the employment by Tertullian of either of these terms, save that in Roman administration various officials were known by the title 'actor...'; for example, the 'actor publicus' managed public property. 'Actores' – the preferable reading notwithstanding the weight of opinion in favour of 'auctores' – almost certainly depicts the clergy as 'shepherds' who are expected to act as responsible 'stewards' of the 'flock' entrusted to them by God. It is a role in which Tertullian believes them to have failed utterly.

Most manuscripts and editors prefer the reading 'auctores' (progenitor, founder, authority, teacher, guarantor) at *De Fuga* 11,1 to that of 'actores' (driver, player, steward, worker) in Tertullian's description of bishops, presbyters and deacons. The only exceptions to this are the *Luxembourg Codex* and *Corpus Christianorum Latinorum*. The former has the singular reading 'actor', the latter 'actores'. The reading 'auctores' seems the more attractive by virtue of majority opinion until one recalls that Tertullian employs it, with the meaning of 'teachers' or 'authorities', of the apostles themselves at *De Praescriptione* 6,4, 'Apostolos Domini habemus auctores' (We have the apostles of the Lord as authorities). It seems unlikely that the New Prophet Tertullian, who refuses the similarly apostolic title of 'antecessor' to the bishops at *De Virginibus Velandis* 1,7, would have conceded the application of 'auctor' to the Catholic clergy. There are also at least two other indicators which support the alternative reading 'actores'. First, at *Adversus Marcionem* IV,29,9 Tertullian says,

Itaque interroganti Petro, in illos an et in omnes parabolam diceret, [id] est illos et ad universos, qui ecclesiis praefuturi essent, proponit actorum similitudinem...

(When, therefore, Peter asked whether [Jesus] had spoken the parable [Luke 12,41f.] to them, or to everyone, that is, to them only or to all who should one day bear rule in the churches, he sets forth the likeness of the stewards...)

It is probable that at *De Fuga* 11,1 Tertullian depicts the clergy as those to whom God has committed the stewardship of his 'property' – the congregations of believers – who nevertheless renounce such responsibility by their failure to hold fast under persecution. Such a meaning would clearly fit the context. Second, the Roman poet Ovid employs the expression 'actor pecoris' to mean 'shepherd' or 'pastor'. The latter is also used of the clergy by Tertullian in the same passage from *De Fuga*, as is 'pecus', meaning a 'flock (of sheep)', of the laity.

'Duces' (generals)

It is only in *De Fuga* that this image is found denoting Christian ministry. There are no obvious biblical, patristic or other precedents for Tertullian's employment of it, save in the frequent use in the scriptures of military images. At *De Ieiunio* 5,3 Tertullian refers to Moses and Aaron as 'duces'. At *Ad Martyras* 4,6 Regulus is called 'dux Romanorum'. At *Adv. Marcionem* III,13,8 Tertullian describes the star which appeared over Bethlehem at the time of the birth of Christ as a 'dux'. At *De Resurrectione* 3,4, *De Anima* 18,12 and *De Patientia* 5,23 'dux' is employed with the meaning 'guide'. At *Adv. Valentinianos* 5,1 the 'self-appointed' (adfectatis) leaders of the Valentinian sect are designated 'duces'. And, most interesting of all, at *De Ieiunio* 10,6 the Paraclete is styled by Tertullian as the 'dux universae veritatis' (the guide of universal truth) a clear allusion to John 14-16.

In his barrage of military imagery at *De Fuga* 11,1 – 'in acie', for example, is a common description of soldiers in battle formation – Tertullian rebukes those Catholic clergy who flee at the first sound of an attack. The term adds little to our appreciation of Tertullian's understanding of Christian ministry, save that it offers another example of what he perceives as the failure by the Catholic clergy to do their duty. He perceives the clergy as a group without whose steadfast example the rank and file of ordinary Christians would be unable to function effectively.

'Honor'

Clement of Rome distinguishes between those who had originally occupied the positions of leadership in the congregation at Corinth and those who had usurped their authority. He speaks of the former as '*hoi entimoi*' (those in honour, that is, those in authority) and of the latter as '*hoi atimoi*' (the worthless, the dishonoured).[13] In secular life 'honor' could be used variously of public honours, an official dignity, an office, a post or preferment (by Sallust), or of a magistrate or other office-holder (by both Juvenal – with whose writings Tertullian was evidently familiar

---

[13] *1 Clement* 3,3.

– and Virgil). It is likely that while Tertullian normally employs the term 'honor' with the plain meaning of the English 'honour', he also frequently employs it to denote ecclesiastical 'office'. This is particularly so when he employs it in connection with the exercise of authority; in *Apologeticum* it is 'der Ehrenamt in der Kirche' and in *De Baptismo* 'kollektiv die Hierarchie'.[14] At both *Apologeticum* 39,5 and *De Monogamia* 12,2 – each from a different period – it is possible to see in the term 'honor' a designation for clerical office and not merely the 'honour' attached to the holding of such office. The identification of 'honor sanctitatis' with 'gradus' and 'officium' is clear. It refers to ecclesiastical office. At *De Virginibus Velandis* 9,1 Tertullian again clearly identifies 'honor sanctitatis' with 'gradus' and 'officium'. Each refers to ecclesiastical office. At *De Baptismo* 17,1 the expression 'ecclesiae honor' is at first glance probably a reference to the dignity – the honour – of the church's life. At *De Exhortatione Castitatis* 7,3, however, there is the suggestion of a somewhat different interpretation for both passages. In the latter, where Tertullian declares that 'differentiam inter ordinem et plebem constituit ecclesiae auctoritas et honor per ordinis consessus sanctificatus deo' (the authority of the church and the honour sanctified by God through the assembly of the Order (sc. of clergy) constitutes the difference between the Order and the people), 'honor' is distinguished from 'auctoritas'. It is not meant as complementary to the latter. 'Auctoritas' here probably means 'decree' in the sense in which 'auctoritas senatus' denoted a decree of the Roman senate.[15] 'Honor' in this context means an ecclesiastical charge constituted by the assembling of the clerical order. This meaning would also suit well the context of the first passage. It is notable also that this usage is as well attested – indeed, even better – in Tertullian's later period as earlier. There is no irony in Tertullian's choice of words.

---

[14] Teeuwen, *Sprachlicher Bedeutungswandel*, p. 69; Van Beneden, *Aux origines*, p. 27. I agree with the latter's assertion that for Tertullian 'honor' means the hierarchy pure and simple.
[15] Van Beneden, *Aux origines*, p. 26.

'Praepositi', 'praesidere' and 'praeesse'

(1)*Praepositi.* At 1 Timothy 5,17 the Greek *'proistemi'* –
corresponding to the Latin 'praepono' – is used of those elders
who 'rule' over a congregation, and, doing this well, are worthy
of a 'double portion' of honour. At Romans 12,8 Paul speaks of
'ho proistamenos' as one who exercises leadership in a congregation.
The word is also employed at 1 Thessalonians 5,12 and at 1
Timothy 3,4-5 of a bishop ruling well his own household and at
3,12 likewise of deacons. The Greek *'proegoumenoi'* – the equivalent
of the Latin 'praepositi' – is similarly used of the church leaders
at Jerusalem;[16] likewise, Clement of Rome says, *'proegoumenous
hémon aidesthomen'* (let us respect those who rule us).[17] In the
Pastor Hermas speaks of *'hoi proegoumenoi tés ekklesias'* (the leaders
of the church), while Clement of Alexandria, in the *Paedagogus*,
says of himself and his fellow Christian teachers that *'poiménes
esmen hoi tón ekklesión proegoumenoi'* (we are shepherds, the leaders
of the churches).[18]

   The employment by Tertullian of 'praepositi' reflects an
oversight/leadership designation for the clergy which he applies
consistently in both periods of his life. It can denote either 'those
placed in authority over...' – as in the sense of the English
words 'overseer' or 'superintendent' – or it can be employed
with a more specific sense as a synonym for either 'pastores' or
'antistites'. It is not used by Tertullian of the civil or secular
authorities (unlike 'praesidere', see below), but is, alone of the
three terms considered here, well attested in early patristic
literature. It has been argued that the 'praepositi' are the 'ordo
sacerdotalis', the 'ordre par excellence' of the church.[19] It was
clearly a descriptive title of long standing in the life of the church
which Tertullian has simply taken over for his own purposes. A
value-neutral term, it reflects the idea present in Tertullian's
thought that the natural order includes both 'leaders' and 'led'
and that the clergy, however unworthy, are part of the former.

   The first use of the term at *De Fuga* 11,3 – 'praepositi ecclesiae'
– denotes those appointed as 'overseers' of the congregation. It is
a neutral term, signifying 'those in authority over...' and

[16] apud Eusebius, *EH* III,32,6.   [17] *1 Clement* 21,6.
[18] *Vis.* 2,2,6; 3,9,7; *Paed.* 1,6.   [19] Van Beneden, *Aux origines*, p. 142.

approximates to the original meaning of the classical Greek '*episkopos*' or English 'overseer'. The second use of the term – '*praepositus gregis*' – is equivalent to 'pastor', which term itself appears in the same chapter. 'Praepositus' is employed at *De Paenitentia* 6,10 as being synonymous with 'antistes', a priest charged with oversight of some ritual or other liturgical action. At *De Monogamia* 12,2 'praepositi' denotes the clergy – called earlier in this same passage the 'clerus' – and stands against the lay designation 'plebs'. It bears a meaning similar to that established for it at *De Fuga* 11,3.

(2)*Praesidere*. There is no clear biblical or patristic precedent by which we can better understand Tertullian's employment of this word and its derivatives. Its background is the administrative life of the Roman world. While capable of being used of administrative oversight generally, with easy application to the notion of Christian '*episkope*', the word and its derivatives were employed specifically in the area of judicial administration. In this may lie, in part, a valuable key to Tertullian's application of it as a description of ecclesiastical oversight. Tertullian employs 'praesides' to denote secular Roman governors at *Scorpiace* 10,11 and speaks at *Apologeticum* 44,2 of those 'qui cottidie iudicandis custodiis praesidetis' (who daily preside at the trials of prisoners). At *De Anima* 33,2 he asserts that 'praesidet humana censura' (human opinion judges).

At *De Resurrectione* 14,9 he speaks in a similar vein of its divine equivalent, 'an utrique substantiae humanae diiudicandae censura divina praesideat' (whether divine opinion determines the judging of the two natures of man), and at 16,4 in the same treatise employs the phrase 'iudicium praesidere' (to offer judgement).

'Praesidere', which appears to refer to an authority exercised in the church both judicially and sacramentally, was a term seen by Tertullian, in both periods of his career, as an appropriate description of the role of Christian clergy, or, at the very least, of the bishop. It is not, as we have seen, found in patristic literature before Tertullian, and has no obvious biblical precedent. It is a word taken directly from its employment in Roman provincial administration which Tertullian uses both of Roman governors and magistrates and of those who exercise authority in the church. Its employment with reference to the 'seniores' of the church congregation at *Apologeticum* 39,5 and to the process of 'excommunication' from the church – at both *Apologeticum* 39,5 (again) and *De Pudicitia* 14,16 – suggests that it might have been used with particular reference to a judicial role exercised by the presbyterate. This latter order played a key part in the church's penitential processes as described at both *De Paenitentia* 9,4 and *De Pudicitia* 13,7. It is likely that presbyters, sitting as a kind of ecclesiastical tribunal, initially heard the charges against those accused of serious offences, and that the bishop acted as a final 'court of appeal'. Tertullian's employment of the term at *De Corona* 3,3 – where it denotes those authorised to administer the eucharistic sacrament – suggests, when taken together with the implications of the two previous passages discussed, that it might also denote a specific liturgical function. It would seem that 'praesidere' was often employed by Tertullian with reference to Christian clergy, especially of the bishop. He uses it of their role as 'judges' within the Christian congregation, particularly in relation to the processes and the rites of penitence and exclusion, as well as of the exercise of their liturgical-sacramental prerogatives. He is consistent in this in both major periods of his career.

At *De Praescriptione* 36,1 Tertullian asserts without equivocation that the teaching of the apostles is authentically transmitted by the churches of apostolic foundation and by those in communion with them. The episcopal 'cathedrae' witness to the unbroken transmission of apostolic doctrine handed down to each generation through an unbroken succession of bishops tracing their foundation, and thus the church's authority to determine the orthodoxy of their doctrine, back to the apostles. 'Praesidere' here refers to authority generally and to orthodoxy specifically, but does not address the questions of penitential or judicial authority; these latter concerns were at this time of no special importance to Tertullian. At *De Pudicitia* 21,6 Tertullian questions the claim of the Catholic bishops to possess the authority to grant indulgence to grievous sinners. He asserts that they have not the 'imperium' – that is, the supreme authority to decide who or what shall be forgiven – but only the 'ministerium', the administration of divine decrees. Tertullian alludes to 1 Peter 5,1f., although what is attacked there is not indulgence on the part of the church leadership, but rather severity. Whatever the specific authority conceded by Tertullian to the clergy, he once more employs 'praesidere' with a judicial signification.

The reference by Tertullian at *De Ieiunio* 17,4 to 1 Timothy 5,17, where the apostle encourages the 'double honouring' of those 'elders' who rule well, is a crude attack on the alleged unworthiness and gluttony of the Catholic clergy. It is a matter of some contention whether the 'elders' in the epistle are to be identified with the presbyterate or with the bishops spoken of at 3,1, or with both; the terms may be synonymous. In *De Ieiunio* it is certain that 'praesidentibus' refers to the clergy generally. Whether 'praesidere' is used here specifically to denote a judicial function is, however, unclear. In the assault by Tertullian at *De Monogamia* 12,3 on some allegedly unworthy Catholic clergy, the context suggests strongly that 'praesident' refers specifically to the bishops. The precise identity of these 'presidents', however, is not crucial for our present purposes. 'Praesidere' again, as in *De Ieiunio*, while possibly denoting a judicial function, may imply no more than general oversight.

(3)*Praeesse*. In his *First Apology* Justin Martyr describes the format of the Christians' weekly worship sessions. After the congregation have gathered together, writings of both prophets and apostles are read. Then, says Justin, '*Eita pausamenou tou anaginoskontos, ho proestos dia logou tēn nouthesian kai proklēsin tēs tōn kalōn toutōn mimnēses poieitai*' (when the reader has finished, the president instructs and exhorts [the congregation] to imitate such good things).[20] In the Latin version '*ho proestos*' is translated 'is qui praeest'. This expression denotes either the bishop or, at the very least, a senior presbyter responsible for teaching. At *Adv. Haer.* 1,10,2 Irenaeus also uses '*proestos*' to denote one of the 'rulers' (A-NCL) of the church. The term is nowhere else attested in patristic literature prior to Tertullian; biblical

[20] 67,3.

precedents can, however, be found at 1 Timothy 5,17, where the writer refers to the 'double-honouring' of those 'elders' who 'rule well' (*kalōs proestōtes*), and at 1 Thessalonians 5,12, where Paul urges the congregation to respect those leaders who are 'over you in the Lord' (*proistamenous humōn en kuriō*). It is also a well attested expression for the exercise of authority in secular literature, being found in the writings of Caesar, Sallust, Cornelius, Nepos and Ovid. Tertullian himself, however, apart from a single reference at *De Fuga* 11,3 which we will discuss below, employs it in neither the secular nor the ecclesiastical sphere as a term designating authority. He employs it frequently to denote impersonal or logical pre-eminence or priority. At *Scorpiace* 6,1 he says 'hic quoque liberalitas magis quam acerbitas dei praeest' (here also the generosity rather than the severity of God holds sway).

At *De Pudicitia* 16,15 he employs 'praeest' to translate the Greek phrase '*kreitton estin*' in the expression '*it is better* (to marry than to burn)' from 1 Corinthians 7,9. At *Apologeticum* 21,11 he declares that 'virtus praesit' (power is over all). At *De Carne Christi* 17,2 he employs 'praefuit' with the sense of something needing logically to be 'first demonstrated', and at *De Resurrectione* 14,3 he asserts that 'causa restitutionis praeesse debebit' (the cause of recovery [that is, of resurrection] ought first to pre-exist).

The phrase 'qui gregi praesunt' at *De Fuga* 11,3 is synonymous with both 'gregis praepositi' from the same passage and 'pastores'. As with both 'pastor' and 'praepositus', Tertullian in both periods of his career concedes the validity of this pastor-exemplar role for Christian clergy. He bitterly repudiates those who fail in such shepherding responsibilities and leave their congregations defenceless and vulnerable in time of turmoil. We are reminded again of Minear's observation that in the New Testament the 'king' and 'shepherd' images frequently coalesce.[21]

'Principes'

'Princeps' was the title by which the Roman emperor was known from Augustan times and is not represented as being

---

[21] Minear, *Images*, p. 86.

applied to Christian leaders in either biblical or patristic literature before Tertullian. It is not clear that Tertullian is referring at *De Ieiunio* 13,5 only to decrees of the Roman senate and mandates of the emperors, and not also, by way of allusion, to the Catholic episcopate. Tertullian has already spoken at length, and critically, about Catholic fasting practices. These seem to him to indulge the weakness and indiscipline of many Catholics. He responds also to some harsh Catholic criticism of the more rigorous New Prophecy practices. Tertullian asks here whether the New Prophets are breaking Roman laws against gatherings of illegal associations and whether this is what actually causes the Catholics so much concern. He thus intimates that the worldly Catholics are perhaps more worried about offending pagan laws and sensibilities than those of God. Tertullian has, only a few lines previous to this, spoken of the 'mandata' issued by the Catholic bishops with respect to special fasting days. 'Senatus' may also be a reference not simply to the official Roman senate, but also an allusion to the Catholic presbyterate.

Other texts
At *De Baptismo* 17,1 the Catholic Tertullian concedes to the bishop the chief right to celebrate the sacrament of baptism; further, the later Tertullian does not repudiate this right, but indeed implicitly confirms it at *De Exhortatione Castitatis* 7,3-6. His designation of the bishop as 'High Priest', by no means intended as sarcasm, will be discussed later. While he also allows this right of celebrating the sacrament to presbyters and deacons – and, in certain circumstances, even to lay persons – it cannot be exercised apart from the bishop's authorisation. This 'high' view of the episcopate, however, is not to be equated with the Ignatian 'not apart from the bishop'.[22] Rather it reproduces Clement of Rome's concern for order. This Tertullian makes clear when he asserts that this episcopal authorisation is not for any sacralist or other theological reason, but rather for the sake of the church's 'honour' and the preservation of 'peace'.

---

[22] See Powell, 'Ordo', p. 293.

At *De Pudicitia* 18,18, from one of Tertullian's most stridently anti-clerical writings, he does not in any way repudiate the validity of the episcopal office (though he does give it somewhat of a battering!). He concedes to the bishop, as chief officer of the congregation, oversight – if not 'power' in any absolute sense[23] – of the reconciliation of 'lesser' sinners; 'grievous' ones must be left to the wisdom and mercy of God alone. While Tertullian will not concede an absolute power or jurisdiction over the penitential process to the bishops – as some had apparently assumed for themselves – he acknowledges that they do have a role to play.

At *De Virginibus Velandis* 9,2 Tertullian is critical of a bishop alleged to have admitted into the order of widows a young woman not yet twenty years of age. Tertullian prefers that such a person should remain in the order of virgins. At no point, however, does he deny to the bishop the authority to make such an appointment. We see here evidence of one of the functions of a bishop – the appointment of persons to certain 'orders' within the life of the church – and one with which, in principle, Tertullian has no quarrel.

At *Adversus Praxean* 1,5 Tertullian first approves and then condemns the actions of a Roman bishop who, having first sought to reconcile the Montanists of Phrygia both with their own regional church and also with the Roman see itself, was then persuaded by the mysterious 'Praxeas' to withdraw this reconciliation and issue in its stead a condemnation. Again Tertullian condemns only the particular decision-cum-action and not the authority which underpins it. It would appear that the Roman bishop exercised a major influence on relations with other churches and on questions of doctrinal and disciplinary orthodoxy. This authority Tertullian does not appear to contest; the particular decisions themselves are the actual cause of his condemnation.

The context of *De Ieiunio* 13,3 lies in Tertullian's criticism of particular Catholic fasting practices – or at least in his rejection

---

[23] See note on 'potestas' in Part II; Rahner's claim, 'Zur Theologie der Busse bei Tertullian', *Abhandlungen über Theologie und Kirche* (1943), p. 152, that even the 'Montanist' Tertullian conceived of the bishops as possessing 'Gewalt' via apostolic succession is not reconcilable with a reading of *De Paenitentia*, let alone of *De Pudicitia*.

of Catholic criticism of Montanist fasts; yet he still does not deny the fundamental right of these bishops to issue instructions to church members concerning their conduct. Indeed, there is every indication that the New Prophecy group both acknowledged and adhered to these instructions; their own fasts were valid extensions – in style, duration and frequency – of these. However, whether the New Prophecy fasts were simply extended adaptations of Catholic ones, or part of a parallel but separate system is not clear. Tertullian at times is so obsessed with ridiculing his opponents that the form of his own practices is not always obvious.

Conclusions

Tertullian acknowledges the pre-eminence of the higher clergy in the life and witness of the congregation; as he is also quick to point out in *De Baptismo* 17, however, this is more for the sake of order and peace in the church than for any strictly theological reasons. Both 'actor' and 'dux', while superficially general leadership terms, reflect in Tertullian the pastoral dimensions of the clergy's role. 'Honor' is a relatively neutral word, though with important precedents in secular literature, and one which may reflect the dignity which even the New Prophet Tertullian attaches to the clerical order. 'Praepositi' denotes general administrative leadership and oversight and has a wide range of significant patristic precedents. The normal ecclesial employment of the word 'praesidere', one drawn from secular administration usage, bears a distinct judicial signification. It reflects the major involvement of the clergy in the penitential processes of the church. The word can also reflect, though this is far from being its most significant use, a sacramental oversight function. Other administrative-cum-leadership functions of the clergy (with particular respect to the episcopate) include the power of appointment to the lower orders (*De Virginibus Velandis*), the regulation and oversight of fasts (*De Ieiunio*), and the conduct of 'foreign' relations with other Christian congregations (*Adv. Praxean*).

Pastoral/nurturing role

'Papa' (Father)/ 'pastor'

The dominical injunction at Matthew 23,9 to call no-one 'father' save God appears initially to have worked against the formal assumption of it by church leaders. From references in Tertullian and others it appears that when it came into use toward the end of the second century, at least in the Latin church, it came in the familiar form of 'papa' rather than the formal 'pater'. In the *Passio Perpetuae et Felicitatis* the martyrs address bishop Optatus – though without irony, despite the tensions evident in the church at Carthage – as follows, 'non tu es papa noster?' (are you not our father?),[24] and do not appear to begrudge him the title.

The chief sources for the image of the minister as 'pastor' are the Johannine writings[25] and the Old Testament. Tertullian employs 'pastor' frequently and in a wide variety of ways; of Christ-as-the-Good Shepherd at *De Anima* 13,3, *De Pudicitia* 7,6;10,13 and at *De Resurrectione* 34,2, of the shepherds to whom Christ's birth was announced at *Adv. Marcionem* v,9,7 and *De Carne Christi* 2,1, of shepherds generally at *Adv. Marcionem* v,7,10, *De Anima* 2,3, *De Paenitentia* 8,5, *De Patientia* 12,6 *Apologeticum* 15,12 and *Ad Nationes* 1,10,45, and, negatively, at *De Corona* 13,30, in an assertion that Moses was a prophet and no poet-shepherd.

Tertullian happily concedes the title of 'pastores' to the Christian clergy. He becomes concerned in those all too frequent situations, however, where the clergy abandon the responsibilities of their 'pastorate' in the face of persecution and leave their congregations defenceless and vulnerable to attack. Tertullian does not deny the 'pastoral' role which is properly a major aspect of the clerical office. He repudiates those 'mali pastores', however, who fail in this responsibility through fear of persecution or slack discipline. For Tertullian the pastoral aspect of the clergy's function is important and one which is most strongly tested in the face of great adversity. In their inadequate performance (or non-performance) of this task Tertullian

---

[24] 13,3.   [25] e.g. John 10,11f.

has nothing but contempt for many of the Catholic clergy. Tertullian addresses his episcopal opponent at *De Pudicitia* 13,7 as 'benedictus papa' and as 'bonus pastor'; this he does sarcastically. He mocks the apparent willingness of the bishop concerned to offer a kindly paternal indulgence to sinners, no matter how grievous the offence. In assuming for themselves the title of 'father' to their congregations, it seems to Tertullian that some bishops mistakenly prefer the role of the merciful parent to the disciplinarian. In *De Fuga* 11 Tertullian makes clear what constitutes for him the archetypal Christian shepherd. He uses, as does the Evangelist John, the image of the shepherd as either faithfully caring for, or, on the other hand, as unfaithfully ignoring, the welfare of his flock. For him the model 'pastor' will be prepared to stay at his post and to suffer when confronted by persecution. He will not leave his congregation leaderless and vulnerable either to external physical assaults or to internal apostasy (11,2). Flight is not only immoral and inappropriate, but also disobedient to the law of Christ and thus subject to divine condemnation (11,3).

Cultic/priestly role

Tertullian draws the image of the priest from Jewish, pagan and early Christian sources. No Christian Father before him, however, refers to Christian ministers specifically as 'priests'. Tertullian employs three words and their derivatives to denote priesthood and priestly function, viz. 'antistes', 'pontifex' and 'sacerdos'.

'Antistes' (priest)

When Tertullian wishes to denote a 'priest' he most often employs 'sacerdos'. On a number of occasions he also employs 'antistes'; this word bears the meanings variously of 'temple overseer', 'high-priest' or 'a priest of a particular rite'. Tertullian employs 'antistes' with both variation and frequency. At *Adv. Marcionem* v,9,9 he refers to Christ as the 'propius et legitimus dei antistes' (the proper and lawful priest of God). He designates Christ as the true High Priest of the Christian 'cult' in the spirit of the letter to the Hebrews. At both *De Ieiunio* 11,4 and *Ad Nationes* I,12,1 he employs 'antistites' of all Christians – clerical and lay – as priests of 'the one creator God and his Christ' and 'of the Cross'; though he does so in a non-liturgical context. The inspiration for both passages is Revelation 1,6. At *De Monogamia* 8,1 he refers to monogamy and continence as the two 'antistites Christianae sanctitatis' (priestesses of Christian sanctity). At *Apologeticum* 1,1 he refers to the magistrates of the Empire, who are the nominal addressees of the treatise, as 'antistites' (though meaning here 'presidents'), and of priests of an Egyptian cult at both *De Monogamia* 17,4 and *De Exhortatione Castitatis* 13,2.

At *De Corona* 3,2 alone Tertullian designates a Catholic cleric as 'antistes', though only as being president of a sacramental rite. Here 'antistes' must denote a member of the clergy, and most probably the bishop, since the passage concerns a sacerdotal function which even the later Tertullian normally preserves as an exclusively clerical prerogative. The use of 'antistes', however, rather than 'sacerdos', would appear to underline Tertullian's view of the officiating priest as being more the 'cultic official' of Clement of Rome than as the 'sacral focus' of the congregation in Ignatius.[26] Tertullian prefers normally, however, to apply 'antistes' either to pagan officials – cultic or administrative – or, occasionally, to all Christians, lay and clergy alike. The context of *De Fuga* 2,1 is the unjust persecution of Christians. The A-NCL translates 'antistites' as 'bishops', but this is only possible if 'sectatores' is meant not to complement 'antistites', but rather to stand over against it. If, however, it is intended as complementary, 'antistites' must denote all Christians.

'Pontifex' (high-priest)

Nowhere in any of the writings of Christian apologists prior to Tertullian is the bishop called by the title of 'Pontifex'. The Pontifex Maximus was the supreme pagan priest of the Roman state cult. Tertullian makes reference to this pagan 'Pontiff' at *De Praescriptione* 40,5 – though here it may be a specific reference to the high-priest of the cult of Mithras – *Apologeticum* 26,2, *De Monogamia* 17,3, *De Exhortatione Castitatis* 13,1 and *Ad Uxorem* 1,7,5. Tertullian is adamant, however, that Christ alone is the

---

[26] See von Campenhausen, *Ecclesiastical authority*, pp. 120f.

authentic 'Pontifex' of the Christian God. At *Adversus Marcionem* IV,13,4 he calls Christ 'Pontifex Patris', at V,35,7 'authenticus Pontifex dei Patris', at V,9,9 'praeputiati (of the uncircumcised) sacerdotii Pontifex' and at *De Carne Christi* 5,10 'salutis Pontifex' (High-Priest of our salvation).

At *De Pudicitia* 1,6 Tertullian mocks the alleged pretensions of at least one Catholic bishop[27] in laying claim to apostolic prerogatives – specifically that of the 'potestas' to remit grievous sins and to issue 'edicts' accordingly – by addressing that bishop derisively as 'Pontifex'. At *Adv. Valentinianos* 37,1 Tertullian likewise condemns the teachings of Valentinus, 'qui ex pontificali sua auctoritate in hunc modum censuit' (who gave determinations even out of his own high priestly authority!). Whether any Catholic bishop had yet begun to claim the title of 'Pontifex' is improbable. In Tertullian's mind some episcopal actions were tantamount to such a claim. Whatever the actual situation, Tertullian's words are a piece of finely crafted abuse, an attack on what he perceived as an impertinent episcopal presumption of apostolic and prophetic prerogatives.

'Sacerdos'

At *De Pallio* 1,2 ('sacerdotium'), *De Spectaculis* 7,1 ('sacerdotia') and *Ad Uxorem* 1,6,3 ('sacerdotia') Tertullian makes clear references to pagan priesthoods. At *Adv. Marcionem* IV, 9,9 he refers to the Jewish priesthood in a quotation from Luke 5,14 and at V,9,9 to the priesthood of both Melchisedek and Christ, designating the latter, 'Christus propius et legitimus dei antistes, praeputiati sacerdotii pontifex' (Christ the proper and lawful priest of God, the chief priest of the priesthood of the uncircumcised). Notwithstanding evidence of both pagan and Jewish influences, Tertullian's references to a specifically Christian 'priesthood' and Christian 'priests' are neither ironic nor mocking. Even in his later 'Montanist' period Tertullian is content to concede

---

[27] Whether he is the Roman or the Carthaginian bishop is not clear from the context. Von Campenhausen's assertion that the polemic in *De Pudicitia* is directed against the penitential authority of episcopal office as such and not against particular incumbents of that office, *Ecclesiastical authority*, p. 229, is only partially true. Tertullian does, on occasion, take aim at particular bishops.

the title of 'priest' to Catholic clergy as under the one High Priest Jesus.[28] When speaking in an ecclesiastical or liturgical context Tertullian's references to Christian 'sacerdotium' are almost invariably to the clergy presiding at the sacraments; there are, of course, exceptions to this. There is not, however, in Tertullian's transition to the New Prophecy a complete change in his attitude towards 'le chrétien sacerdoce'.[29] Even in his pre-Montanist days Tertullian held to no sacral priestly office, 'holy per se'.[30] The contention that the references to 'sacerdotes' in *De Exhortatione Castitatis* 7 are not complementary, but rather the very opposite, is not borne out by a close reading of the text.[31] The assertion that in *De Baptismo* 17 baptism is given the value of 'une ordination sacerdotal'[32] is acceptable possibly only in the most general terms – namely, of a universal priesthood which Tertullian sometimes endorses when it suits his purposes. Tertullian is content to concede to the Catholic clergy the title of 'priests', but with the proviso that it is understood as one always of 'ministerium', and never, except God grant it, of 'potestas'.[33]

It is only when Tertullian wishes to impose the disciplinary obligations of the clergy upon the laity that he reverts to the concept of the universal priesthood of Revelation 1,6.[34] At both *De Monogamia* 12,2 and *De Exhortatione Castitatis* 7,4 he condemns those lay persons who claim the privileges of priesthood while repudiating its attendant discipline of monogamy. At *De Monogamia* 7,8 he also states firmly that all Christian priesthood derives from the High Priesthood of Jesus, 'de suo vestiens'. This is crucial for his understanding of Christian priesthood in both periods of his life. At *De Exhortatione Castitatis* 7,3, 'Nonne et laici

---

[28] See *Adv. Marcionem* v,9,9.

[29] D'Alès, *La théologie de Tertullien*, p. 323, wrongly suggests the lesser role given the clergy in Tertullian's later period, especially as regards the penitential process, indicates this. Tertullian does not, he asserts, seem to regard this process as a sacrament requiring priestly oversight. This was not so.

[30] Von Campenhausen, *Ecclesiastical authority*, p. 228.

[31] Bévenot, 'Tertullian's thoughts', p. 137.

[32] Van Beneden, *Aux origines*, p. 34, places too much emphasis on Tertullian's alleged elevation of the status of the laity in his later period. In both periods of his career Tertullian consistently displays a very low opinion of the capacity and competence of lay persons in general.

[33] See above *De Pudicitia* 21,6 under the discussion of 'praesidere'.

[34] See *De Monogamia* 7,8f.

sacerdotes sumus?' (Are we lay persons not also priests?) Tertullian reverts again to the concept of the priesthood of the laity, superficially to affirm the formal right of the laity to perform sacerdotal functions, but in reality to impose upon them the monogamous obligations of the clergy. The reference to the bishop as 'high-priest' at *De Baptismo* 17,1f. is not intended as either ironical or derisory. It is made to underscore the chief right of the bishop to preside over the sacrament of baptism, and to distinguish him in this matter from other Christian 'priests', the presbyters and deacons who may preside only with episcopal authorisation. That this title is nowhere else applied by Tertullian to the bishop – in his 'Montanist' period, at *De Monogamia* 7,8, for example, he refers to Christ as the 'summus sacerdos' – does not invalidate its use by him here, nor exclude the possibility that the 'later' Tertullian could have sat comfortably with it. What Tertullian clearly had in mind was the pattern of the Jewish ritual priesthood and within the terms of this model the bishop is properly the High Priest. The lower priests derive their authority to a ritual presidency solely from him.

At both *De Praescriptione* 29,3 and 41,8 Tertullian asserts that there are specific 'priestly' functions to be carried out normally only by the clergy. While these functions are not specified in either passage, it is clear that they refer to particular sacramental prerogatives. These functions distinguish the respective roles of the clergy and the laity, and at 41,8 Tertullian strongly condemns unnamed heretical groups partly on the ground of their assigning 'priestly' tasks to lay persons. That Tertullian could also not envisage the propriety of women being permitted to engage in 'priestly' tasks – in the matter of sacramental administration at least – is demonstrated explicitly at *De Virginibus Velandis* 9,1 when he repudiates any attempt by women to undertake the role of the 'sacerdotium' proper; this would include teaching, baptising, presiding at the Eucharist, and any other 'manly task' (virilis muneris). Tertullian supports his position by reference to 1 Corinthians 14,34. He is elsewhere forced, however, by both the words of the Apostle (1 Corinthians 11,5) and Montanist practice to concede to women the right to prophesy.

The Christian clergy exercise, in part, the function of priests –
patterned to some extent perhaps on the Jewish temple model –
as liturgical officers or overseers of the congregations under their
pastoral care. While Tertullian is concerned to restrict this
prerogative to the clergy in times free of persecution and to
males at all times, he does so for reasons principally of order and
peace (at least in the first instance) rather than for specifically
theological ones. In his understanding of the clergy as priests/cultic
leaders he is greatly influenced by Clement of Rome and not by
the Ignatian model. In the end all Christian priesthood, as
mediating between God and man, stands not on its own
authority, but derives all authority from that true High-Priesthood
which is Christ's alone.

Other functions

De Anima 51,6 reveals that the clergy conducted funerals. It is
not clear whether this was the specific prerogative of the
presbyterate, which thus begins to look more like a college of
'parish priests', or whether 'presbyter' is employed in a more
general sense. If the latter were the case, however, one might
expect 'sacerdos' rather than 'presbyter' to be used. *De Paenitentia*
9,4 and *De Pudicitia* 13,7 provide interesting insights into the
specific role of the presbyters within the disciplinary process.
Quasten even suggests that the prostration before the presbyters
by a person undertaking '*exomologesis*' means that penance in
this context was a formal ecclesiastical rite.[35] The *De Paenitentia*
passage could certainly entertain such a construction. The
wording of the passage from *De Pudicitia*, however, which
unquestionably describes a similar rite, suggests otherwise. The
church at most gives witness and support by intercessory prayer.
It is before the whole church that the penitent gives witness to
his (or her) reformed intent. Supplication, according to *De
Paenitentia* 9,4, is made generally before the 'cari dei',[36] as well as

---

[35] Quasten, *Patrology II*, p. 301; I consider the major concerns of *De Paenitentia* to be more
penitential than ritual.

[36] I prefer the reading 'caris' to the less likely 'aris' (Cod. Vaticanus and Cod. Florent.
Magl.). See Vokes, *SP* 14 (1976), p.74; W. P. Le Saint, *Tertullian: treatises on penance*,
ACW 28 (London, 1959), p.174, note 159.

specifically before the presbyterate. Tertullian here gives no hint of any presbyteral or other ecclesiastical 'judgement'. The only suggestion of clerical prerogatives in judicial deliberations is found in an authority conceded to bishops by Tertullian of granting absolution to minor offenders at *De Pudicitia* 18,18 and to the 'seniores' at *Apologeticum* 39,5 in the 'excommunication' from the church of grievous sinners.

Conclusions

The background to Tertullian's understanding of the major Christian offices is, in part, his perception of their history and development to his day. The episcopate in particular, as established by the apostles, provides continuity for the life of the church, particularly for the faithful transmission of authentic apostolic teaching. In this Tertullian is influenced mainly by Clement of Rome and Irenaeus of Lyons, but not by Ignatius of Antioch. Tertullian never employs scriptural texts (e.g. Isaiah 60,17; Philippians 1,1; 1 Timothy 3,1f.; Titus 1,6f.) to confirm this understanding and presentation of the episcopate or the other clerical offices.

Even as a New Prophet Tertullian does not repudiate the basic tripartite system of the Catholic ministry headed by the bishop. He sees the major clergy as exercising a ministry involving (though not always exclusively) leadership, pastoral and cultic-priestly dimensions. At no time in his career, not even in the early period, did Tertullian hold a sacral-absolutist view of episcopacy which he later was required, as a New Prophet, to throw over. It seems likely that it was the increasingly presumptuous claims of some Catholic bishops to a greater 'potestas' than had ever properly been theirs, particularly in the area of the remission of sin, which prompted Tertullian to question the theological-ecclesiastical framework in which he had previously operated. The behaviour and attitudes of some Catholic clergy also led him to question both their fitness for such office and the system which had afforded them their positions of prominence in the first place.

In his long-standing battle with heresy – one fought primarily

over questions of doctrine, although often over that of discipline
as well – the episcopal order was a useful and authoritative
witness to the authenticity of the Catholic position. In the
struggle concerning the jurisdiction over the penitential processes
of the church, however, much more was at stake. In the conflict
over correct doctrine, the question was, 'Who or what witnesses
most authoritatively to authentic apostolic doctrine?'; in that
over the authority to remit sin, the central question became,
'Who or what possesses the apostolic (and therefore divine)
power to forgive?'. It seemed to Tertullian, at least with respect
to the latter question, that evidence of an active indwelling by
the Spirit (i.e. that same Spirit who indwelt the apostles and the
prophets) was necessary in addition to any other measure of
apostolicity; mere election to an institutional office, however
apostolic in origin, could not suffice, and support for this view
was close at hand in the manifest unfitness of many of the clergy.
The authenticity of the church as the Body of Christ was largely
dependent upon the evidence of the Spirit's indwelling; such was
equally appropriate in relation to the exercise of ministry within
that Body. The observation is accurate that Tertullian 'wants to
respect them (i.e. the bishops); and if in the end he comes into
conflict with them all the same, this at any rate does not imply to
his mind that external authority as such should not in any
circumstances be normative within the church. It is only against
the truth that such authority has no rights'.[37]

The term 'presbyter' was, in Tertullian's time, the one
remaining 'official' title left over from primitive Palestinian
Jewish-Christianity, having come into Christian usage from the
synagogue.[38] The 'early' Tertullian, most particularly when he
uses the term in the generic sense of 'clergy', may well employ it
in its pristine sense. Otherwise, it must be said that apart from
the office of presbyter occupying second place in the three ranks

[37] Von Campenhausen, *Ecclesiastical authority*, p. 212.
[38] I am conscious that at Acts 1,20 – with reference to Psalm 109,8 and the replacement
of Judas Iscariot by Matthias in the Twelve – the Greek word '*episkope*' is employed to
denote the 'office' assumed, and that the word '*diakonia*' is also used in a number of
places (e.g. Acts 1,17;6,4 et al.) to denote Christian 'ministry' generally. In none of
these cases, however, do the terms denote anything remotely like the later formal
episcopal or diaconal offices as they emerge in the course of the second century.

of major Christian offices, it does not figure prominently in Tertullian's consideration of Christian ministry. In keeping with the spirit of the age, when the monarchical bishop had finally broken away from the presbyteral 'pack' in the West, Tertullian is concerned specifically with the episcopate and its functions and authority. The other two ranks of clergy are seen mainly in terms of their relationship to this principal ecclesiastical office. It is possible, as we have seen, that presbyters exercised 'lower court' oversight of the penitential processes of the church – with the bishop acting as an appellate court – and carried out ministry tasks such as baptisms and the conduct of funerals. Yet some distance has been moved from the position of honour and dignity afforded the collegial presbyterate in the early church. From its considerable authority in that time, from its identification by Ignatius of Antioch as successor to the great Council of the Apostles[39] and from the position of effective interchangeability with the episcopate in the thought of Irenaeus, it has become a modest 'vice-presidential' body under the authority of an all-powerful single bishop. Tertullian's predilection for the age of the primitive church is not discomforted by the bishop emerging triumphant from the presbyteral college. As Catholic or as New Prophet, Tertullian's understanding betrays no significant shift.

The office of deacon plays a very minor role in Tertullian's understanding of ministry. It is the third-ranked, both in dignity and authority, of the major Christian offices. Its status as sacerdotal, however, gives it precedence over the non-sacerdotal orders of widows, virgins, doctors and lectors. According to apostolic injunction, deacons were required to be monogamous, along with bishops and presbyters, which requirement met with Tertullian's complete approval. The precise role of the diaconate is not clear, though it is evident that the deacons shared with the bishop and presbyters the pastoral oversight of the congregation. As regards the liturgical life of the congregation a deacon might baptise with episcopal approval, though the circumstances under which such authorisation might be granted are not made

---

[39] *Smyrnaeans* 8,1.

clear. It is probable that the diaconate furnished personal assistants to the bishop as certainly became the practice in later times. Although it is not explicitly stated as so, deacons were probably also responsible, very much in the primitive tradition, for some of the day-to-day pastoral needs of the congregation. Tertullian's understanding of the function of the diaconate, as of the episcopate and presbyterate, undergoes no discernible change in his transition from Catholic to New Prophet. Tertullian saw the major clergy as leaders occupying an honourable and apostolically founded office; as pastors who could reasonably be expected to lead their people by faithful example (which often they did not) and to afford those people protection from harm (which often they did not); as priests of the Christian cult who held certain near-exclusive prerogatives of liturgical action, but who ultimately held such by the grace of God through the one High-Priest Jesus Christ.

MINOR OFFICES

Tertullian also speaks of two minor offices within the North African church – apart from those of widow, virgin, prophet and martyr (see below) – both of which may have been open to lay persons.

'Doctor' ('the teacher')

The office of teacher (Lat. 'doctor'; Gk. '*didaskalos*') is well established in both the New Testament and the Fathers before Tertullian. It is listed alongside, though clearly of lesser dignity and authority than the offices of apostle and prophet at 1 Corinthians 12,28f. and Ephesians 4,11. It is mentioned alongside that of prophet at Acts 13,1. The office of teacher is probably first linked specifically to that of the bishop at 1 Timothy 3,2f. Although the actual term '*didaskalos*' is not used, the bishop is required to be '*didaktikos*' (apt at teaching). In the *Martyrdom of Polycarp* that venerable bishop is referred to as 'apostolic and prophetic teacher'.[40] In the *Shepherd* Hermas refers to 'apostles,

---

[40] 16,2.

bishops, teachers and deacons'.[41] This suggests that the presbyterate may have possessed a major teaching function in the
Roman church and that the words 'presbyter' and 'teacher'
were interchangeable. In the *Didache* it is said that the bishops
and deacons of the local congregation may exercise a 'ministry'
(*leitourgia*) of prophecy and teaching, although this is still
ordinarily the function of itinerant prophets and teachers.[42]
Hippolytus of Rome and Clement of Alexandria both speak of
an office of teacher, but with no indication that it is linked to
another office.[43] Finally, in the *Passio Perpetuae et Felicitatis*
Aspasius is referred to as 'presbyter doctor', although this may
indicate more his learning than any specific teaching function.[44]

At *De Pudicitia* 14,27 Tertullian refers to Paul as the 'doctor
nationum'. At *De Baptismo* 1,3 he speaks of 'illa monstrosissima
cui nec integre quidem docendi ius erat' (that most monstrous
woman, for whom there is no right even to teach right doctrine),
a reference to a female of the heretical Cainite sect whom
Tertullian would have barred from teaching at the very least on
the grounds of her gender. 'Ius docendi' will refer to a prerogative
or office of teaching. At 17,5 of the same treatise Tertullian
speaks of a wrongful assumption of 'licentia mulierum docendi
tinguendique' (a licence for women teaching and baptising),
which presumptuous claim is based on the spurious writings of a
presbyter from Asia Minor (*Acta Pauli et Theclae*). This 'docendi
et tinguendi feminae potestas' Tertullian repudiates. This is
another reference to an office of teacher, but no more can be
drawn from it save Tertullian's resolute opposition to women
occupying such office. The sole reference in Tertullian to a
specific office of teacher at *De Praescriptione* 3,5 suggests for it a
somewhat lowly ranking, if such a description as 'ranking' is
appropriate here. The list, is, however, neither comprehensive
nor exhaustive – neither presbyter nor prophet is mentioned –
and one might assume that actual 'rankings' are not in fact
indicated. Tertullian offers no clue as to the particular function
of the office; it is possible, however, that a lay teaching 'order'
had developed at Carthage, much as it had at Alexandria, and

---

[41] *Vis.*, 3.5.1. [42] 15,1.2. [43] *Trad. Apost.* 19,1; *Eccles.* 23. [44] 13,1.

that this order had assumed some of the teaching functions hitherto undertaken by the bishop and/or the presbyterate. Irenaeus had associated the office of bishop (and that of the presbyterate) with the role of teacher. Tertullian does not explicitly do so. His association of the succession of the episcopal office with the authentic handing down of unadulterated apostolic doctrine does not require the conclusion of a specific teaching role either for the bishop or for either of the other major clerical offices.

The 'lector'

The office of lector – as one who reads the scriptures at worship – is not mentioned specifically in the Scriptures and, of the Fathers before Tertullian, only Hippolytus and Justin Martyr refer to it (Gk. *'anagnōstēs'*).[45] At *De Praescriptione* 41,8 we find Tertullian's sole reference to such an office. He 'pairs' it with the office of deacon in his condemnation of the heretical practice of alternating clerical and lay roles indiscriminately. Thus, he evidently regards it as a 'lay' office.

[45] *Trad. Apost.* 12; *1 Apology* 67,3.

CHAPTER 8

Women in ministry

It is clear that Tertullian denies certain specific ministerial functions to women. At *De Baptismo* 1,3 he denies to the Cainite woman, on grounds of her sex, the right even to teach orthodox doctrine, and at 17,5 he repudiates the authority of the apocryphal *Acta Pauli et Theclae* for the assumption of the right of women to baptise or to teach. At *De Virginibus Velandis* 9,1 Tertullian states without equivocation,

'Non permittitur mulieri in ecclesia loqui' (1 Corinthians 14,34f.; 1 Timothy 2,12) sed nec docere, nec tinguere, nec offerre, nec ullius muneris, nedum sacerdotalis officii sortem sibi vindicare.

('It is not permitted for a woman to speak in church', but neither to teach nor baptise nor offer [the elements], nor to claim for herself the allocation of any duty, much less that of priestly office.)

and repudiates a virgin's claim to any 'praerogativa virilis aut gradus aut officium' (any masculine prerogative or rank or duty) (ibid.).

In the writings of Tertullian the 'ordo sacerdotalis' (*De Exhortatione Castitatis* 7,2) or 'ordo ecclesiasticus' (*De Idololatria* 7,3) – that order of the church which exercised the exclusive right to administer the Eucharist – is reserved to males.[1] At *Adv. Marcionem* v,8,11 Tertullian reaffirms the apostolic ban on women teaching in the church, but acknowledges, partly on the basis of apostolic injunction, the right of women to prophesy (1 Corinthians 11,5f.). This right he reaffirms in his account of the 'sister' who prophesies on the corporeality of the soul at *De*

See section on 'ordo' above.

Anima 9,4 and also accepts as part of established Montanist history and practice. Tertullian also recognises two orders which are exclusively female, those of the widow and the virgin.

The widow

Tertullian's understanding and representation of the 'order' of widows is based principally on his perception of the history and present situation of the church of his day rather than on particular theological insights; it is nevertheless true that these are also informed by the biblical witness.[2] While at Acts 6,1 and 1 Timothy 5,3 there are references to the practice of providing for destitute Christian widows, and at 1 Corinthians 7,8, without additional comment, one to widows (and virgins), there is at Acts 9,39f. a suggestion of a distinct, though undefined, 'order' of widows. At 1 Timothy 5,9f., where it is required that widows whose needs are genuine, are over sixty years of age and only once-married should be 'enrolled' (*katalegēsthō*), the reference is more specific. While this is the first unambiguous indication of an 'order' proper, it is clear that enrolment is solely for the purpose of assessing those who properly qualify for church maintenance. There is no suggestion that widows thus supported are to exercise a specific ministry function. In the writings of Hermas, Ignatius, Polycarp and Justin Martyr widows are mentioned, but mainly with reference to the provision of congregational support, and not to a specific ministry to be exercised by them.[3]

At *De Praescriptione* 3,5 we have a clear indication that Tertullian considered 'widows' as belonging to a formal 'order' and church 'office', when he lists them alongside other offices. A passage at *De Virginibus Velandis* 9,2 tells very little about contemporary practice or about Tertullian's own preferences, save that he considered it usual practice for a woman to be of mature age (the apostolic stipulation of sixty years was probably enforced) before being admitted to the order. Such admissions were apparently the sole prerogative of the bishop. This passage says nothing about any specific role for the order. A passage at

[2] See also B.B. Thurston, *The widows: a women's ministry in the early church* (Fortress, 1989).
[3] *Mand.* 8,10; *Sim.* 1,8; 5.3.7; *Smyrn.* 6,2; *1 Apol.* 67,6.

De Pudicitia 13,7 adds little to our discussion except for the information that the widows sat as a group during this penitential rite (and probably at other times as well). Tertullian gives no information on the particular role, if any, played by them in the penitential process. *De Monogamia* 11,1 employs for the first and only time in Tertullian's writings an institutional designation for this group. The use of the term 'secta' – a word usually employed by Tertullian to designate the church itself as a type of philosophical 'school' – is probably employed here to distinguish the widows' order from the specifically sacerdotal orders.[4] The passage also confirms the prerequisite of monogamy for admission to the order. At *Ad Uxorem* 1,7,4 there is a direct reference to the apostolic injunction at 1 Timothy 5,9f. concerning admission to the roll of widows which demonstrates Tertullian's belief that this order was of apostolic foundation. It is possible that admission into the order was effected by a formal rite.[5]

Of the eight occasions on which Tertullian employs the term 'ordo' to denote an 'order' proper seven clearly indicate the clerical 'ordo' and at least one of these explicitly excludes non-sacerdotal ministries.[6] Tertullian appears normally to restrict the use of the term to those who belong to that 'order' which has had conceded to it the exclusive right to exercise sacerdotal functions – that comprising bishop, presbyters and deacons. He does on occasion, however, include the widows (and virgins?) in his representation of ecclesiastical 'orders'.[7] This flexible employment of the term leads to some confusion and inconsistency, although Tertullian's position is usually clear. Though the reading 'quantae' at *De Exhortatione Castitatis* 13,4 with reference to ecclesiastical orders is the one favoured by the editors of CCL, it is not the most widely preferred. The majority of MSS, as we saw earlier, prefer the reading 'quae' to 'quantae'. If the latter is accepted, however, this passage raises certain issues for us. Van Beneden contends, for example, that the reference to an 'ordo ecclesiae' at *De Monogamia* 11,4, which he maintains sets the

---

[4] See the discussion of 'secta' and that on 'ordo' above.
[5] See below for a discussion of the terms 'adlegere' and 'adlectio'.
[6] See discussion on 'ordo' above.
[7] See *De Exhortatione Castitatis* 13,14.

clerical 'order' over against that of the laity, must include the order of widows.[8] The latter was included later in the same chapter alongside the three normative, traditional offices listed among those committed to a monogamous state. Yet, he also contends that the 'ordo ecclesiasticus' at *De Idololatria* 7,3 is a sacerdotal reference – and thus exclusive to men – and cannot therefore be identified with the 'ordo ecclesiae'. It cannot, therefore, include the widows.[9] He continues, 'Ce rapprochement entre le service des veuves à l'autel et celui des prêtres n'implique pas que ce service des veuves ait été d'ordre liturgique.[10] He argues, however, that this 'ordo ecclesiasticus' must have included widows (and virgins?), since the reading 'quantae' can admit of no other construction than that which is inclusive of women. Whatever the reading preferred, however, there is no implied sacerdotal function for the female order(s).

Tertullian probably does on occasion include the widows within the category of 'clergy', in the sense of them belonging to a church order for entrance into which there was a formal rite of admission. Yet he offers no clues as to any specific ministry function for them, save their appearance during the penitential rite in *De Pudicitia*. The widows were clearly part of a well-defined and prestigious group within the life of the church. Their role, however, may have been a largely passive one. It is not in question that they were materially supported by the congregation and that consideration of financial strain on the church 'budget' may explain some of the reluctance to concede too easy an entry into the order. This might also, however, be as readily explained by Tertullian's desire to maintain a quality of person and a value of service within such a high-profile class of church members.

The virgin

As with the order of widows, that of the virgins is understood by Tertullian not from a strictly theological standpoint, but from the history and present condition of the church. Paul refers to 'virgins' at 1 Corinthians 7,8f., but not as designating a specific,

---

[8] Van Beneden, *Aux origines*, p. 22.   [9] Ibid., p. 38.   [10] Ibid., p. 41.

formalised order. Both Polycarp and Ignatius of Antioch refer to virgins, but with no suggestion that they exercised a particular role apart from that status.[11] They were, for the early church, as for Tertullian, important symbols of the holiness of the church and of the virtuous Christian life. Tertullian provides no specificity as to any actual role for this 'order'; their primary function may indeed have been simply to be. Their very existence is eloquent testimony to Christian holiness and to union with Christ. It is at best a non-sacerdotal 'order' which Tertullian regards, moreover, as inferior in dignity and status to that of the widows.

At *De Praescriptione* 3,5 no more is suggested than that the 'virgins' belonged among other ecclesiastical 'offices' or 'orders'; it says nothing about a specific ministry function. At *De Exhortatione Castitatis* 13,4 it is possible that the virgins might be included among the women referred to as members of the 'ordines ecclesiastici'.[12] And yet, as acknowledged above with reference to the widows, the reading 'quantae' is not generally preferred. The reference to those who choose to 'marry' God is, however, an apt description of Christian virgins who are described as 'espoused' to Christ at *De Resurrectione Carnis* 61,6. Here the language of Tertullian suggests an order of virgins for which there is a formal process of admission; by this process members of the 'order' are said to marry Christ as does the church. Thus the virgins represent an aspect of the authentic church, that of its essential holiness. As the church is the Virgin Bride of Christ, so these young women give concrete expression to that image.

Conclusions

Tertullian regarded the ministries of teaching, baptising and presiding at the Eucharist and other unspecified priestly functions as closed to women. For this there were for him sufficient apostolic directives in 1 Corinthians and 1 Timothy. He did, however, consistent with other apostolic advice and New

[11] *Ep.* 5,3; *Smyrn.* 13,1.
[12] Van Beneden, *Aux origines*, p. 38; see above the discussion on the widows.

Prophecy practice, concede the right of women to prophesy. Tertullian acknowledges, in addition, two female orders, that of the widows and that of the virgins. The first, of undoubted apostolic foundation, was maintained by the church and subject to stringent admission requirements similar in part to those laid upon the male clergy (e.g. monogamy). And yet, apart from a possible involvement by them in the penitential process, the nature of any particular ministry function is unclear. The role of the second group appears to have consisted of little more than retaining their virginal status and leading otherwise exemplary and blameless lives. They provided a significant symbol for the church, particularly as giving embodiment to the church as the Virgin Bride of Christ. Admission to both groups seems to have involved some form of ritual-liturgical action, perhaps through some form of consecration. The form of this, however, is nowhere made explicit.

CHAPTER 9

Other ministries

Some of the ministries about which Tertullian speaks cannot be categorised as 'offices' in any formal sense. These include the martyr-confessors and the prophets. There is no formal process or rite of appointment or admission to either group, though ecclesiastical recognition in either case is by no means unconditional or unqualified.

The martyr-confessor

Although the position of 'martyr' was never an ecclesiastical office in a formal sense, many in the early church, particularly towards the end of the second century, believed the martyr-confessor to be endowed with special authority. At Acts 7,55f. the proto-martyr Stephen received a glimpse of the glory of God on the occasion of his martyrdom, though this does not suggest any special endowment. At Revelation 2,10 those at Smyrna who stand firm in the face of persecution are promised that if they are 'faithful unto death . . . I will give you the crown of life'. While this suggests that their faithfulness will bring them special blessing, it does not carry the implication that they will thereby be granted in the meantime a special authority in the church. Yet in time, especially when penitential discipline became a major issue for the church, the notion that the confessor-martyr was endowed with an extraordinary authority to grant absolution came to the fore. This was certainly so among sections of the church at Carthage. It seems that even Tertullian, in his earliest writings at least, was prepared to entertain the idea. Tertullian remains consistent in his advocacy of martyrdom into his later period. Indeed, his commitment to the idea of the high 'calling' of martyrdom is even more emphatic. Yet he also believes that laxity is encouraged through the indiscriminate granting of absolution by confessors who are obviously flattered by the attendant adulation. Tertullian wants them to be highly regarded, but not at the price of a relaxation of discipline. Whether, however, one can call the position of martyr an 'office', except in the broad sense of a specific ministry of witness to which a person may be called, is unclear. There is, of course, no sense of any ordering by the wider church to elect or otherwise appoint to such a position. The confessors chose or elected themselves simply by virtue of their activity; it is also true, however, that for Tertullian recognition as an authentic confessor was by no means automatic. Pristinus, the Catholic martyr denied the status of martyr by Tertullian on account of his alleged gluttony (*De Ieiunio* 12,3) (Tertullian regarded fasting as highly as chastity), was one whom he clearly regarded as unworthy of the title because his alleged lifestyle did not match the demands of holiness. As the church must become now that which it is called to be, so must the individual Christian. The demands of sanctification and Tertullian's whole eschatologically informed outlook required no less.

The position of the martyr at the end of the list of church offices at *De Praescriptione* 3,5 should not be seen as a reflection upon its dignity or status. For even as a New Prophet, when he was wont to repudiate, even ridicule, some of the claims of the Catholic martyrs,[1] Tertullian regarded martyrdom very highly. In *Ad Martyras* the addressees are confessors presently detained in prison. Tertullian writes both to encourage them and to lift their spirits, depicting prison life in a most positive light as an experience for which they should actually be appreciative! At 1,6 it is probable that the 'peace' of which he speaks is the forgiveness of sins and the reconciliation to the church of those who had lapsed. We have evidence, then, of a widespread practice, of which Tertullian himself does not here disapprove, whereby lapsed Christians, unable to effect forgiveness through traditional church channels, seek it instead at the hands of the

[1] See *De Pudicitia* 22.

confessors. This suggests that confessors – by virtue of their willingness to undergo martyrdom – are endowed with an extraordinary authority to absolve sin. At *Scorpiace* 6,10 Tertullian speaks of martyrdom wiping clean the sinner's slate. Martyrs were regarded as having obtained forgiveness for their sins – no matter how serious – by virtue of this 'second baptism'. Yet this applied only to their own sins and did not empower them to remit those of others.

The prophet

The high regard in which the Christian prophet is held in the New Testament is demonstrated by passages such as Acts 11,27f. – Agabus and his companions coming from Jerusalem to Antioch – Acts 13,1 – prophets and teachers holding the chief positions of authority in the congregation at Antioch – 1 Corinthians and Ephesians 4,11 – prophets named as second only to the apostles in authority and prestige – and Revelation 18,20f. – where the eminent standing of the Christian prophet is affirmed by John. This high regard for the prophet is also maintained beyond the time of the New Testament as witness the *Didache*, the *Shepherd* of Hermas and the *Adversus Haereses* of Irenaeus.[2] Towards the end of the second century, however, this regard was widely questioned in the increasingly institutionalised Catholic church. This is reflected, in part, in the reaction against the enthusiastic, though unquestionably doctrinally orthodox, Montanist movement in Phrygia. The regard in which prophecy was held in less sophisticated circles persisted undiminished, however, alongside a dutiful, but far less enthusiastic, respect for the emerging 'episcopal' church. Tertullian's main concern in promoting both the gift of prophecy and the ministry of the prophet was not to undermine the priority of the apostles. His commitment to the concept of an apostolically founded church and orthodox (i.e. apostolically authorised) teaching would not allow him to do this. He wished, however, to both defend and promote the New Prophecy and to point out to the church the dangers of unqualified claims to an authority based on an

---

[2] *Didache* 11-15; *Pastor*, passim; *Haer.* III,11,9; IV,33,6.

ambiguous 'apostolicity'. This he maintains with respect both to the question of church order and to that of Christian doctrine. He seeks therefore to safeguard the ambiguous Scriptures from heretical misuse by reference initially to an apostolic Rule of Faith and later to a form of prophetic supplement. He was concerned to demonstrate that godly prophecy had not ceased with John the Baptist but was alive and flourishing in the New Prophecy movement. He also sought to defend the more rigorous disciplinary practices of this movement against Catholic objections, particularly against those who would hold forth their 'apostolic' authority in such a way as would undermine this renewed rigour. He also acted to distance himself from the implications of many of his earlier pronouncements which were now being used against him.

Tertullian is keen at *Adversus Marcionem* v,17,16 to point out that Christ left not only apostles but also prophets in the church which he founded. Not only, then, is the church founded on the witness of the apostles, but also on the testimony of the prophets whose successors continue to proclaim the word of God. Tertullian argues against Marcion who would hold a 'modified' Paul as the sole, valid human channel of divine truth. He asserts that the Gospel continues to be revealed and interpreted anew through Christian prophecy in the present age. At *De Anima* 2,3 Tertullian might be seen to argue for a virtual New Prophecy power of veto over Christian doctrinal development. This does not mean, however, that the New Prophecy has replaced Scripture as providing doctrinal norms, but rather that the outpourings of the New Prophecy might play the authentic, interpretive role of the Spirit of Truth foretold in John 14-16. Likewise does Tertullian claim for the New Prophecy at *De Pudicitia* 21,7 the function of the Paraclete in John 14-16: to interpret for a new age the teachings of Jesus. He asserts also that he stands solidly within the tradition of this New Prophecy and acknowledges a reliance on its witness. This parallels his claim elsewhere to be a legitimate 'heir' to the apostles (*De Praescriptione* 37,5).

At *Adversus Marcionem* v,8,11 Tertullian concedes the 'right' of prophesying granted to women by Paul. This he did despite his reservations concerning active ministry roles for women. *De Anima* 9,4 concerns a Montanist 'sister' who experiences visions during worship; this confirms for Tertullian this right of women to prophesy.[3] At *De Pudicitia* 21,5 Tertullian implies that 'divinity', that is, the divine Spirit, indwelt both the prophets of old and the Christian prophets of the early church.[4] This indwelling, he further implies, authorised them to grant absolution from serious sin. Those who claim an authority to remit sin by virtue of a historical connection to the apostles – here Tertullian addresses principally the Catholic bishops, the apostolic origin of whose office he does not dispute – must also demonstrate the presence of that Spirit which indwelt and empowered the early prophets. At 21,6 Tertullian asserts that the Catholic bishops, qua bishops, cannot demonstrate this indwelling of the Spirit as can the prophets. The former can show nothing of the presence of that empowering Spirit which indwelt both the prophets and the apostles, notwithstanding that their office was established by the latter.

[3] See 'Women in ministry' above.
[4] Despite the development among the Montanists of the concept of a prophetic succession from primitive times (Eusebius, *Ecclesiastical History* v,17,4), 'Tertullian seems consistently to ignore all prophecy between the Baptist, or at any rate the Apostles, and Montanus', H. J. Lawlor, 'The heresy of the Phrygians', *JTS* 9 (1908), p. 488.

CHAPTER 10

Appointment to office

There are a number of terms which Tertullian employs to denote either appointment or election to church office or promotion from lesser to higher office. We will now look at these and consider what they might tell us about Tertullian's understanding of Christian office.

'Adlectio' and 'adlegere'

In Roman law 'adlectio' originally denoted the election of a person to the Senate, and later the bestowal of citizen rights on entire communities.[1] Tertullian uses it seven times in settings both pagan and Judaeo-Christian. At *Adv.Marcionem* II,24,2 he employs it of the 'election' of Saul as king by God, at II,25,4 of the 'election' of man into divinity (i.e. of the Incarnation), at III,21,3 of the 'election 'of the 'nations', at III,21,4 of the 'election' of the 'elders' of the Jews, and at V,17,10 of the 'election' of the Fathers of the Jews. At *De Baptismo* 12,8 Tertullian employs 'adlectio' to denote Christ's 'choosing' of the first disciples. The verb 'adlegere' is also used extensively by Tertullian with a variety of meanings. He employs it normally, however, to denote a divine choosing, such as that of Saul at *Adv. Marcionem* II,24,2, of Peter by Christ at IV,11,1, of the other apostles and the Seventy by Christ at IV,24,1, of the 'nations' by God at *De Resurrectione* 22,4, and, finally, of the animals in the Ark by Noah at *De Monogamia* 4,5.

The employment of 'adlectio' or 'adlegere' in an ecclesiastical setting appears to be confined by Tertullian to admission to the

---

[1] Teeuwen, *Sprachlicher Bedeutungswandel*, p. 70.

'official' classes of bishops, presbyters, deacons and widows. They were not used for the 'minor' grades of 'virgin', 'lector' and 'doctor', nor for recognition as a 'prophet'. The traditional employment of 'adlectio' in a secular setting to denote election to the Senate clearly influenced Tertullian. Thus he employs it to denote election to the Christian 'senate'. Its usage by Tertullian also reminds us that 'adlectio-adlegere' denotes a special kind of 'choosing', one with the suggestion of divine endorsement. Thus, for Tertullian, abuse of the trust of ecclesiastical office is an abuse of the trust and endorsement of God. Included among Tertullian's chief complaints against heretical groups was the irregularity of their ministerial order and the ease with which a person might pass from one office to another, especially when this concerned a transfer from lay to clerical status (and back again!). One of the marks of a God-fearing – that is, orthodox and authentic – Christian fellowship was for Tertullian, as witness his remarks at *De Praescriptione* 43,5, an appropriateness in the regulation of admissions to clerical ranks and of transfers between such ranks. Since the order of widows was not included in that church order to which was exclusively conceded the right to preside at the Eucharist – the 'ordo sacerdotalis' – *Ad Uxorem* 1,7,4 demonstrates that 'adlegere' does not for Tertullian denote exclusively election to the sacerdotal order; it could be applied more widely.

Tertullian is concerned at *De Monogamia* 12,1, *De Idololatria* 7,3 and *De Exhortatione Castitatis* 7,2 with election to a 'sacerdotal order' which was exclusive to men – though only in one (*De Exhortatione Castitatis* 7,2) is this order explicitly so named. As with the previous two passages dealt with they provide no information concerning the actual process of election. The reference to 'presbyteri' at *De Exhortatione Castitatis* 7,6 is probably to occupants of that particular office, though it is possible that it is intended as a general term to include all clergy. If the former, then it may be an indication that the presbyters were not 'promoted' from the ranks of the diaconate but rather direct from the laity.

'Eligere' (choose)

This is a word commonly employed by Latin writers of the classical period to denote 'choosing' or 'selecting'. It is employed by Tertullian more than a hundred times in this general sense. Its employment to denote an act of formal or ritual 'election' to office is unusual. At *De Virginibus Velandis* 9,3 Tertullian suggests that all eligible persons, that is, all once-married widows, may be qualified for admission to membership of this order. There is no fixed number of 'seats' in the order and no 'election' proper. This does not rule out, as we saw above, a formal rite of admission. The use of this word to denote 'election' to office in the church is exceptional. Tertullian normally prefers the less profane 'adlegere'. The employment of 'eligere' may simply indicate that election to the order of widows was a less formal matter – concerned more with eligibility than with vocation – than the more formal elections to the higher offices.

'Promotio' (advancement)

This particular word is not found in any of the Latin writers of Tertullian's period. It bears the sense of 'advancement' or of 'movement forward'. Tertullian employs it but once. As noted in our discussion of the word 'adlectio' from the same passage, a God-fearing Christian church, was, in Tertullian's view, one which had a well-ordered approach to appointments and promotion within its ministerial ranks. For Tertullian, 'promotion' or 'advancement' within the different clerical ranks – as distinct from 'admission', denoted by 'adlectio' – was a matter of merit and qualification, and not one of whim. It is possible that 'promotio' at *De Praescriptione* 43,5 is a word virtually invented by Tertullian from the root-word 'promoveo' for use in the immediate context. It is found nowhere else in contemporary usage and Tertullian uses it only here. It reflects clearly his commitment to order within the church, a keenness for which never deserted him, not even as a New Prophet.

Conclusions

There is nothing that the terms which Tertullian employs for election/appointment to ministerial office can tell us about the actual process of election itself or about any rite of admission or consecration. The employment of 'adlectio' and 'adlegere' to denote election to the higher offices of the church seems merely to confirm the view that Tertullian sees the clergy as a type of Christian senate. He clearly viewed such election as one principally by human decision, albeit with a suggestion of divine endorsement. He makes no reference whatever to a formal recognition of someone as an authentic prophet, but this suggests only that he regarded appointment to such a ministry as the sole prerogative of God through his Spirit.

Conclusions

Tertullian consistently acknowledged the tripartite system of
ecclesiastical leadership headed by a monarchical bishop as
providing an appropriate, historical basis for Christian ministry.
He believed that this system was founded by the apostles. This
he affirmed in both his early and late periods (*De Praescriptione*
32,3; *Adv. Marcionem* IV,5,2). He argued, too, that although there
was no theological reason for lay persons not exercising a
sacramental ministry, concern for the order of the church
demanded that, in normal circumstances, only the 'priestly'
order should do so (see *De Baptismo* 17 and *De Exhortatione
Castitatis* 7). Although he appears to some as a confirmed – even
zealous – laicist, his particular brand of laicism was concerned
mainly to impose upon the laity those disciplinary obligations
(e.g. monogamy) which were laid upon the clergy (see *De
Exhortatione Castitatis* 7). The only divergence from this original
affirmation of the episcopal system was his later emphasis on the
gift of prophecy – the only 'charismatic' gift which he explicitly
identifies – by which he, inter alia, promoted the rigorous
demands of the New Prophecy. His later attacks on the assumed
'powers' of the episcopate (see e.g. *De Pudicitia* 21,5 and *De
Virginibus Velandis* 1,7) were not in fact major deviations from a
previously held position. For it was probable that the Catholic
clergy had begun in the late second century to assume for
themselves new powers and not that Tertullian had repudiated
a previous position. He consistently regarded the clergy as
superior in dignity to the laity (see e.g 'minor' and 'maior locus'
at *De Fuga* 11,1; 'plebs' (for the laity) at *De Anima* 9,4 and *De
Exhortatione Castitatis* 7,3; 'ordo' (for the clergy) at *De Corona*

13,1; *De Monogamia* 8,4.11,4.12,2; *De Exhortatione Castitatis* 7,3.13,4 and *De Idololatria* 7,3). The resentment which he later displayed towards the Catholic clergy was, in part at least, motivated by his perception of their failure to provide the pastoral protection to which he regarded 'lesser' Christians as entitled (see e.g. *De Fuga* 11,1). The clergy were to be like the 'patrons' of Roman society; they formed a Christian nobility of sorts (see 'seniores' at *Apologeticum* 39,5). They were to provide the key leadership for the Christian community (see 'actores' at *De Fuga* 11,1, 'duces' at *De Fuga* 11,1, 'praepositi' at *De Fuga* 11,3 and *De Monogamia* 12,2 and 'praesidentes' at *De Pudicitia* 14,16 and *De Corona* 3,3, this last term drawing its inspiration from secular judicial usage); they were to be the pastors, the nurturers and the protectors of the 'simplices'; they were to act, evidently following the Jewish temple model, as priests of the Christian cult (see *De Corona* 3,2, *De Virginibus Velandis* 9,1 and *De Exhortatione Castitatis* 7,4). They drew such authority, however, by grace of the one High Priest Jesus, and, where it suited other concerns of the Tertullianic agenda (e.g. the imposition on the laity of the priestly obligations of monogamy), shared this 'priesthood' with other Christians. They also conducted funerals (see *De Anima* 51,6). The bishops regulated admissions to the lower orders (see *De Virginibus Velandis* 9,2), determined the timing and conduct of Christian fasts (see *De Ieiunio* 13,3), and apparently oversaw relations with other Christian congregations (see *Adv. Prax.* 1,5). It was in fact his 'high' view of this priestly-pastoral ministry, rather than any contempt for it, which drove him bitterly to attack the Catholic leadership. Their failure to maintain proper standards of discipline and morality among Christian people was for him a grievous dereliction of duty. He never doubted the legitimate, apostolic origin of the episcopate. Many bishops, however, had failed to live up to the obligations placed upon them by such a foundation.

In his early period Tertullian's main concerns were doctrinal. A writing such as *De Praescriptione Haereticorum* demonstrates this clearly. The existence of the apostolic-episcopal order provided valuable testimony, via its apostolic foundations, for upholding orthodox doctrine; in this sense the bishops were assuredly apostolic. In the later period, when he placed greater emphasis on the question of discipline, the episcopal order appeared as a possible obstacle to the implementation of his rigorist programme and had therefore to be neutralised.

Tertullian's understanding of ministry is argued, at least initially, on historical rather than on scriptural or purely theological grounds. For example, Tertullian acknowledged that the Pastoral Epistles, long regarded as an important scriptural proof for the validity of the episcopate, 'de ecclesiastico statu compositas' (deal with ecclesiastical discipline) (*Adv. Marcionem* v,21,1). Yet, although he does cite passages from them with regard to other matters,[1] he never draws on them in presenting his understanding of church office. It seems that, for Tertullian, the bishop-presbyter-deacon structure was 'given' and something that had simply to be accepted. This explains his apparent reluctance to repudiate this three-tier structure even in his most vitriolic anti-clerical outbursts.

Von Campenhausen sees in Tertullian's thought the age-old tension between the claims of office and the demands of the Spirit.[2] Van den Eynde challenges this view, denying that there is in Tertullian any suggestion of a necessary conflict between office and Spirit.[3] The former, however, does not conceive of this tension as necessarily or mutually exclusive. What Tertullian 'felt strongly', he maintains, was the need for the 'old free men of the Spirit' to be acknowledged by the church alongside the more formal office-holders;[4] such as was apparently the case, for example, in the congregation addressed by the writer of the *Didache*.

Some Catholic scholars applaud the 'earlier' Tertullian as a champion of the historic episcopate. Michaelides, for example, suggests that the role of the bishop, in Tertullian's thought, 'est indispensable à l'esse de l'Eglise'.[5] Some Protestants, on the

---

[1] D. I. Rankin, 'Tertullian's use of the Pastoral Epistles in his doctrine of ministry', *Australian Biblical Review* 32 (1984), pp. 18-37.
[2] Von Campenhausen, *Ecclesiastical authority*, p. 178.
[3] D. van den Eynde, *Les normes de l'enseignement chrétien dans la littérature patristique des trois premiers siècles* (Paris, 1933), p. 322.
[4] Von Campenhausen, *Ecclesiastical authority*, p. 178.
[5] Michaelides, *Foi, écritures*, p. 81.

other hand, applaud the 'later' model as the author of a series of 'exposés' on clerical unworthiness and on the illegitimacy of the so-called 'holy orders'. Others, from both camps, though often for entirely different reasons, see in writings from both periods of his career, and thus in his transition from Catholic to New Prophet, no fundamental change in his view of ministry and, particularly, of ecclesiastical office. Adam calls Tertullian 'das Formalprinzip des Protestantismus'.[6]

For von Campenhausen, while office as an institution indispensable to the church's order and dignity is a feature of Tertullian's thought, there is no place for a sacral priestly office, holy per se, not even in his pre-Montanist period.[7] The Catholic van Beneden takes issue with those scholars who choose to see only a doctrine of ministerial 'functionalism' in, for example, *De Exhortatione Castitatis*. He argues that there are in this treatise, as also in his earlier ones, evidences of juridical elements.[8]

It is in the sometimes vicious debate concerning the oversight of the penitential process that we see what is often taken for Tertullian's alleged 'breach' with the Catholic leadership. Whatever the nature of this breach – either schism, or conflict which stopped short of actual division – the question remains: who or what changed? The traditional response has been to lay the accusation squarely at the feet of the African himself. There are clear indications, however, and not just from Tertullian, that a significant transformation was taking place during his lifetime within the church itself. This concerned the Catholic church's understanding of itself and of its leaders, their status, authority and prerogatives. We see this in Tertullian's refusal to acknowledge the apostolic title of 'antecessor' as appropriate for bishops (*De Virginibus Velandis* 1,7); in his characterisation of the

---

[6] Adam, *Kirchenbegriff*, p. 229.
[7] Von Campenhausen, *Ecclesiastical authority*, p.228. Altendorf, *Einheit und Heiligkeit*, p. 27, sees Tertullian as presenting a consistent and functional view of ministry. Flessmann-van Leer, *Tradition and scripture*, p. 154, agrees, calling the traditional view of Tertullian's (early) 'hierarchical' concept of the church a 'fallacy'. De Labriolle, *De Paenitentia*, p. 411, points out that even *De Paenitentia*, a sacralist proof for many, is actually concerned more with penitential than ecclesiological questions.
[8] Van Beneden, *Aux origines*, p. 143. Rahner, 'Zur Theologie der Busse', argues that Tertullian's bishops had 'Gewalt' and not only 'Funktion' (p.152), and yet sees no radical change in Tertullian's thinking between *De Paenitentia* and *De Pudicitia* (p. 158).

bishop in *De Pudicitia* 1,6 as 'Pontifex Maximus' and as 'episcopus
episcoporum'; and, in his barbed reference to this same bishop as
'apostolice' at 21,5, even when he still acknowledges the
episcopate to be of genuine apostolic foundation. Each of these,
whatever Tertullian's penchant for exaggeration, must reflect a
measure of veracity with respect to the nature of Catholic
claims.

Irenaeus of Lyons, by whom Tertullian is greatly influenced
on the question of episcopal succession and of apostolicity,
ascribes a special 'charisma veritatis' to the office of bishop.[9]
Tertullian does not endorse such a concept; such 'charisma' is
for him linked to the question of the guaranteed transmission of
an unadulterated apostolic teaching and not to that of penitential
authority. A reassessment of episcopal prerogatives was, however,
taking place during the latter part of the second century.
Consequently, 'tangible supremacy over sin' became 'of decisive
importance for the nature and the definition of all spiritual
authority within the church, and this includes the authority of
the organised ecclesiastical offices'.[10] Tertullian may have
perceived, rightly or wrongly, a move by the Catholic episcopate
to assume for itself a power granted by God through Christ only
to the apostles or to those appointed by them; and to claim this
as a 'charisma' attaching to a particular office within the
church, regardless of the worthiness of a particular incumbent.
He perhaps feared the setting up of an authority 'which might
rival the importance of the valid law of God'.[11] Both Origen and
Jerome quote Marcion, from his *Antitheses*, when they also
protest against the increasing assumption of a special episcopal
charisma.[12] Tertullian was not, therefore, the only one to sense a
fundamental change in Catholic claims. While it is not correct
that Tertullian's polemic in *De Pudicitia* was not directed against
a particular bishop,[13] it is true that Tertullian was primarily
concerned with claims to a penitential authority presumed by
the Catholics to be inherent in the episcopal office.

As has been stated elsewhere, Tertullian was more than

[9] *Haer.* IV, 26, 2.   [10] Von Campenhausen, *Ecclesiastical authority*, p.214.
[11] Ibid., p. 232.   [12] *On Galatians* 6,6.
[13] Von Campenhausen, *Ecclesiastical authority*, p. 229.

willing, and consistently so, to affirm the apostolic foundation of the episcopate and its subordinate offices. This he regarded both as historically verifiable and as necessary to guarantee both the authenticity of transmitted orthodox teaching and the right ordering of the sacramental and organisational life of the church. Thus the higher clergy, under the direction of the bishop, held a near-exclusive right to administer the sacraments, to oversee the penitential rites of the church – even to pronounce absolution in relation to minor offences – and to regulate admissions to the lower orders. For all intents and purposes the higher clergy were the patrician-senatorial-magisterial class of the church. But they were not, however dignified their office, the apostles; neither were they, in terms of any absolute authority (the 'potestas'), their true successors. If anyone could claim this for themselves (and it is doubtful that any could) it was only those who could demonstrate an indwelling by the same Spirit as the Scriptures witness to have indwelt the apostles and prophets. When the bishops claimed the right to enunciate correct doctrine they could claim a valid apostolic pedigree as physical witnesses and symbols of apostolic continuity; when they claimed the same for the authority to determine and to regulate the process of divine forgiveness, such pedigree, in and of itself, was shown to be inadequate as regards any spiritual endorsement of such power. Historically derived apostolicity had its limits.

Apostolicity was not, however, the sole criterion for determining the authenticity of a charismatic, prophetic ministry; notwithstanding the impression that the latter was largely determined in Tertullian's eyes by the status of one's attitude towards the New Prophecy, he contends that such authenticity is demonstrable solely by spiritual evidences. In his later period it could be said, not unfairly, that the prophets of the early church join the apostles as ministers of the first rank appointed by Christ. Tertullian stands within the Latin tradition of an ecclesial order centred around and witnessed to by an historical episcopate established by the apostles; this tradition is exemplified principally by the writings of Clement of Rome and Irenaeus of Lyons before him, and not by the Eastern tradition of Ignatius of

Antioch.[14] Office, for Tertullian, validates cultic role, but is not indispensable, and is not a substitute for the apostles, nor, through them, for the person of Christ.

We saw in Part II the extent to which Tertullian anticipated that later credal formula which affirmed the true church as 'one, holy, catholic and apostolic'. He affirmed the necessary unity of the true church as embodying the one, undivided Body of Christ which cannot be other than that which it is; he affirmed, too, the necessary holiness of the true church as being the Virgin Bride of Christ which must be that which it is called to be in the present age, and not only in future promise. The vows of the church's virgins, the consecrated continence of its widows and the sanctified monogamy of its clergy all testify to this fact of holiness. Tertullian could not countenance the proposition that the clergy, being fallible human persons, might not at all times and in all places maintain the perfection which the demands of sanctification and his own eschatological framework place upon them in the present age, any more than he could the proposition that the holy church as the Virgin Bride of Christ might not remain unsullied in that imperfect reality reflected in the present, sinful condition of the world. He could not countenance the thought that the true church might yet be 'simul iustus et peccator' and that absolute perfection might come only at the End; likewise he could not condone the frailty and human foibles of her clergy. Holiness, for Tertullian, demanded no less.

There is also, in Tertullian's eschatological framework, yet another implication for his view of Christian ministry. And that is the provisional nature of church order. At *Apologeticum* 39,5 Tertullian speaks of the disciplinary judgements of the ruling 'seniores' 'apud certos de dei conspectu, summumque futuri iudicii praeiudicium est' (among men certain that God sees them; and a notable foretaste of the judgement to come), which von Campenhausen calls a 'provisional judgement'.[15] As the decisions of the ecclesiastical tribunals are provisional, so, too, must be the church's own existence. Church order is, for the Tertullian of both periods, an integral part of Christian ministry;

---

[14] Contrary to Powell, 'Ordo', p. 293.
[15] Von Campenhausen, *Ecclesiastical authority*, p. 217.

but it is not forever and at the End will be gathered up into the eternal ministry of its Lord and High Priest. In the final analysis the true church is in no way dependent upon its formal ordering. It is the Spirit and the Word which are indispensable to the church, and not office nor even charisma. The Rule of Faith is witnessed to by the tradition of the church and its order, but neither established nor legitimised in the final analysis by them.[16] The ministry of the church derives from that of Jesus Christ, as prophet, priest and king; it could not fail to be equal to that commission. Tertullian can only have been a most disappointed observer!

[16] R. F. Evans, *One and holy*, p. 12, describes Tertullian's 'vision of the church as a people set apart awaiting the end of the age'. Bray, at *Holiness*, p. 150, speaks of Tertullian seeing the imminence of the parousia necessitating 'the church's immediate and total sanctificaton before it arrived'. Tertullian had no doubt that the End would come and that it would be soon. The purpose of the church's order and its ministry was to help the church prepare for the End in the time left to it. When the End would come such an order's primary and sole reason for existence would itself be at an end. Tertullian's major concern with the Catholic leadership was the impression that the latter was settling in for the 'long haul' and thus taking its eyes off that moment which stood not far off in time and which should have determined its programme. This was a time not for a consolidation into a timeless future, but for an earnest preparation for the fast-approaching and decisive moment in history.

PART IV

General conclusions

It has been demonstrated at numerous places already that Tertullian for the most part maintained throughout his career consistent doctrines of both church and ministry, both as a Catholic and as a New Prophet. We have seen how he maintained a consistent position on the necessary unity, holiness and apostolicity of the authentic church – the question of catholicity is perhaps another matter – employing a number of images which, inter alia, underlined these notes of the true church. We have seen, too, how he maintained, even through into his New Prophecy period, a fundamental belief in the importance of a lawful, ordered Christian ministry and in the appropriateness and legitimacy of the three ranks of sacerdotal offices. This he did notwithstanding his violent disagreement with several holders of such offices.

He did, of course, lay greater emphasis in his New Prophecy period than he had in the Catholic on the 'charismata', both on the 'charisma' of Christian prophecy, and consequently on the New Prophecy movement itself. This is true also of his pronouncements concerning the role of the Spirit in the life of the church and the process by which the apostolicity of the true church might be properly authenticated; this is particularly so with reference to the requirements of discipline and the penitential process, with that which Tertullian perceived as the valid demands of sanctification. In none of these matters, however, is there a substantial repudiation of positions he had held in the earlier period. In the later part of Tertullian's career the church was confronted with issues with which it had not had to contend seriously in the earlier. These issues included the rapid militarisation of the empire under the Severans; the increased influx into the church of greater numbers of persons from the upper classes of Roman society; demands both for accommodation to social pressures in light of these developments and for a more liberal administration of the penitential process; and, increasing persecution between periods of relative toleration and uneasy peace.

We have seen how Tertullian's own emphasis shifted from a primary concern for doctrine to one for discipline; this may account for subtle changes of emphasis but does not involve a necessary contradiction or repudiation of previously held views. The Tertullian of either period never questioned the necessary unity of the true church; he consistently throughout his career believed that church to be the one, undivided and authentic Body of Christ. Likewise he never questioned the necessary holiness of the true church which he believed to be the Virgin Bride of Christ; it was only when he perceived that the church was failing to reflect such holiness in its life and witness in the present age that he began to rail against the institution and vehemently to denounce her clergy whose sacred task it was, in his view, to administer the church with such holiness unsullied. For both his understanding of the demands of sanctification and his eschatologically formed outlook led him to the firm view that this was a both/and present-future reality and not an either/or. The historical apostolicity of the church and its official ministry were also never doubted; it was only when Tertullian sensed that such a pedigree was being used to drive a wedge between the reality of the church's present nature and its ultimate reality – which for Tertullian were identical – that he sought to restrict the scope of these historical claims and to place more emphasis on prophecy and on men of the Spirit both in his ecclesiology and in his understanding of authentic Christian ministry.

The question whether the concepts on which Tertullian based his doctrines of church and ministry underwent any significant change in his transition from apologist for the Catholic church to propagandist for the New Prophecy movement is vital to a proper consideration of those doctrines; likewise important are the questions whether Tertullian's alleged 'laicism' was as evident in his early period as in his later one; whether there is any real evidence to support the well-cherished notion that Tertullian actually repudiated the Catholic episcopal system; and whether indeed the only 'changes' which did occur for the most part were those brought about by the demands of a particular polemical context. A fundamental question must be: 'Is Tertullian consistent?'

Notwithstanding the wide array of material available, reference to key selected passages from two of his works, from the 'Catholic' treatise *De Baptismo* and from the later *De Exhortatione Castitatis*, should provide a basis for a definitive answer to this question.[1] In the passages concerned Tertullian addresses key aspects of authentic Christian ministry and office.

The texts

i. *De Baptismo 17*: The immediate purpose of Tertullian in this chapter is to consider the proper administration of the sacrament of baptism: 'Superest ad concludendam materiolam de observatione quoque dandi et accipiendi baptismi commonefacere.'(1) (In concluding our brief subject, it remains only to bring to mind the matter of the observance of the giving and receiving of baptism.)

ii. *De Exhortatione Castitatis 7*: The immediate purpose of Tertullian in this chapter is to consider whether the monogamist discipline laid as a necessary obligation upon all Christian clergy should not equally be applied to Christian lay persons; 'Inde igitur apostolus plenius atque strictius praescribit unius matrimonii esse oportere qui allegantur in ordinem sacerdotalem ... (3) Nonne et laici sacerdotes sumus?' (2.3) (Hence, therefore, the Apostle fully and clearly laid down that it was obligatory for those elected to the priestly order to be once-only married ... (3) For are we lay persons not also priests?)

The texts as responses to the questions raised
i. *De Baptismo*: In this treatise Tertullian's starting-point is the need for order in the sacramental and disciplinary life of the

---

[1] Some of these passages have already been discussed at various points in preceding parts of this book.

church, so that the 'peace' of the church might be safeguarded. Hence,

...dandi quidem summum habet ius summus sacerdos, si qui est, episcopus; dehinc presbyteri et diaconi, non tamen sine auctoritate episcopi, propter ecclesiae honorem, quo salvo, salva pax est.(2)

(...indeed the High Priest, who is the bishop, has the chief right [of baptising]; and after him the presbyters and deacons, though not without the authority of the bishop, on account of the honour of the church, which honour being preserved, peace is preserved.)

'Peace', order and the absence of schism are the primary concerns.

This is not all, however, for Tertullian concedes that in certain circumstances a lay person may celebrate the sacrament, 'alioquin etiam laicis ius est'(2) (otherwise even to lay persons the right [to baptise] belongs) on the basis that 'quod enim ex aequo accipitur ex aequo dari potest' (ibid.) (for what is received can equally be given) and, 'baptismus, aeque dei census, ab omnibus exerceri potest'(ibid.) (baptism, as much as [sc. the Word of the Lord] the property of God, can be administered by all) and, in the following circumstances, 'sufficit scilicet [et] in necessitatibus utaris, sicubi aut loci aut temporis aut personae condicio compellit' (3) (let it be sufficient that you avail yourself in times of necessity of this right [to baptise], if at any time circumstance of time or person compel you).

In this period, however, Tertullian would normally restrict the exercise of the sacramental ministry, at least with regard to that of baptism, to the 'maiores',[2] to the 'dicatum (consecrated) episcopi officium' (and hence also to its subordinate clerical offices), since, 'Episcopatus aemulatio scismatum mater est' (2) (envy of the bishop's office is the mother of schisms) and, 'omnia licere dixit sanctissimus apostolus, sed non omnia expedire' (ibid.) (the most blessed Apostle has said that all things are lawful, but not all are expedient).

The 'bottom-line' for Tertullian here, however, is that, notwithstanding his 'high' view of episcopo-clerical prerogatives, he yet offers what is a non-sacralist view of sacramental ministry; one open to lay persons and clergy alike, the immediate

---

[2] Tertullian also refers to the clergy as 'maiores' in his 'Montanist' treatise *De Fuga* (11,1).

basis for which is neither theological nor sacral in character, but rather one governed by the requirements of order.

ii. *De Exhortatione Castitatis* 7: In this treatise, on the other hand, Tertullian offers a 'from below' view of 'sacerdotium' and 'ministerium'. His starting-point and basic premise is that the fundamental obligations of Christian discipline (here particularly the rule of monogamy) should be applied not only to the clergy, but also to the laity from whose ranks the former come. He asserts that the 'difference' between the clergy and the laity is one of human (and therefore presumably not of divine) sanction; that 'differentiam inter ordinem et plebem constituit ecclesiae auctoritas et honor per ordinis consessus sanctificatos deo' (3) (the authority of the church and the honour of the gathering of the Order sanctified to God determines the difference between that Order and the people). And thus, 'ubi ecclesiastici ordinis non est concessus, et offers et tinguis et sacerdos es tibi solus' (ibid.) (where there is no gathering of the ecclesiastical order, you offer [the elements] and baptise and be a priest to yourself alone) since, 'unusquisque enim, secundum quod et apostolus dicit, "vivit fide sua, nec est personarum acceptio apud Deum"' (4) (for each person, according to what the Apostle says, 'lives by his own faith, and neither is there is any partiality of persons with God').

Further, influenced by Revelation 1,6 – 'he has made us priests to God and to His Father' – Tertullian asks rhetorically, 'Nonne et laici sacerdotes sumus?' (3) (For are we lay persons not also priests?), an observation which leads him to lay out what he regards as the implications of this for the disciplinary life of his fellow lay persons thus addressed, 'Igitur si habes ius sacerdotis in temetipso, ubi necesse est, habeas oportet etiam disciplinam sacerdotis' (4) (Therefore, if you have the right of a priest [sc. to celebrate the sacraments] in yourself, when it is necessary, it is only proper that you have also the discipline of a priest) that is, in this case, the obligation of monogamy.

And yet, while the 'bottom-line' and underlying premise here is again that of a non-sacralist view of sacramental ministry, one based on human (and hence by implication of non-divine) discretion and sanction, there is also, as in *De Baptismo*, a 'high' view of the prerogatives of the clergy over against the laity. Lay administration here is, as in *De Baptismo*, allowable only 'ubi necesse est'. The 'ordo sacerdotalis' referred to in this passage is 'l'ordre par excellence de l'Eglise'.[3] Further, the 'honor' referred to at 7,3 may not simply be a reference to the esteem and dignity attached to the sacerdotal office, for it is well attested that this term can also denote the actual 'office' itself to which such 'honour' is attached[4]. It suggests an elevated, if not quite exalted, view of the sacerdotal ministry and one common to both treatises and thus both periods of his career.

Further evidence of Tertullian's consistency

The references to 'auctoritas' in the passages quoted from both treatises also demonstrate further common ground between the two. Both may have been used in the sense of 'authorisation', 'sanction' or 'approval', although the suggestion that 'ecclesiae auctoritas' (*De Exhortatione Castitatis* 7,3) could have the meaning 'decree of the church' in the sense in which the expression 'senatus auctoritas' denoted a resolution of the Roman senate is attractive.[5]

Tertullian employs the word 'ius' throughout his writings with a great variety of meaning. However, in both the passages dealt with Tertullian uses it with a similar meaning, that of the 'sanctioned right to exercise some prerogative'. He also employs it with like meaning at *De Baptismo* 1,3 of the 'docendi ius' (right to teach), at 17,4 of the 'ius docere', at *Adv. Marcionem* v,8,11 of the 'prophetandi ius' (right to prophesy), at *De Pudicitia* 21,9 and 17 of the 'ius donare delicta' (right to forgive sins), and at *De Oratione* 10,1 of the 'ius petitiones' (right of offering petitions). 'Ius sacerdotis' at *De Exhortatione Castitatis* 7,4 refers to the prerogative of administering the sacraments, and 'ius dandi' at

---

[3] Van Beneden, *Aux origines*, p. 30.

[4] See the discussion of 'honor' in Part III. See also *De Baptismo* 17, where Tertullian speaks of the 'ecclesiae honor'.

[5] While 'senatus auctoritas' tended to denote an informal rather than a formal resolution of the Roman senate – 'consultum' more often denoted the latter – Tertullian employs 'senatus auctoritas' to denote an official edict of the Senate at *Ad Nationes* 1,10,16.

De Baptismo 17,1 to the prerogative of administering baptism. Tertullian's attitude to the administration of the Eucharist in his early period is not clear, but it is probable (see the references to 'offerre' in *De Exhortatione Castitatis* 7,3) that he would have also allowed lay administration of communion under circumstances similar to those under which he allowed lay baptism.

SUMMARY

In both *De Baptismo* and *De Exhortatione Castitatis* Tertullian envisaged the normal situation to be that whereby the 'priestly order' – expressly so called in the latter treatise and acknowledged as a 'priestly' body under the oversight of the 'high-priest' bishop in the former – exercised the 'rights' of the sacramental ministry, that is the prerogative of administration. In neither, however, is this recognised as theologically or as sacrally the exclusive 'right' of the clergy whatever the circumstance, but only as a matter of an appropriately provisional church order. When necessary – in *De Baptismo* 'in necessitatibus' and in *De Exhortatione Castitatis* 'ubi necesse est' – such a 'right' belonged by right also to the laity. The difference between the approach in *De Baptismo* and that in *De Exhortatione Castitatis* is that in the former Tertullian is seeking to guarantee order in congregational life. He begins 'from above', with the assumption of episcopal and clerical prerogatives, moving 'downwards' only, by way of necessary concession, to the inalienable and incontestable 'rights' of the laity, once the maintenance of 'peace' is firmly secured. In the later treatise Tertullian seeks to establish the equality of clergy and laity in the disciplinary demands of the Christian life. He begins therefore 'from below' with the assumption that all Christians – lay and clergy alike – are 'priests', since in theory all are entitled to exercise the prerogatives of the 'priestly' sacramental ministry. He only begins to work his way 'upwards' from this commonly held 'right' to exercise 'priestly' functions to the more exclusive, ordered position represented by actual practice, once he has firmly established the inescapable conclusion that all who claim such prerogatives must also accept the accompanying disciplinary obligations.

It is not true that the Montanist writings of Tertullian indicate a complete change in his attitude towards 'le chrétien sacerdoce', and that the role of the bishop, for Tertullian's early period at least, 'est indispensable à l'esse de l'Eglise'.[6] It was never so. On the other hand, it is true that even for the Catholic Tertullian there is never a sacral priestly office, holy per se, but at best one indispensable to church order.[7] In *De Baptismo* 17 and *De Exhortatione Castitatis* 7 we have 'une doctrine analogue', the only difference being one of 'le ton', and that brought about by the differing requirements of context.[8] What we see in both treatises is essentially the same picture; it is only the angles that are different. This is the case for most aspects of Tertullian's doctrines of church and ministry. The emphases are sometimes wholly different, but the essential concepts underlying them are the same in both periods of Tertullian's Christian life. Tertullian is accused properly of many things; inconsistency here, however, cannot be one of them.

Tertullian of North Africa played a major role in the development both of Western ecclesiology and of the understanding of Christian ministry in the Latin church in its transformation from the functionalist approach of the mid-to-late second century to the absolutist sacerdotalism which emerged under Cyprian of Carthage in North Africa in the mid-third century.

Tertullian was influenced undoubtedly by the writings of both Clement of Rome and Irenaeus of Lyons – by the former in the need for order in election and promotion within Christian ministry, and by the latter in the perception of an apostolically founded episcopal succession. He was also influenced by his own understanding of Christian history, by his pronounced tendency towards rigorism and by the perceived need for the maintenance of ecclesiastical order. He in turn greatly influenced, among others, Cyprian of Carthage, the latter effectively establishing

---

[6] Michaelides, *Foi écritures*, p.81. See note 10 in chapter 8 above for a fuller statement of the arguments here.

[7] Von Campenhausen, *Ecclesiastical authority*, p. 228.

[8] De Labriolle, 'Tertullien, était-il prêtre?, *Bulletin d'ancienne littérature et d'archéologie chrétienne* 3 (1913) p. 169.

the absolutist claims of the Western Catholic episcopate. The influence of Tertullian's thought in the area of the proper ordering of Christian ministry and in that of ecclesiological and ministerial terminology and imagery cannot be disputed, and the impact of his thought, even to this day, can be strongly felt.

As was said in the General Introduction, the late second to early third century was a watershed period in the development of Western ecclesiology and ministry, culminating in the Cyprianic episcopate in the mid-third century. In that period the thought of Q. Septimius Florens Tertullianus, Christian Father of North Africa, was a crucial factor.

Appendix

Tertullian is no systematic theologian. He writes to specific issues. In his extant writings he offers no systematic treatment either of the church or of Christian office and ministry. Those writings in which he deals with these questions – for the nature of the church in *De Praescriptione*, *Apologeticum* and *De Pudicitia*, and for that of Christian ministry in *De Baptismo* and *De Exhortatione Castitatis* – are primarily concerned with other issues. Those sections which touch on the nature of church and Christian ministry are largely subordinate to these other concerns. None of this leads to the conclusion either that Tertullian has nothing of value to contribute to questions of church and ministry, or that there is not in his writings a rich storehouse of ecclesiological thought; these writings in fact reflect the development of a significant ecclesiological tradition. There is very little on the surface for the casual prospector, nor is there below that surface a hidden seam of gold, which, once struck, might produce a source of valuable insights. The valuable deposits to be found scattered along the shafts of Tertullian's thought processes must be mined by patient excavation. I have done this, in part, by an examination of those images employed by Tertullian with reference both to the church and to Christian ministry.

I have adopted a lexical approach to these questions. Such word studies are common in Tertullian scholarship and have received general, though by no means uncritical approval. The method is problematic and full of potential pitfalls for the unwary. Criticisms of the method include the charge that such an approach tends unnecessarily to remove passages from their context; that it tends to isolate key terms from others which are related, but do not conform to the same terminological form; and that it is a non-holistic approach which seeks to understand a thing from its parts rather than its whole, thus failing to give appropriate expression to the essential character of that whole. The criticism that the lexical approach becomes unduly repetitive is valid but unavoidable if it is to be comprehensive. It is surely preferable to be comprehensive than to provide reading which, while interesting, omits vital material. It is clear that the method can produce a tendency to isolate historical context from discussion of the text and the latter from its literary context. Yet these dangers can be mitigated by giving, in the right place, appropriate attention to such historical and literary contexts. The introductory and concluding sections offer important opportunities for drawing together otherwise isolated and ahistorical series of fragmentary textual analyses. Another criticism, that the lexical approach might make all the terms equally important, can be met by making it clear, particularly in the conclusion, that this is not so. These concerns are valid, but the possible consequences are not automatically concomitant with the lexical method. They must be acknowledged, however, and any scholar employing this method must use great caution so that the dangers might be avoided, or at least minimised.

Tertullian of Carthage possessed a fertile imagination. He wrote predominantly in images and in this was very much a man both of the Bible and of his own philosophical background and training. Tertullian's understanding of the nature of the church and of Christian ministry is not expressed exclusively in images. The exploration of such images is, however, an appropriate starting point. Do these scattered images present a first picture of Tertullian's understanding of church and ministry? The lexical approach involves a consideration of specific texts and of particular words within those texts. A 'holistic' approach might promise a broader view of the issues, but by dealing with texts in an unstructured way, it can impose views on Tertullian rather than come to terms with Tertullian's complex thought.

It is important to place Tertullian within specific historical, cultural and political contexts. I therefore offer brief accounts of the following: the city of Carthage; the history of the North African church prior to Tertullian; the impact of the Severan dynasty and its militarisation of provincial life seen in Tertullian's frequent employment of military imagery; and the cult of Mithras as a serious pagan challenge to the Christian faith. It is appropriate also to place Tertullian in the context of the New Prophecy movement (Montanism) and of the Catholic church of his day.

Gosta Claesson's *Index Tertullianeus* offers a handy reference for the various usages by Tertullian of particular words and/or images for the church. In exploring Tertullian's understanding of the nature of the church, I begin with these images. These are listed exhaustively, with detailed discussion. Similar images are kept together; 'schola' with 'secta', 'virgo' with 'sponsa', 'Christus' with 'corpus', 'spiritus' and 'trinitas'. In considering each image I have discussed the following questions: the biblical, patristic or other precedents for Tertullian's usage; whether his use of a particular image, for example, conforms to a biblical model; the consistency in his use of an image from his early (Catholic) through to his later (New Prophecy) period; whether some images are employed in one period and not in the other, and with what degrees of intensity; whether his employment of particular images provides grounds for seeing the development in Tertullian of an understanding of the church linked to the traditional 'notes' of the church – unity, holiness, catholicity and apostolicity; whether his employment of particular images conforms to other later ecclesial 'notes', e.g. those of the Reformed tradition – preaching truly, administering the sacraments rightly, maintaining godly discipline – or other more recent models – the Church as Institution, as Mystical Communion, as Sacrament, as Herald, as Servant (Dulles); whether his ecclesiological thought conforms to what Minear calls the four Master Images for the church in the New Testament – the People of God, the New Creation, the Fellowship in Faith, and perhaps most important of all, the Body of Christ; whether it reflects anything of modern ecclesiological preoccupations with the tensions/dichotomies said to be present between the church as priestly or as prophetic, as vertically or as horizontally determined or constituted, as institution or as event. It is appropriate also to consider Tertullian's employment of the same images in contexts other than the ecclesial to gauge to what extent such usage informs the broader ecclesiological question. These images are, of course, not all that Tertullian has to say on the subject. It is also important to consider his understanding of the church in the matters of penitential discipline (*De Pudicitia*), in the transmission of the apostolic tradition (*De Praescriptione*), and in the development of an effective apologetic (*Apologeticum*).

In any discussion of Tertullian's understanding of the nature of Christian ministry Claesson's *Index* is again a useful resource. The lexical approach is again employed as starting point. Every reference by Tertullian to any of the 'official ministries' – clerical and lay – as well as those to ministry generally (ministerium) and to ministry gifts (charismata and spiritualia) has been examined. Then there are those illustrative expressions which Tertullian employs with reference to aspects of Christian ministry and leadership.

As previously, I have considered the biblical, patristic and secular precedents for Tertullian's employment of these terms and images and the extent to which he is influenced by them. As with the issue of the nature of the church, the extent to which Tertullian has remained consistent from early through to later periods has also been explored. There are some writings which, in part at least, deal more extensively with the nature and function of Christian ministry, either in relation to liturgical leadership and oversight (*De Baptismo* and *De Exhortatione Castitatis*) or to the administration of the church discipline (*De Paenitentia* and *De Pudicitia*).

Select Bibliography

1. CRITICAL EDITIONS AND TRANSLATIONS OF TERTULLIAN'S WORKS

Tertullian's opera I (Opera Catholica, Adversus Marcionem) II (Opera Montanistica) Corpus Christianorum. Series Latina I-II, Turnhout, 1954.

Ante-Nicene Christian Library, 7 (1878),11 (1878), 15(1880), 18 (1884).

Becker, C., *Tertullians Apologeticum, Werden und Leistung*, Munich, 1954.

Evans, E., *Against Praxeas*. Text, translation, and commentary, London, 1948.

On the Incarnation. Text, translation and commentary, London, 1956.

De Oratione. Text and notes. London, 1953.

On the Resurrection. Text, translation and commentary, London, 1960.

Tertullian's *Homily on Baptism*. Text, translation and commentary. London, 1964.

Adversus Marcionem. Text and commentary. 2 vols.Oxford, 1972.

De Labriolle, P., Tertullien. *De Paenitentia, De Pudicitia*. Texte et tradition, 1906.

Le Saint, W. P., *Treatises on Marriage and Remarriage*, (ACW 13).

Treatises on Penance (ACW 28). London, 1958.

Waszink, J. H., *Tertullian's De Anima*, Amsterdam, 1947.

Treatise against Hermogenes (ACW 24). London, 1956.

Tertullian, *Apology & De Spectaculis*, ed. T.R. Glover; Minucius Felix, *Octavius*, trans. G.H. Rendall (LCL 250), Cambridge, Mass, 1877.

Meijering, E. P.,*Tertullian Contra Marcionem*, Leiden, 1977.

2. INDICES

Biblia Patristica. Index des citations et allusions bibliques dans la littérature patristique, Paris, 1975-7.

Vol. 1, Des origines à Clement d'Alexandrie et Tertullien
Vol. 2, Le troisième siècle (Origène excepté).
Claesson. G., *Index Tertullianeus*, Paris, 1974/75.
Lampe, G. W. H. (ed.), *Patristic Greek Lexicon*, Oxford, 1961-8.
Quellet, H., *Concordance verbale du De Corona de Tertullien*, New York, 1975.

3. TEXTS AND TRANSLATIONS OF OTHER PRIMARY SOURCES

Aelius Spartianus, *Scriptores Historiae Augustae*, LCL
Apostolic Fathers, LCL 24 and 25 (1912-13).
Eusebius, *Ecclesiastical History*, LCL 153 and 265 (1926-32).
Justin: *The Apologies of Justin Martyr* (Cambridge Patristic Texts; ed. A.
     W. F. Blunt, Cambridge, 1911).
Irenaeus: (Sources Chrétiennes 1965-82).
Clement of Alexandria: Stahlin's Edition, ed. O. Stahlin GCS.
Cyprian: *Opera* (CCL 3,3A – 1972-76).
Dio Cassius, *A Roman History*, LCL.
Herodian, *History*, LCL.
Novatian: Fausset, W. Y., *Novatian's treatise on the Trinity*, Cambridge,
     1909.
Musurillo, H., *The Acts of the Christian martyrs: introduction, texts and
     translations*, Oxford, 1972.
Passio Perpetuae et Felicitatis (Cambridge Patristic Texts; ed. J. A.
     Robinson, 1891).

4. MODERN WORKS SPECIFICALLY ON TERTULLIAN

Abramowski, L.,'Tertullian: sacramento ampliat(i)o, fides integra,
     metus integer', *VC* 31 (1977) pp. 191-5.
Adam, K., *Der Kirchenbegriff Tertullians*, Paderborn, 1907.
D'Alès, A., *La théologie de Tertullien*, Paris, 1905.
     'Tertullien helléniste', *REG* 50 (1937), pp. 329-62.
Andresen, C., 'Ubi tres, ecclesia est, licet laici: Kirchengeschichtliche
     Reflexionen zu einem Satz des Montanisten Tertullians.
     (Matt.18:20)', *Vom Amt des Laien in Kirche und Theologie*, ed. H.
     Schroer, 1982, pp. 103-21.
Ayers, R. H., 'Tertullian's "paradox" and "contempt for reason"
     reconsidered', *ExpT* 87 (1976), p. 308-11.
     *Language, logic and reason in the Church Fathers: a study of Tertullian,
     Augustine and Aquinas*, Olms, 1979.
Balfour, I. L. S.,'Tertullian's description of the heathen', *SP* 17 (1979),
     pp. 785-9.

Baney, M. B., *Some reflexions of life in North Africa in the writings of Tertullian*, Washington, 1948.

Barnes, T. D., 'Tertullian's Scorpiace', *JTS* ns 20 (1969), pp.105-32.
'Tertullian the antiquarian', *SP* 14 (1976), pp. 3-20.
Tertullian: a historical and literary study, 2nd edition, London, 1985.

Bastiaensen, A. A. R., 'Tertullian's argumentation in De Praescriptione Haereticorum', *VC* 31 (1977), pp. 35-46.
'Tertullian's reference to the Passio Perpetuae in De Anima 55.4', *SP* 17 (1979), pp. 790-5.

Bévenot, M., 'Tertullian's thoughts about the Christian priesthood', in *Corona Gratiarum*, 1975.

Blum, G. G., 'Der Begriff des Apostolischen im theologischen Denken Tertullians', *KerDo* 9 (1963), pp. 102-21.

Braun, R., *Deus Christianorum*, Paris, 1962 (2nd edn)
'Note sur Tertullian, De Cultu Feminarum II, 6.4. Histoire d'un texte obscur', *SE* 7 (1955), pp.35-48.
'Tertullien et les poètes latins', *AnFLetN* 2/4 (1967), pp. 21-33.
'Tertullien et les séditions contres les empereurs (*Apol*.35,8-9)', *REAug*. 26 (1980), pp. 18-28.

Bray, G., 'Legal concept of ratio in Tertullian', *VC* 31 (1977), pp.94-116.
Holiness and the will of God: perspectives on the theology of Tertullian, London, 1979.

Campenhausen, H. von, 'Tertullien', in *Gestalten der Kirchengeschichte*, Alte Kirche I, pp. 97-121.

Carnelley, E., 'Tertullian and feminism', *Theology* 92 (1989), pp.31-5.

Countryman, L. W. M., 'Tertullian and the Regula Fidei', *Second Century* 2 (1982), pp. 208-27.

Daniel, R. W., 'A note on Tertullian's De Idololatria', *VC* 39 (1985), pp. 63-4.

Davies, J. G., 'Tertullian, De Resurrectione Carnis 63: a note on the origins of Montanism', *JTS* ns 6 (1955), pp. 90-4.

Decarie, V., 'Le paradoxe de Tertullien', *VC* 15 (1961), pp. 23-31.

Eno, R., 'Ecclesia docens; structures of doctrinal authority in Tertullian and Vincent', *Thomist* 40 (1976), pp. 96-115.

Evans, E., 'Tertullian's theological terminology', *CQR* 277 (1944), pp. 56-77.

Evans, R. F., *One and holy: the Church in Latin patristic thought*, London, 1972.
'On the problem of Church and empire in Tertullian's Apologeticum', *SP* 14 (1976), pp. 21-36.

Fredouille, J.-C., *Tertullien et la conversion de la culture antique*, Paris, 1972.

Frend, W. H .C., 'Their word to our day; Tertullian' *ExpT* 81 (1970), pp. 136-41.
'A note on Tertullian and the Jews', *SP* 10 (1970), pp. 291-6.

Bibliography 215

Gero, S., 'Miles gloriosus; the Christian and military service according to Tertullian', *CH* 39 (1970), pp. 285-98.

Gonzales, J. L., 'Athens and Jerusalem revisited: reason and authority in Tertullian', *CH* 43 (1974), pp. 17-25.

Grant, R. McQ., 'Two notes on Tertullian (his account of Greek philosophical views on God)', *VC* 5 (1951), pp. 113-15.

Groh, D.E., 'Tertullian's polemic against social co-optation', *CH* 40 (1971), pp. 7-14.

'Upper-class Christians in Tertullian's Africa', *SP* 14 (1976), pp. 41-7.

'Christian community in the writings of Tertullian. An inquiry into the nature and problems of community in North African Christianity' (PhD diss., N/W Univ.), Evanston, 1979.

Guignebert, Ch., *Tertullien. Etude sur ses sentiments à l'égard de l'Empire et de la société civile*, Paris, 1901.

Hallonsten, G., 'Some aspects of the so-called Verdienstbegriff of Tertullian', *SP* 17 (1979), pp. 799-802.

Satisfactio bei Tertullian, Malmo, 1984.

Hanson, R .P .C., 'Notes on Tertullian's interpretation of scripture', *JTS* ns 12 (1961), pp. 273-9.

Harnack, A., 'Tertullian Bibliothek christlicher Schriften', *Sitzungsberichte der Deutschen Akademie der Wissenschaften zu Berlin* (1914), pp. 306-7.

Hornus, J. M., 'Etude sur la pensée politique de Tertullien', *Revue d'histoire et de philosophie religeuses* 38 (1958), pp. 1-38.

Jansen, J. F., 'Tertullian and the New Testament', *Second Century* 2 (1982), pp. 191-207.

Karpp, H., *Schrift und Geist bei Tertullian*, Gütersloh, 1955.

Keresztes, P., 'Tertullian's apologeticus: a historical and literary study', *Latomus* 25 (1966), pp. 124-33.

Klein, R., *Tertullian und das römische Reich*, Heidelberg, 1968.

de Labriolle, P., 'Tertullien jurisconsulte', *Nouvelle revue historique de droit français et etranger* 30 (1906), pp. 5-27.

'Tertullien: était-il prêtre?', *Bulletin d'ancienne littérature et d'archéologie chrétiennes* 3 (1913), pp. 1-61.

'Tertullien, auteur du prologue et de la conclusion de la passion de Perpétue et de Félicité', *Bulletin d'ancienne littérature et d'archéologie chrétiennes* 3 (1913), p. 129.

History and literature of Christianity from Tertullian to Boethius, London, 1924.

Langstadt, E., 'Tertullian's doctrine of sin and the power of absolution in "de pudicitia"', *SP* 2 (1957), pp. 251-7.

McDonnell, K., 'Communion ecclesiology and baptism in the spirit: Tertullian and the early church', *Theological Studies* 49 (1988), pp. 671-93.

MacMullen, R., 'Tertullian and "national gods"', *JTS* 26 (1975), pp. 405-10.

Mahé, J.-P., 'Tertullien et l'épistule Marcionis', *RScRel*, 45 (1971), pp. 358-71.

Meijering, E. P., 'Bemerkungen zu Tertullians Polemik gegen Marcion (Adv. Marc.1, 1-25)', *VC* 30 (1976), pp. 81-108.

Michaelides, D., *Foi, écritures et tradition, ou les 'praescriptions' chez Tertullien*, Paris, 1969.
    Sacramentum chez Tertullien, Paris, 1969.

Mohrmann, C., 'Tertullian, De Baptismo 2,2', *VC* 5 (1951), p. 49.
    'Observations sur la langue et le style de Tertullian', *Nuovo Didaskaleion (Cantania)* 4 (1950/51), pp. 41-54.
    'Saint Jerome et Saint Augustin sur Tertullien', *VC* 5 (1951), pp. 111-12.

Moingt, J., *Théologie trinitaire de Tertullien* (vols,i-iv), Paris, 1966-9.
    'La problème du Dieu unique chez Tertullien', *RScRel* 44 (1970), pp. 337-62.

Morel, V., 'Le développement de la "disciplina" sous l'action du Saint Esprit chez Tertullien', *RHE* 35 (1939), pp. 243-65.
    'Disciplina: le mot et l'idée representée par lui dans les oeuvres de Tertullien', *RHE* 40 (1944-5), pp. 5-46.

Morgan, J., *The importance of Tertullian in the development of Christian dogma*, London, 1928.

Nisters, B., *Tertullian: seine Persönlichkeit und sein Schicksal*, Münster, 1950.

O'Malley, T. P., *Tertullian and the Bible: language-imagery-exegesis*, Utrecht, 1967.

Pelikan, J., 'The eschatology of Tertullian', *CH* 21 (1952), pp.108-22.

Powell, D., 'Tertullianists and Cataphrygians', *VC* 29 (1975), pp.33-54.

Quasten, J., 'Tertullian and "tradition"', *Tradition* 2 (1944), pp.481-4.

Rahner, K., 'Zur Theologie der Busse bei Tertullian', *Abhandlungen über Theologie und Kirche*, 1943, pp. 139-167.

Rankin, D. I., 'Tertullian's use of the Pastoral Epistles in his doctrine of ministry', *Australian Biblical Review* 32 (1984), pp. 18-37.
    'Was Tertullian a schismatic?', *Prudentia* 18 (1986), pp. 73-80.
    'Tertullian's consistency of thought on ministry', *SP* 21 (1989), pp. 271-6.

Roberts, R. E., *The theology of Tertullian*, London, 1924.

Rordorf, W., 'Tertullians Beurteilung des Soldatenstandes', *VC* 23 (1969), pp. 105-41.
    'Dossier sur l'ad Martyras de Tertullien', *REAug.* 26 (1980), pp. 3-17.

Schoellegen, G., *Ecclesia Sordida? Zur Frage der sozialen Schichtung frühchristlicher Gemeinden am Beispiel Karthagos zur Zeit Tertullians*. Münster, 1985.

Sedgwick, W. B., 'Conjectures on the text of Tertullian (De Pallio)', *VC* 22 (1968), pp. 94-5.

Sider, R. D., 'Structure and design in the De Resurrectione of Tertullian', *VC* 23 (1969), pp. 177-96.

Ancient rhetoric and the art of Tertullian, Oxford, 1971.

'On symmetrical composition in Tertullian', *JTS* ns 24 (1973), pp. 405-23.

'Tertullian, On the Shows: an analysis', *JTS* ns 24 (1973), pp. 339-65.

'Approaches to Tertullian: a study of recent scholarship', *Second Century* 2 (1982), pp. 228-60.

Stager, L., *Das Leben im römischen Afrika im Spiegel der Schriften Tertullians*, Zurich, 1973.

Stead, G. C., 'Divine substance in Tertullian', *JTS* ns 14 (1963), pp. 46-66.

Stockmeier, P., 'Gottesverständnis und Saturnkult bei Tertullian', *SP* 17 (1979), pp. 829-35.

Strauss, J., 'Des christlichen Kaisers secunda maiestas: Tertullian und die Konstantinische Wende', *ZKG* 90 (1979), pp. 293-303.

Swift, L. J., 'Forensic rhetoric in Tertullian's Apologeticum', *Latomus* 27 (1968), pp. 864-77.

Teeuwen, St W. J., 'De voce paenitentia apud Tertullianum', *Mnemosyne* 55 (1927), pp. 410f.

Sprachlicher Bedeutungswandel bei Tertullian, Paderborn, 1926.

Torjesen, K. J., 'Tertullian's "political ecclesiology" and women's leadership', *SP* 21 (1989), pp. 277-82.

van der Geest, J. E .L., *Le Christ et l'ancien Testament chez Tertullien*, Nijmegen, 1972.

van der Nat, P. G., 'Observations on Tertullian's treatise on idolatry', *VC* 17 (1963), pp. 71-84.

'Tertullianea', *VC* 18 (1964), pp. 14-31, 129-43.

van Winden, J. C. M., 'Idolum and idololatria in Tertullian', *VC* 36 (1982), pp. 108-14.

Vermander, J. M., 'La polémique de Tertullien contre les dieux du paganisme', *RScRel* 53 (1979), pp. 111-23.

Waszink, J. H., 'Tertullian's principles and methods of exegesis' in *Early Christian literature*, ed. W. Schoedel, Utrecht-Anvers, 1979, pp.17-31.

and van Winden, J. C. M., 'A particular kind of idolatry – an exegesis of Tertullian, de Idolol. 23', *VC* 36 (1982), pp. 15-23.

Wilken, R. L. , 'Tertullian and the early Christian view of tradition', *Concordia* 38 (1967), pp. 221-33.

Wolfl, K., *Das Heilswirken Gottes durch den Sohn nach Tertullian*, Rome, 1960.

5. OTHER

Altendorf, E., *Einheit und Heiligkeit der Kirche*, Leipzig, 1932.

Aune, D. E., *Prophecy in early Christianity and the ancient Mediterranean world*, Grand Rapids, 1983.

Bakhuisen van den Brink, J., 'Traditio in theologischen Sinne',*VC* 13 (1959), pp. 65-86.

'Tradition and authority in the early Church', *SP* 7 (1961), pp. 3-22.

Barnes, T. D., 'The family and career of Septimius Severus', *Historia* 16 (1967), pp. 87-107.

'Pre-Decian Act Martyrum', *JTS* ns 19 (1968), pp. 509-31.

'Legislation against the Christians', *JRS* 58 (1968), pp. 32-50.

'The chronology of Montanism', *JTS* ns 21 (1970), pp. 403-8.

Barton, I. M., *Africa in the Roman Empire*, Accra, 1972.

Beare, R., 'The meaning of the oath by the safety of the Roman emperor', *AJPhil* 99 (1978) pp. 106-10.

Benabou, M., *La résistance africaine à la romanisation*, Paris, 1976.

Benarro, H. W., 'Rome of the Severi', *Latomus* 17 (1958), p. 712.

Bender, W., *Die Lehre über den Heiligen Geist*, Munich, 1961.

Berkouwer, C., *The Church*, Michigan, 1976.

Bethune-Baker, J. F., *An introduction to the early history of Christian doctrine to the time of the Council of Chalcedon*, London, 1933.

Bietenhard, H., 'The millennial hope in the early church', *ScotJTh* 6 (1953) pp. 12-30.

Birley, A. R., *Septimius Severus, the African emperor*, London, 1971.

Blackman, E. C., *Marcion and his influence*, London, 1948.

Brandon, S. G. F., 'Mithraism and its challenge to Christianity', *Hibbert Journal* 53 (1954/55) pp. 107-14.

Braun, R., 'Nouvelles observations linguistiques sur le rédacteur de la "Passio Perpetuae"', *VC* 33 (1979), pp. 105-17.

Burleigh, J. H. S., 'The Holy Spirit in the Latin Fathers', *ScotJTh* 7 (1954), pp. 113-32.

Campenhausen, H. von, 'Tradition und Geist im Urchristentum', *Studium Generale* 4 (1951), pp. 351-7.

Ecclesiastical authority and spiritual power in the Church of the first three centuries, London, 1969.

Caron, P.G., 'Les seniores laici de l'Eglise africaine', *Revue Internationale des droits de l'antiquité* 6 (1951), p. 7.

Charles-Picard, G., *La civilisation de l'afrique Romaine*, Paris, 1959.

Cohn, N., *The pursuit of the millennium*, London, 1970.

Danielou, J., *The origins of Latin Christianity*, London, 1977.

Davies, J. G., 'Was the devotion of Septimius Severus to Serapis the cause of the persecution of 202-3?', *JTS* ns 5 (1954), pp. 73-6.

Dolger, F. J., 'Achtung des Ehebruches in der Kultsatzung', *AC* 3 (1932), pp. 132-47.

Donaldson, S. A., *Church life and thought in North Africa, AD 200*, Cambridge, 1909.

Dulles, A., *Models of the church*, Dublin, 1976.

Flessmann-van Leer, E., *Tradition and scripture in the early Church*, Assen, 1954.

Ford, J. M., 'Was Montanism a Jewish-Christian heresy?', *JEH* 17 (1966), pp. 145-58.

Frend, W. H. C., *The Donatist Church*, Oxford, 1952.

'The seniores laici and the origins of the Church in North Africa', *JTS* ns 12 (1961), pp. 280-4.

Martyrdom and persecution in the early Church, Oxford, 1965.

'The North African cult of martyrs: from apocalyptic to hero-worship [plates]' in *Jenseitsvorstellungen in Antike* ed. T. Klausner and E. Dassmann, 1982, pp. 154-67.

Garnsey, P. D. A., 'The Lex Julia and appeal under the empire', *JRS* 57 (1967), pp. 56ff.

Greenslade, S. L., *Schism in the early Church*, London, 1953.

'Ordo', *ScotJTh* 9 (1956), pp. 161-74.

Hammond, M., 'Septimius Severus, Roman bureaucrat', *Harvard Studies in Classical Philology* 51 (1940), pp. 137-73.

'Review of G. J. Murphy, *The reign of the emperor Lucius Septimius Severus from the evidence of the inscriptions*, 1947', *AJPh* 71 (1950), pp. 193-202.

Hannestad, K., 'Septimius Severus in Egypt', *Classica et Mediaevalia* 6 (1944), pp. 194-222.

Harnack, A., *History of dogma*, London, 1897.

Militia Christi: the Christian religion and the military in the first three centuries, Philadelphia, 1981.

Marcion, Des Evangelium von fremden Gott, Darmstadt, 1924.

Haywood, R. M., 'The African policy of Septimius Severus', *Transactions of the American Philological Association* 71 (1940), pp. 175-85.

Helgeland, J., 'Christians and the Roman army AD 173-337', *CH* 43 (1974), pp. 149-161.

'Christians and the Roman army from Marcus Aurelius to Constantine' (bibliog.) in *Principat* vol. 23/1, ed. W. Hasse, 1979, pp. 724-834.

Kelly, J. N. D., *Jerome*, London, 1975.

Kirkpatrick, D. (ed.), *The doctrine of the church*, London, 1964.

Knox, J., *Marcion and the New Testament*, Chicago, 1942.

Knox, R. A., *Enthusiasm: a chapter in the history of religion*, Oxford, 1950.

de Labriolle, P., 'Mulieres in ecclesia taceant', *Bulletin d'ancienne littérature et d'archéologie chrétiennes* 1 (1911), pp. 3-24, 103-22.

La crise montaniste, Paris, 1913.

Les sources de l'histoire du Montanisme, Paris, 1913.

Lampe, G. W. H., 'Christian theology in the patristic period' in *A History of Christian doctrine*, ed. H. Cunliffe-Jones, Edinburgh, 1978.

Leclerq, H., *L'Afrique chrétienne*, Paris, 1904.

Le Saint, W. P., 'Traditio und Exomologesis', *SP* 8 (1966), pp. 414-19.

Leske, E., 'Montanism', *Lutheran Theological Journal* 15 (1981), pp. 79-85.

Marrou, H. I., 'Doctrina et discipline dans la langue des Pères de l'Eglise', *ALMA* 9 (1934), pp. 5-25.

A history of education in antiquity, London, 1956.

Mauch, O., *Der lateinische Begriff 'disciplina'. Eine Wortuntersuchung*, Basel, 1941.

McCann, A. M., *The portraits of Septimius Severus*, Rome, 1968.

Merkelbach, R., *Mithras*, Königstein, 1984.

Minear, P. S., *Images of the church in the New Testament*, London, 1960.

Moltmann, J., *The church in the power of the Spirit*, London, 1977.

Monceaux, P., *Histoire littéraire de l'Afrique chrétienne*, vol. 1, Paris, 1901.

'Les seniores laici', *Bulletin. Société Nationale des Antiquaires de France* (1903), pp. 283-6.

Murphy, G. J., *The reign of the emperor Lucius Septimius Severus from the evidence of the inscriptions*, Philadelphia, 1945.

Newbigin, L., *The household of God*, London, 1957.

Norris, R. A., *God and world in early Christian theology*, London, 1966.

Osborn, E. F., *The beginnings of Christian philosophy*, Cambridge, 1981.

'The love command in second-century Christian writing', *Second Century* 1 (1981), pp. 223-38.

Pannenberg, W., *The church*, Philadelphia, 1983.

Parker, H. M. D., *A history of the Roman world from AD 138-337*, London, 1935.

Parks, E. P., *The Roman rhetorical schools: a preparation for the courts under the early empire*, Baltimore, 1945.

Pelikan, J., 'Montanism and its trinitarian significance', *CH* 25 (1956), pp. 99-109.

Platnauer, J., *The life and reign of the emperor Lucius Septimius Severus*, Oxford, 1918.

Poschmann, B., *Penance and the anointing of the sick*, London, 1964.

Powell, D., 'Ordo Presbyteri', *JTS* ns 26 (1975), pp. 290-328.

Prestige, G. L., *God in patristic thought*, London, 1952.

Quasten, J., *Patrology II – the ante-Nicene literature after Irenaeus*, Maryland, 1984.

Quispel, G., 'African Christianity before Tertullian' in *Romanitas et Christianitas*, Studia J.H. Waszink oblata, Amsterdam, 1973, pp. 275-9.

Robinson, J. A .T., *The body: a study in Pauline theology*, London, 1952.

Schillebeeckx, E., *The church with a human face*, London, 1985.

Simon, M., 'Mithras, rival du Christ?', *Etudes Mithraiques*, Leiden, 1978, pp.457-78.

Speidel, M. P., *Mithras – Orion: Greek hero and Roman army god*, Leiden, 1980.

Telfer, W., *The Forgiveness of Sins*, SCM, London, 1959.

'The origins of Christianity in Africa', *SP* 4 (1961), pp. 512f.

The Office of Bishop, London, 1962.

Turcan, R., *Mithra et le mithraicisme*, Paris, 1981.

van Beneden, P., 'Ordo. Über den Ursprung einer kirchlichen Terminologie', *VC* 23 (1969), pp. 161-76.

Aux origines d'une terminologie sacramentelle, Louvain, 1974.

van den Eynde, D., *Les normes de l'enseignement chrétien dans la littérature patristique des trois premiers siècles*, Paris, 1933.

Vermaseren, M. J., *Mithras, the secret god*, London, 1963.

Vokes, F. E., 'Montanism and the ministry', *SP* 9 (1966), pp.306-15.

'Penitential discipline in Montanism', *SP* 14 (1976), pp. 62-76.

Welch, C., *The reality of the church*. New York, 1958.

Westermann, W. L. and Schiller A. A., *Apokrimata: decisions of Septimius Severus on legal matters*, New York, 1954.

Williams, C. W., *The church*, London, 1969.

General Index

Julia Domna (wife of Septimius Severus), 23
Justin Martyr, 93, 158, 174, 176

'laicus', 128–31
'lector', 174

Marcion (heretic), 5, 81, 83, 93, 125, 184, 194
Marcus Aurelius (emperor), 11
'martyr', 181–3
Minucius Felix (author of the *Octavius*), 18f.
Minutius Timinianus (proconsul), 13
Mithras, 19, 24f., 69f.

Nero (emperor), 23
New Prophecy, the (Montanism), 11, 30, 38, 41–51, 102f., 138, 141, 159, 160, 161, 167, 183f.
Novatian (heretic), 83, 96

'officium', 141–2
'ordo', 132, 134–8, 142f., 145, 177f.
Origen of Alexandria, 93, 111, 194
Ovid (poet), 158

Papinian (jurist), 21
Passio Perpetuae et Felicitatis, 12f., 17, 51, 131, 139, 162, 173
'pastor', 162–3
'pecus', 133, 151
Pius Antoninus (emperor), 23
Plautianus (Praetorian commander), 21
'plebs', 131–2

Pliny (the Younger), 11
Polycarp (bp. of Smyrna), 93, 104, 144, 176, 179
'pontifex', 164–5
'praeesse', 157–8
'praepositi', 154–5
'praesidere', 155–7
presbyterate, 143–72 passim, 156, 168–9, 170–1, 173, 187
'principes', 158–9
'promotio', 188
prophecy, 183–5
'psychici', 28, 29, 31f., 37f., 45, 49, 124f., 150

'sacerdos', 163–8
Scapula Tertullus (proconsul), 14, 23
'senatus', 138–40, 159, 187
'seniores', 18, 139–41, 169
Septimius Severus (emperor), 12–13, 20f., 68
Serapis, 13, 20, 24, 25f.
Shepherd (Pastor), The, (of Hermas), 32, 71, 91, 103, 140, 144, 154, 172f., 176, 183
Socrates (philosopher), 22, 87
Stoicism, 68, 71, 114, 145

Tertullianistai, 37
Trajan (emperor), 11

Valentinus, 5, 87, 125
Vigellius Saturninus (proconsul), 10
virgin, 178–80
widow, 176–8, 179f.

Index of citations from Tertullian

225